QUEER SPACES

An Atlas of LGBTQIA+
Places and Stories

Edited by Adam Nathaniel Furman
and Joshua Mardell

RIBA ᚻ Publishing

SPONSORS

ALLFORD HALL MONAGHAN MORRIS

Allford Hall Monaghan Morris is an architecture practice founded in 1989. It has offices in London, Bristol and Oklahoma City, and works across the UK and around the world on projects across sectors and scales, from a transformative mixed use masterplan to a small therapeutic space for a charity. The practice won the RIBA Stirling Prize for Burntwood School in 2015, and has won many other awards and critical acclaim for its work over the last thirty years. Since 2017 AHMM has been majority owned by its employees through an Employee Ownership Trust.

ANOMⱯLY

Anomaly is a collection of London based architects, interior designers and creative minds who are driven by more than just creating exciting space. This isn't your run-of-the mill architecture practice. We see ourselves as the outsiders in the best way possible. Aspects of traditional architecture can be archaic, they don't need to be. We believe the perfect balance for creating unforgettable environments is through speaking our clients' language; we build amazing relationships through breaking bread. We thrive off collaborative and engaging discussion with the drive to challenge every brief. We ensure our approach revolves around a distinct concept built on a shared idea and delivered with Anomaly's defined passion and commitment for spatial experience.

GRIMSHAW

Grimshaw is an award-winning internationally renowned practice recognised for delivering buildings, infrastructure and places that are underpinned by the principles of humane, enduring and sustainable design. Our collaborative approach works to ensure that there is opportunity for all voices – including LGBTQIA+ – to influence the future of our public spaces and places. With studios in Los Angeles, New York, London, Paris, Dubai, Melbourne and Sydney we bring this approach to the clients and projects we work on across multiple sectors, including transport, aviation, infrastructure, workplace, culture, education and sports.

PLP/ARCHITECTURE

PLP Architecture is a collective of architects, designers and researchers who value the transformative role of ideas and architecture's ability to inspire. Based in London, the practice is led by an experienced and dedicated group of partners who have worked together for more than three decades. Together, they have designed and delivered a wide range of projects around the world, producing intelligent, ground-breaking, and exciting designs through a profound commitment to social, economic and environmental ideals. PLP Architecture has created some of the greenest buildings on the planet and is now designing and building projects on three continents.

RIBA ∰

The Royal Institute of British Architects is a global professional membership body driving excellence in architecture. We serve our members and society in order to deliver better buildings and places, stronger communities and a sustainable environment. Being inclusive, ethical, environmentally aware and collaborative underpins all that we do.

© RIBA Publishing, 2022

Published by RIBA Publishing, 66 Portland Place, London, W1B 1AD

ISBN 9781 91412 421 1

Reprinted 2022

The rights of Adam Nathaniel Furman and Joshua Mardell to be identified as the Authors of this Work have been asserted in accordance with the Copyright, Designs and Patents Act 1988 sections 77 and 78.

British Library Cataloguing-in-Publication Data
A catalogue record for this book is available from the British Library.

Commissioning Editor: Clare Holloway
Project Manager and picture researcher: Caroline Ellerby
Production: Jane Rogers
Designed and typeset by Alex Synge / The First 47
Printed and bound by TJ Books, Cornwall
Cover design: Alex Synge / The First 47
Endpapers design: Adam Nathaniel Furman

While every effort has been made to check the accuracy and quality of the information given in this publication, neither the Author nor the Publisher accept any responsibility for the subsequent use of this information, for any errors or omissions that it may contain, or for any misunderstandings arising from it.

All quotes from external sources in the book were made in private correspondence with the author.

www.ribapublishing.com

Dedicated to the memory of Leah Nobuko, whose wisdom and beauty was carried by an oceanic pleasure in the world around her, Paula, whose creative fire forged and then sustained the spirits of those of us lucky enough to have been touched by her, and Donald, a galvanising mentor, wit and collector: the dearly missed Cousin Pons of Portobello.

Acknowledgements

Editing this book, we have met incredible people, discovered and learned so much, and been floored with awe and respect both for the amazing work going on in the field and by those who created the spaces we have highlighted, as well as so many others that we were not able to include. Embarking on this journey together, we have both been markedly changed by it. We would like to pass our heartfelt thanks to Clare Holloway for commissioning the book and pushing for it to be the very best it could possibly be, Helen Castle for being so supportive on behalf of the RIBA, Caroline Ellerby, whose incredible organisational skills, eye for detail and constant support were vital in enabling this to all come together, Jane Rogers for all her hard work and creativity in putting it all together and making it a physical reality, and Alex Synge who is responsible for making it look absolutely stunning. A huge thank you also goes to Olivia Laing, whose writing has been a formative and important inspiration to both editors, and for whom their foreword has profound meaning.

We would like to extend a huge thank you to all the contributors. We were completely moved by the degree of love and passion for the subject shown by every single one of those who have had their words published in this book, and we wish to extend an equal thank you to those photographers, institutions and individuals who have so kindly helped us in presenting visuals of all these spaces that we felt were so important to include. We are also extremely grateful to the practices who financially supported the book, and hope this support is indicative of an architectural context that is becoming more open to queerness in all its wonderfully myriad forms.

Adam Nathaniel Furman:
I would like to express thanks to my long-suffering and ridiculously supportive partner Marco Ginex. Thanks to Eusebio Penha, who went out and took the most incredible photographs of Mexico City for the book, and Katsushi Goto and Vishwa Shroff for so generously opening up their awe-inspiring network of creatives to the research journey we undertook before ever thinking we could create this publication. A very broad, but important, extension of gratitude to those queer spaces, now mostly gone, which very much saved me as a teenager from an abusive, and then entirely absent school environment, and taught me strength and self-belief, as well as helping me to get a couple of A-Levels (thank you King Willy for all the tea, and Costa OCS for the loo codes); from my perspective this has very much all been done in their honour. I would like to, also a bit broadly, thank the younger generation of queer designers and architects, who over the past few years have given me so much hope and joy in seeing how confidently they are taking up space in the profession, demanding to be heard, and beginning to transform it for the better, from the ground up. I hope this book will in some small way, together with the many other brilliant publications being created and recently written on the subject, provide their activities and actions with a deep and proud, confidence-boosting, shared foundation. I would like to thank Timothy Brittain-Catlin for being a bright, friendly light in an often intellectually dark and lonely architectural education, being my mentor, critic, inspiration and true friend. Finally, I would like to extend a perpetual and unbearably tight hug of undying gratitude and love to Joshua Mardell, and his alter ego Dom Josh, who has made the (omg so long) journey of making this book into one that has been so much bloody fun, a voyage of growth, learning, gossip and great conversation, a glorious queer space in its own right...

Joshua Mardell:
I would like to express my thanks to: James Boaden, Karin Daan, Kit Heyam, Torsten Lange, Charlotte Malterre-Barthes, Sarah Nichols, Barbara Penner and Thaddeus Zupančič for so obligingly suffering enquiries, gifting illustrations or helping me plug vital gaps in my existing knowledge and network. I am particularly grateful to Peter Swaab, editor of the *Journal of the Sylvia Townsend Warner Society*, whose passion and generosity helped us overcome obstacles in illustrating the charming, unassuming literary abodes of Townsend Warner and Valentine Ackland. I would also like to acknowledge the encouragement I have received from my fellow historians in the Society of Architectural Historians of Great Britain's LGBTQIA+ network, who all work hard to effect positive change in our discipline. At York, I would like to acknowledge the unsparing warmth and ongoing support of Anthony Geraghty and Liz Prettejohn, which has been a great strength to me academically and personally, and my students, all of whom have found queer spaces on their syllabi, and entered into the subject with enthusiasm and understanding. I wish to extend my gratitude to several of my friends, to Bethany Marett, Oliver Simpson and – especially – Jure Kirbiš, all of whom, for reasons unbeknownst to me, have continually put up with me. Above all, I wish to thank Adam. Their persistent belief in the sheer significance of this project, their demands for the absolute best, combined with their extraordinary erudition, has so considerably strengthened what this book was able to become – talking to them every day for nearly two years was never anything less than an absolute pleasure.

Contents

PUBLIC

Foreword

Olivia Laing

There's a line from a Pet Shop Boys track that's been looping around my head lately. It's from 'Being Boring', that strange, elegiac pop song to those lost to AIDS. 'I never dreamt,' Neil Tennant sings in his confiding, reticent way, 'that I would get to be / the creature that I always meant to be.' There's something central to queer identity encapsulated in this statement: the idea of a hidden self, a mysterious creature that can emerge from its chrysalis, given the right conditions.

What this magnificent book reveals is the near-unbelievable ingenuity, courage and skill of queer people in creating these conditions for themselves. Through history and across the globe, queers have been supplying their own needs for nurture, education, safety, pleasure and erotic play in what are often outspokenly hostile, if not lethal environments, from internment camps to totalitarian states.

The idea that queerness requires an ecosystem to flourish helps clarify the fundamental importance of queer space. It's not just a physical building in which to hook up or hang out. Instead, it's an alternate universe, a secret network that runs right round the world. Queer space might be a private home, built to new architectural specifications, like the windowless, open-plan house nicknamed Dracula's Den in Japan. It might celebrate an idiosyncratic aesthetic, from the shell-encrusted domesticity of A la Ronde in England to Ludwig II of Bavaria's lavish and melancholy unfinished castles.

Queer space can be private, intimate and secretive, or it can be communal, public and shared. It could be a Hijra in Bangladesh, a sanctuary for a community of gender-nonconforming people, or a community centre, an archive, a bathhouse or a museum. Queer space comes and goes, sometimes enduring in the same site for decades, like London's

Royal Vauxhall Tavern or New York's Stonewall Inn, and sometimes so transient it lasts only for a single encounter. As Ailo Ribas says in the essay that opens this book, 'it is making use of space in a queer way.'

And oh, the ingenuity of those reclamations! Did you know the last carriage on the Mexico City Metro, El Último Vagón, was appropriated by the queer community back in the 1970s and is now commonly understood to be a cruising zone, nicknamed 'the happy box'? Or that in Stalinist Russia, the safest space for gay sex was the men's toilets in the Central V.I. Lenin Museum in Moscow? Homosexuality had been decriminalised by Lenin's government, and, during the far more repressive Stalin years, cruising in towns tended to take place by Lenin monuments, campily nicknamed 'Grandma Lena'.

Reading this book has taught me about sites I'd never heard of, as well as making me reflect on queer space in my own life. I grew up the trans kid of a lesbian parent, under the malign influences of the homophobic Section 28 and the AIDS crisis. For my mother's closeted generation there was the legendary Gateways Club in London, as well as the private homes where lesbian life has always existed beneath the radar. On her shelves were books describing the havens carved out by predecessors, from the Ladies of Llangollen to Vita Sackville-West. But even the private house was an insecure refuge. We ran away from one after my mother was outed, and left another in a moonlit flit, escaping an alcoholic partner, whose rages were partially fuelled by the intense homophobia she experienced at work.

The annual extravaganza of Pride was an antidote to this forced invisibility, a queering of public space that in the late 1980s was far wilder and more angry than today's corporate outing. As a teenager I moved

to Brighton and in my thirties drifted on to New York, settling in the East Village. Both were predominantly queer zones, where expression was at least legal, if not always safe. Here I set about investigating queer spaces of the past, from the piss-stinking Hudson piers immortalised by David Wojnarowicz to the Institut für Sexualwissenschaft, a queer/trans sanctuary established by Magnus Hirschfeld in Weimar Berlin.

In many countries around the world, homosexuality and divergent gender expression are still illegal and subject to harsh sanctions, including life imprisonment in Uganda. It's hard to describe how moving it is to read about the bars and centres established in these hostile environments. Even in countries with much more inclusive laws, struggle remains. In Argentina, the first country in Latin America to legalise same-sex marriage, a national census of the *travesti*-trans population in 2007 'showed a life expectancy of 35 years and a common desire: access to education.' This led to the founding of Mocha Celis, a school for the LGBTQ+ population. Also in Argentina is the Archivo de la Memoria Trans, which has collected over 10,000 documents, digitising photos, letters and keepsakes of those who died prematurely and as a result of violence and state neglect.

The archive is a powerful space of queer resistance. The queer lives that have been historised tend overwhelmingly to be white, male, wealthy and upper class. Unrecorded lives exist as holes in the record, whose presence can later be denied. As Helen Smith tartly observes with regard to 1950s Sheffield, 'working class, queer domestic spaces don't carry blue or rainbow plaques.' Among the wonders of this book is how it grapples with this problem, finding evidence for diverse queer existence through time as well as space. It's a luminous queer archive-cum-party in its own right, avowedly diverse, multiple and full of life.

Another thing that's stayed with me is the ongoing sense that any space can be turned queer. As Doron von Beider explains in an essay describing romantic and sexual encounters in Jerusalem and Tel Aviv: 'I learned that some special people were self-manifesting infrastructures of queerness; they kept bravely, or stupidly, changing the use and entire meaning of the spaces they occupied, or had access to.'

How beautiful this is. It makes me think that queering space is not so dissimilar to rewilding it. Look, it's happening right now. A way of life that has been brutally repressed is flooding back in, to reclaim and beautify what was actually always our own space.

Olivia Laing (pronoun fluid) is the author of four works of non-fiction, *To the River*, *The Trip to Echo Spring*, *The Lonely City* and *Everybody*, as well as an essay collection, *Funny Weather*, and a novel, *Crudo*.

Introduction

Adam Nathaniel Furman and Joshua Mardell

When you – for whatever reason – have to modify your behaviour or hide aspects, or indeed the better part of yourself to 'fit in'; or when you can't ever actually 'fit' anywhere because you're somehow different in a visible, unconcealable way, you seek out spaces where you can simply be yourself, unmediated and unfettered. Spaces where you can express yourself without fear or shame. Spaces where you can act freely in a manner that is truly consonant with your inner self.

Places like this, where you can mingle with others usually burdened and now similarly released from the constant pressure to modify oneself, hide oneself, or the ceaseless need to justify one's very existence, are not only important; in many instances they are life-giving, and often life-saving.

Queer spaces that create these vitally important environments have been created, and continue to be created, in a spectrum of different forms, shaped by and catering for a range of different queer communities and individuals in countries and cultures across the world and throughout time. Each has its own unique and specific circumstances, its own story, urban and architectural contexts, needs, aesthetics, tribulations and joys. Mindful of these specificities, the editors have been careful to respect each individual contributor's own valued voice, including their preferred use of queer acronyms.

Growing up queer means experiencing the destabilising absence of a broad and accessible queer history, most notably, in our case, in relation to spatial design. The many generations who came before us have given proof and examples of our right to inhabit, create, design and transform spaces. This book is our contribution to the work being done by so many to enable access to a shared queer heritage, one that has previously been sidelined and ridiculed. Here we show how it is strong, vibrant, vigorous and worthy of its own space in the public sphere of recognised memory. Thus, for a section of society that does not benefit from the ubiquitous and oppressively reactionary canon of architectural and design history, we hope this book will be an act of queer heirlooming, a gifting by simple example, through generations of accumulated strength, of spaces of affirmation.

The very fact that this book has been published by the professional body of architects of the British Isles indicates that times are changing, as does the fact that several architecture practices have financially supported its creation. The current possibilities in mainstream publication that we have as editors are only possible because of those who created work in far less supportive contexts before us, trailblazers who built the foundations for a generation of publications and exhibitions that are bringing the queer spaces past and present to a general audience, including, of course, the seminal 'Queer Space' exhibition at the Storefront for Art and Architecture in New York (1994) and Aaron Betsky's iconic *Queer Space: Architecture and Same-Sex Desire* (1997).

To re-narrativise our history depends to some extent on where we look, and the spaces in this book are intended to highlight the ingenuity, scope and diversity of places created by those within the queer coalition, all of which are valid and important. What we have been able to include, however, is fragmentary. We have done our best to highlight as broad a spectrum of diverse examples from as many parts of the world as possible, but there were nonetheless limits created by the size of the book, the extents of our networks and knowledge, and the timeframe within which this was put together. An important limiting factor was that in many parts of the world queer spaces, communities and individuals require secrecy for their continued safety, and could not yet participate in a publication of this nature.

Sadly, the erasure and absence of official records of queer experience and history continues; as Facundo Revuelta has poignantly put it in reference to trans communities in Argentina, 'Many things from the past were lost as documenting life was so difficult when existence itself took up all of one's energy'. Often the only remaining evidence for documenting certain queer histories is peripheral and peculiar, such as criminal records. Yet queer identity should not be defined by the form of its evidence, which is so often simply a function of where the normative gaze of an antagonistic society was cast. As Helen Smith has put it, 'Queer historians can subvert this material and use it to fill the silences,' or in Katarina Bonnevier's words: queer stories should no longer 'hide behind straight curtains'.

We have organised the abundance of spaces in this book in three scales: 'domestic', 'communal' and 'public'. Within these categories we were keen to form contrasts between vignettes, highlighting the variety of people and places across time and space, while enabling them to forge continuities across those distances, and across social strata. Therefore one finds a decadent monarch in 19th-century Bavaria alongside the working-class inhabitants of a typical 'two-up, two-down' terrace in 1950s Sheffield, and an LA-based LGBTQIA+ rights organisation alongside a short-lived queer bar in Kampala.

Emerging from the collection of spaces selected, a set of clear typologies can be recognised. Educational spaces, in all their diversity, demonstrate the quite singular needs of the queer community, for instance, the development of basic life skills not transferred when one loses one's family, or in the case of the Mocha Celis school for queer youth in Buenos Aires, 'methods of productive self-expression and the cultivation of pride and self-esteem'.

Above
The apartment of Dan
Friedman, queer educator,
graphic and furniture
designer, 1982–88.

There are several important instances of the reappropriation of historically heteronormative spaces in the book, too, including institutional ones. The transformation of the Santiago Apóstol Cathedral in Nicaragua is one such example, which, not deemed fit for 'normal' occupation, became a space for homosociality and cruising. Comparably, at Holy Trinity Church in York, the lesbian landowner and businesswoman Anne Lister solemnised her union with her lover Ann Walker in the Easter of 1834.

The archives we have included are examples of particular approaches to the preservation, discovery and rediscovery of queer history; for instance, at the Museum of Transology in London, contributors to the collection, coming from their own embodied experience, have been in complete control of their stories. Archiving is a form of activism. Other typologies include queer kinship groups, havens for queer writers, bookshops, community centres, activist spaces, bars and nightclubs, public and cruising spaces and much besides.

Queer people have always found ways to exist and be together, and there will always be a need for queer spaces. The community of contributors to this book in themselves are an inspiring example of the will to occupy and support such spaces, as well as document and remember them, with each being a rich example of queer life especially within the world of architecture and design. We hope that this book will act as a spur to further investigate the spaces shown, ones similar to them, as well as the other works and writings of the contributing authors themselves.

We hope it will help readers contemplate what form these spaces of affirmation and memory might take in the future so that they may become active participants in forging them. Hints and visions have been offered in this book, including: by Stalled! for safe, gender non-binary bathrooms; by Queer House Party, for a new model of collaboration, solidarity and accessibility in nightlife; and by Museo Q, which champions a radical, nomadic queer museology.

We hope, furthermore, that readers will continue the ongoing and collective work of uplifting all the brilliant queer lives and queer histories in architecture to which this book makes a small, but meaningful, contribution.

DOMES

The space of the domestic for those able to pool resources communally, or those in possession of wealth by virtue of class, was often where queer individuals, couples and kinship groups were primarily able to create lasting and meaningful environments. These alternative domesticities were little queer worlds that catered for those whose lifestyles were disallowed in the public sphere, where memories could be accumulated, milestones in life be celebrated, and their value as humans to one another be affirmed and marked in physical form. Several types of domestic spaces are explored in this section, from homes and alternative forms of queer kinship to personal journeys of queerness.

Train Journey

BETWEEN PREMIÀ DE MAR AND BARCELONA, CATALONIA, SPAIN

Ailo Ribas

In the summer of 2017, I discovered the beauty and pain of intentional adaptation. Reconciling my dissent from the sex-gender system with my desire to have breasts, I went online and purchased my first pair of tits.

After an initial period of adjustment, I wore them almost every day without fail – at work, at university, in my flat, at my parents' house, out with friends, in the street, to go to the supermarket. The newfound thrills and anxieties of being visibly trans – and the personal and collective survival strategies I had to learn – were juxtaposed by the newfound difficulties and discomforts of muting my transness in familiar spaces in which I was yet to come out. Living in London, I would visit my Catalan hometown, Premià de Mar, throughout the year. This was one such space where, for many years, I would hide my transness out of fear of being outed to my family. Despite having a progressive, gentle family and group of friends, navigating the layers of small-town hypervisibility – especially in a country that remains inflected by the lingering tenets of National Catholicism – was something I was not ready to face. For readers who may not know, National Catholicism was the totalitarian merging of church and state with which Franco governed Spain between 1939 and 1975.

Having to present as a boy, I would remove my breasts while I was there. Under my shirt, my phantom tits were a wound that would not heal. The modification of our bodies is a trans survival strategy: the splicing and suturing of our flesh; the incorporation and removal of prostheses and other appendages; the chemical hacking of our endocrine system to induce physiological changes; the use of cosmetics, clothes, accessories, piercings to shape our appearance. By survival strategy I mean first and foremost a mode of adapting, evolving and transforming so that we might thrive, both individually and collectively. Changing, removing, assimilating, hiding, emphasising: these are our tools. Being trans is existing in constant relation to change.

How does changing how we inhabit our body change how we are able to inhabit and move through our environments?

If presenting as a boy – while necessary for me to retain control over when and how I chose to reveal myself to my town – was drowning, then taking the train to Barcelona was coming up for air. As the threshold between the constant threat of disclosure in my hometown and the resuscitating, life-giving anonymity of the city, the train became a space of transition, of transformation. I would board the train, equipped with a bra underneath my shirt, my breasts and make-up in my bag; apply them subtly in my seat as if it were the most ordinary thing, and step off the train in Barcelona fully metamorphosed. I used the train as a changing room, an escape pod: it is a locked bedroom door; a public bathroom; being home alone; a queer bar; a new outfit; a pair of breasts; a packer; a friend's house; a support group. It allowed me to be who I needed to be to survive in both environments, as well as in myself. It is a mode of transportation, a way of getting the fuck out and of extending deep within. Queer space is simply that which allows us to be in right relationship with change;[1] that which allows us to move between worlds, to shapeshift, to learn and teach the skills necessary to gestate and conceive our own worlds. It is making use of space in a queer way: learning to forage for, assimilate and wield spaces as prostheses, as tools for personal transformation and social change.

Opposite, top
Putting in breasts on the train from Premià de Mar to Barcelona, November 2020. Still from video by the author.

Opposite, bottom
Applying make-up.

Fonthill Abbey

WILTSHIRE, ENGLAND

Whitney Davis

Fonthill Abbey, the Neo-Gothic residence erected in Fonthill Gifford in Wiltshire by William Beckford (1760–1844), was built in stages between 1793 and 1813. Topped with an enormous tower, it was mostly destroyed in a windstorm in 1823 and is now known through contemporary descriptions and representations. Beckford's architect, James Wyatt, drew on his experiments in medievalism and on European prototypes admired by Beckford. The Abbey would house Beckford's vast collections of books, *objets d'art* and artworks. The estate was popularly understood to exemplify the protagonist's obsessions with towers and gardens in Beckford's celebrated Orientalist novel *Vathek*, drafted in 1782. But Beckford himself was known to his contemporaries as much as an infamous 'sodomite' as a writer, builder and collector. In 1784, when he was 24, the newspapers had exposed his sexual intimacies with 16-year-old William Courtenay, when Beckford was a guest at the younger man's family home. As the son of the powerful Alderman William Beckford (twice Mayor of London) and one of England's richest men, Beckford was expected to have a glittering public career. But the scandal foreclosed it. After a decade of self-imposed exile on the Continent, he mostly retreated to Fonthill, though still seeking out liaisons with 'butterflies' – pretty young men. As he wrote to a friend, at Fonthill he consoled his unhappiness by building. Shunned by local gentry, he saw the place as a 'limbo', a place of waiting and suffering in hope of redemption at the Last Judgment. Gazing out from the tower, he longed for a 'beatific vision' in which a beautiful angelic youth would come forth from the heavens to embrace him with love and understanding.

Indeed, sodomy was built into the very lineage and fabric of the Abbey, which was meant, Beckford said, to commemorate the Mervyns, Elizabethan gentry who had first built a manor house on the estate. In 1631, Mervyn, Lord Audley, had been tried and executed for rape and sodomy in England's best-known sodomy trial before Oscar Wilde's. Ordinarily this would have been a dangerous affiliation to proclaim. But Fonthill Abbey was what might be called a 'queer family romance', reimagining its owner's consanguinities in terms of cultural ancestors who shared his sexuality.

Beckford detested the gimcrack house Fonthill Splendens, built by his father in the then-popular Palladian style beside Fonthill Lake. As the site for the Abbey, Beckford settled on the higher ground opposite Beacon Hill, and in 1807 tore Splendens down and reused its stone. Indeed, he did everything he could to block out the memory – even the visibility – of Splendens (marked as 'Site of the Former Mansion' on the estate map). The Abbey was clearly designed to face a beholder viewing it from Beacon Hill to the southwest. Prospects *from* and vistas *within* the building – stage-managed by its fenestration and use of glass, mirrors and lustrous multicoloured *objets d'art* – were organised in the complementary direction, looking out to the west and south. At the same time, almost every possible view to the north and east was avoided – views, that is, to the estate's kitchen garden and workmen's housing, to Splendens and to Fonthill church and village, the unaesthetic worlds of labour, money, family and society. Notably, in the long galleries of the Abbey one would expect to find large windows on the eastern wall matching those on the western wall, but instead Beckford installed mirrors, paintings and book cabinets.

Effectively this turned the Abbey into a kind of stage set – a space for the play of imagination and projection.

Escaping the 'mean' parental home and form of life, it attached Beckford to many imagined communities. But for all that, it could not realise the 'beatific vision' of blissful erotic transformation and social redemption – transfigurations available only in the metaphors of art and architecture.

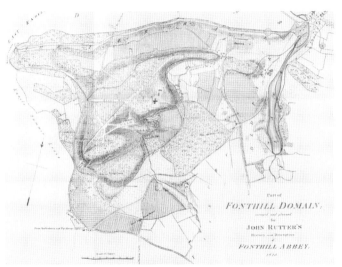

Clockwise from top-left

Part of Fonthill Domain, surveyed by S Paull for John Rutter (all images are from John Rutter, *Delineations of Fonthill and Its Abbey*, 1823).

View of Fonthill Abbey from the north and west.

King Edward's Gallery, looking south.

Longitudinal section, looking east.

View from the southwest, from Beacon Hill.

Former Knockaloe Internment Camp

ISLE OF MAN

Kit Heyam

Today, little trace remains of Knockaloe Internment Camp: the site has been levelled and returned to its original use as farmland, though archaeological traces of the camp can still be found.[2]

But from 17 November 1914 until October 1919, Knockaloe held up to 22,769 civilian internees, mostly of German, Austro-Hungarian and Turkish descent. It was a camp solely occupied by people assigned male at birth (AMAB), who were present in Britain at the start of the First World War and considered by the authorities to be of military age.

It became a queer space of gender nonconformity which illustrates a central challenge in the investigation and interpretation of trans history.

As civilian internees rather than prisoners of war – imprisoned under a policy that Britain pursued from the start of the First World War – the inhabitants of Knockaloe were exempt from forced labour under international law. As a result, in a (sometimes futile) quest to avoid boredom and depression, they organised a wide variety of activities, from sports tournaments to potato-peeling businesses.[3] Central among these activities was theatre: the camp had as many as 20 separate theatres across its four compounds, in which the internees staged on average one show per week. As in other civilian and military prison camps of the period, all roles were played by AMAB internees, necessitating onstage gender nonconformity. In addition, some internees lived full-time as female, continuing to use female names and pronouns offstage in non-theatrical contexts, and wearing practical as well as theatrical female-coded clothing. Their fellow internees embraced, validated and bolstered their female identities, describing them in sometimes sexualised feminine terms, and sending them fan mail and messages of romantic interest.[4]

Historians have interpreted the internees who lived as female at Knockaloe and other camps in three ways: as 'substitute women', mitigating the isolation caused by internment (a period during which many internees did not encounter any cisgender women) and helping to create a sense of home within

the camp; as helping to make their onstage female presentation more realistic by 'sustaining the illusion' offstage; and/or as legitimising same-sex love and attraction. In addition to this, we can consider that some female-presenting internees were motivated by trans experience: identification as female or a sense of comfort or rightness with female presentation.[5]

At its peak, Knockaloe housed about two-thirds of the total number of civilians interned in Britain. The huge numbers involved make it likely that all of the above motivations coexisted between, and indeed within, individuals. But absent any substantial testimony from female-presenting internees, this presents us with a methodological challenge. A queer approach, which seeks to make space for trans possibilities while refusing to definitively fix the internees in modern identity categories, requires us to acknowledge the multiple simultaneous experiences of gender nonconformity which coexisted at Knockaloe – and to recognise that to call the female-presenting internees 'cross-dressing men' or 'male impersonators' is itself to constrain the possibilities of their experience. This speaks to a wider issue in the investigation of trans history. Historical investigation often demands personal testimony and/or certainty of motivation – knowledge of *why* someone is behaving in a gender-nonconforming way – from people or periods when such testimony is lacking. This leads to denial of trans possibilities. The queer space of Knockaloe Internment Camp, and the widespread gender nonconformity it witnessed, points to the need to develop new historiographical methodologies to avoid erasing trans histories.

Above
Site of the former Knockaloe Internment Camp, Isle of Man.

Opposite, clockwise from top-left

Internees at Knockaloe presenting as female in non-theatrical and theatrical contexts.

View of a POW Camp, Isle of Man, 1915–1919, George Kenner. (Although the date 1915 is given here, some internees arrived in late 1914.)

View of P.o.W. Camp, Isle of Man, 1915-1919

Light Coffin – Dracula's Den

CHIBA, JAPAN

Alyssa Ueno

A male couple, a barber and a painter, went to architect Osamu Ishiyama and said, 'We want to live in a bare-looking space without any windows, somewhere that resembles an old aeroplane hangar.' The architect proceeded to design a big coffin-like box.

The two-storey, 6m-tall mass of steel was built in the cold, rugged landscape of Chiba. It has neither windows nor an entrance, instead the inhabitants use the shutters for loading and unloading artworks as a doorway. The residence of this same-sex couple did not require partitions, nor did it require children's rooms. Furthermore, they said that they did not need a bedroom or a living room.

The site had been known as 'Dracula's Den' even before the house was built, but the name was adopted by the couple as a nickname for the house as it suited their lifestyle.

The circulation of the large, one-room space starts from the shutter, then proceeds to the bed, the toilet, kitchen and bath in a straight line. When looking up, one sees a metal mesh catwalk crossing the space above. The architect was forced to create some skylight windows because the local building regulations did not allow for a completely windowless construction, so the light pours down from above and evokes the image of a 'light coffin'. A coffin is an object associated with the image of death. However, from the photographic documents and episodes recounted by the owners and guests who were able to enjoy a unique lifestyle inside this box, we can see the building as an architectural paradox in which a supposedly claustrophobic space is precisely what allows for and fosters the freedoms they enjoy within.

This project became a successful antithesis to the mass-produced nLDK housing units that are so ubiquitous in Japan. 'nLDK' is an abbreviation for Living Dining Kitchen and usually comes alongside the bedroom number 'n' as a standardised form of domestic real estate that also defines a certain standardised lifestyle. In contrast, the 'Light Coffin' emphasises the fact that it is possible to have different forms of 'family' living in a 'house', questioning what a 'family unit', and its accompanying container, should be. The architect himself recalls that he felt that 'the concept of "domestic floor plans" that we learn and are taught as common-sense collapsed, just because a homosexual couple asked me for a house'.[6]

As a context to this architectural project, the 1990s was a decade in which the gay liberation movement was gaining momentum in Japan. Furthermore, a media phenomenon that could be described as a 'gay boom', coupled with the expressive and newly high-profile activities of gay people themselves, led to a further flourishing of gay visibility in the latter half of the decade.[7]

However, even today, with negative attitudes towards LGBTQ+ people having eased considerably, it is still rare to see private information about, let alone the home set-up of, any same-sex couple disclosed in public.[8] This architectural project can be seen as a very rare case, not just for its spatial uniqueness, but also from the perspective of multiple contrasting forms of privacy, with the couple requiring the feeling of protection from the immediate surroundings and the prying eyes of neighbours, but wanting total openness in their interior in all activities towards one another and guests, and with the project and images of it being shared and discussed widely as a fascinating new form of housing in the architectural media. The duality of being architecturally closed to the external physical world while being open towards the media may somewhat resonate with the unique situation of how queerness expresses itself, closed yet open, in Japanese society even today.

Top-left
External view of the house with windowless walls.

Top-right
The two owners on the catwalk.

Opposite
The one-room space is inhabited by an artist and a barber.

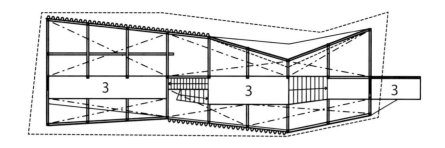

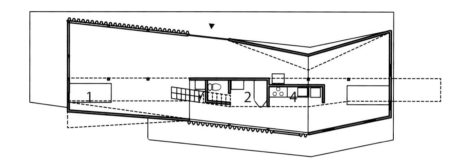

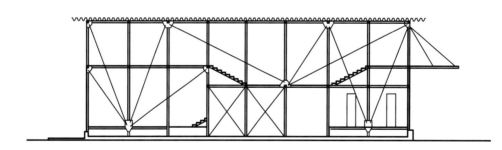

1. bed
2. bathroom
3. catwalk
4. kitchen

Scale 1:200

Opposite
Plans and section drawings
of the house.

Top
The residents and guests
enjoy the bohemian
atmosphere that is made
possible within the protected
and sealed-off space of the
house.

Bottom
Bathroom with two vanity
mirrors. The space is
seamlessly connected with
the living space.

Plas Newydd

LLANGOLLEN, WALES

Freya Gowrley

Plas Newydd, an eclectically decorated cottage *orné*, is best known as the home of the so-called 'Ladies of Llangollen', Lady Eleanor Butler (1739–1829) and the Hon Sarah Ponsonby (1755–1831).[9] Having met in County Kilkenny in Ireland in around 1769, Butler and Ponsonby struck up an uncommonly intense friendship despite their age gap of around 16 years. Faced with the threat of unwanted marriages, their early story is one of frustration and anguish. With their first attempt at elopement failing in 1778, their fate seemed destined to be determined by their tyrannical guardians and the governing social milieu of the 18th-century Irish elite: Ponsonby would marry, while Butler would be sent to a convent. Eventually, however, their families relented, permitting them first to see each other again, and finally to move to Britain to set up life together. While London had been their initial choice for a future residence, they eventually settled on Llangollen in Wales, a location with which Ponsonby was particularly enchanted. Llangollen commanded intensely beautiful prospects and possessed a number of striking landmarks, such as the ruined castle of Dinas Brân and the long-crumbling Valle Crucis Abbey, both of which were to become hubs for Romantic writers and artists during the late 18th and early 19th centuries. The pair would live together at the property from 1779 until Butler's death in 1829, which was followed by Ponsonby's own demise, just a few years later, in 1831.

During Butler and Ponsonby's time at Plas Newydd, they became celebrated as models of rural retirement, creativity and innocent intimacy by individuals as diverse as the writer and politician Edmund Burke and the poet William Wordsworth. This level of fame resulted in an enduring consumer culture based on images of their house and their own likenesses, which included printed images, portraits and postcards. Yet despite the thriving visual and material culture that emerged around the women, much of the fabric and collections of Plas Newydd do not survive intact, with the house having been significantly remodelled in the Victorian period, and many of their personal effects dispersed in the house sale that followed their deaths.

Although the precise date of its establishment is unknown, a modest cottage certainly stood on the spot by the time of the women's arrival. It is not an overstatement to say that the women transformed Plas Newydd following their arrival at the property: throughout the duration of their custodianship of the house, it was systematically turned from a fairly substantial square stone building, roofed with plain tiles, into an ornate spectacle. By the time of Butler's death, gone was the Georgian elegance of the front of the original building, with its simple symmetry and relatively plain façade, and in its place was a Gothic fantasy of grotesque carvings and shimmering coloured glass collected by the women.

Its interiors were likewise ornamented with an extensive programme of oak carvings, which were arranged patchwork-like throughout several areas of the house. These spaces were extensively hung with drawings of the surrounding landscape, and portraits of their friends and relatives, many of which were gifted to the women as material testament to their affective relationships, now lost to history.

Butler and Ponsonby are celebrated by many today as early lesbian heroines, and Plas Newydd functions as a monument to their life of idyllic retirement and the profound relationship they shared at the house.

Above
Plas Newydd, near Llangollen: the seat of the late Lady Eleanor Butler and Miss Ponsonby, WL Walton, after Edwin Jacques, 1840.

Opposite
The Rt Hon Lady Eleanor Butler and Miss Ponsonby, 'The Ladies of Llangollen', RJ Lane, after Mary Parker (later Lady Leighton), 1828.

Proof

The Rᵗ. Honᵇˡᵉ Lady Eleanor Butler and Miss Ponsonby.
"The Ladies of Llangollen."

The Palaces of Ludwig II

KINGDOM OF BAVARIA, GERMANY

Sean F Edgecomb

In 1864, at the age of 18, Prince Ludwig Otto Friedrich Wilhelm of the House of Wittelsbach (1845–86) ascended to the throne of the Kingdom of Bavaria. The life of Ludwig II was shaped by a complicated childhood split between militaristic training required by his father and his penchant for Teutonic legends instilled, in part, by his doting mother. As modern Germany began to take shape in the mid-19th century through its unification (1871), Ludwig's title became little more than symbolic. Following this event, the young monarch became obsessed with divine rule, driven by an obsession with Louis XIV of France.

With limited power, Ludwig was merely performing his monarchical role and ordered palaces that he considered worthy of this imagined status.

In the late 1860s, he began conversations with the designers of composer Richard Wagner's fantastical operas at the court in Munich. Rather than structures of defence, like the castles of medieval origin, he yearned for palaces as performance venues, confections that brought to life his favourite folklore with theatrical tricks (forced perspective, faux finishes and trompe l'oeil) and with the most up-to-date technology. These were places where he could perform an imaginary sovereignty. Ludwig oversaw the construction of three palaces in the Alpine regions of Lower Bavaria: Neuschwanstein (1869), Linderhof (1874) and Herrenchiemsee (1878). While glorious to gaze upon, these extravagant constructions were little more than stage sets. While Ludwig lived in a period prior to the socio-cultural establishment of same-sex desire as a queer identity (after Oscar Wilde), florid personal letters and anecdotes point to his obsession with several men, including Wagner and a handsome young Austrian actor named Josef Kainz.[10]

The three palaces of Ludwig constitute queer spaces because they were built as sites where the king could isolate himself from the court and aspire to pursue his same-sex desires, even though it is impossible to know if his longings were fulfilled. Ludwig would be deposed from the throne in 1886, accused of 'hereditary insanity' by the court doctor.[11] Only days after being taken into custody, the king's body was found, drowned in the waters of Lake Starnberg. The circumstances surrounding the king's death are sketchy at best, but his legacy for queer imagination and world-making remains steadfast in the palaces, which are among Germany's most visited tourist destinations today.

Above
Trade cards from the Liebig's Company, Antwerp, featuring Romantic depictions of Hohenschwangau and Neuschwanstein, c 1898.

Opposite
The main hall of Neuschwanstein.

Neuschwanstein Castle

In Richard Wagner's opera *Lohengrin* (1848), the titular character protects the Holy Grail as the Swan Knight. Adolescent Ludwig, who first saw the work performed in Munich, was obsessed. The Bavarian royal family had long associated their dynasty with the symbol of the swan, most evident at their summer palace of Hohenschwangau Schloss (Upper Swan Castle), where the avian symbol was ubiquitous in the heraldic décor, from chandeliers and upholstery to Romantic murals. As king, Ludwig longed for a more dramatic location and edifice to play out his childhood fantasies as a 19th-century embodiment of *Lohengrin*.

Choosing a high, rocky outcrop overlooking a gorge as a building site (farther up the mountain than Hohenschwangau), Ludwig imagined Schloss Neuschwanstein (New Swan on the Rock Castle) with a design that anachronistically juxtaposed the imposing bulk of the Romanesque with the airy decoration of the Gothic. Opera designer Christian Jank drafted the initial plans for the castle, which was subsequently actualised by architects Eduard Riedel and Georg von Dollman. Their collaboration brought Ludwig's fantastical vision to life and even employed theatrical techniques to heighten the atmosphere. Neuschwanstein was constructed around a steel frame, and though it was never fully completed, this stability allowed for a startling monolith that seemed to grow phallus-like from the mountain peaks. The interior design was equally cohesive in its symbolic value – an immense Byzantine Throne Hall, which ironically held no throne, a Singers' Hall built for an immense chorus, which only saw solo performances for the solitary king, and a shadowy grotto room with faux stalagmites and the whisper of running water.

While the castle mimicked the spaces of civic spectacle and state occasions that are a signature of Wagner's operas, they were used only by the reclusive Ludwig, who was known to wear a mask, concealing his face, whenever anyone else was present. The historical and aesthetic queerness of Neuschwanstein might be related to the often bizarre behaviour of its hermit-like sovereign – the castle itself acting as a kind of self-imposed closet in which to hide his sexuality. Perhaps the castle is, in fact, a fantastical interpretation of Ludwig's most intimate dreams and queer desires and never intended for the public access that is now essential to its preservation. Ironically, Neuschwanstein would also serve as inspiration for Walt Disney's theme park castles, making it a pervasive, if misunderstood, cultural symbol.

Linderhof Palace

In a picturesque valley near the southwestern Bavarian village of Ettal, Ludwig's father, King Maximillian II, had inherited a hunting lodge. After a period of enlarging the original building, in 1874 Ludwig chose to raze it to make room for a new, queerer vision – a miniature Rococo palace where he could play the role of Moon King, a less than subtle homage to his idol, Louis XIV, *le Roi Soleil* (the Sun King). So enamoured was Ludwig with the French king that he almost named Linderhof 'Meicost Ettal', a made-up word that combines the palace's location and an anagram of Louis' famous declaration of monarchical absolutism: *'l'etat, c'est moi'* (I am the state).[12] A lover of nocturnal pleasures, Ludwig would rise to eat his breakfast at sunset and was known to retire from the palace under the cover of night, riding through crystalline winters in a gilt carved sleigh.

In designing Linderhof, architect Georg von Dollman was inspired by Versailles and the Petit Trianon, scaling down these *châteaux enfilade* (castles where doorways are formally aligned through a series of rooms rather than an exterior corridor) and designing a Hall of Mirrors, a formal bedchamber (to mimic the French court etiquette of the *grand lever* – the morning rising ritual of a monarch made famous by Louis XIV), an audience chamber and a formal dining room. These luxurious interiors were designed to allow Ludwig to indulge his eccentricities and obsessions – another curated space in pursuit of his queer desires. For example, the dining room featured a custom mechanical 'wishing table'. This device had a crank that allowed the table to be lowered to the kitchen and set without any human interaction between the king and servants. According to Theodor Hiernes, a Linderhof cook, Ludwig demanded that the table would be set for four, so that he could play host to the Bourbon ghosts of the kings Louis XIV, Louis XV and their mistresses Madame de Pompadour and Madame Maintenon.[13]

Perhaps even more fantastical than the palace itself are the manicured grounds – dotted with more theatrical venues for the king to play out his fantasies beyond the cabinet of curiosities or *Wunderkammer* that was the miniature palace. If the palace was French, its environs were most certainly German. A Nordic hut, inspired by Wagner's *Die Walkure*, was a place for the king to read legends and feast while lounging on animal furs. The Moorish Kiosk (famous for its peacock throne) and the Moroccan House were colonial interpretations of Orientalist decadence. The Gurnemanz Hermitage, plucked from Wagner's *Parsifal*, was constructed specifically for Ludwig to visit on Good Friday (and the king demanded a wildflower meadow on that day, whether painted by a cooperative mother nature, or the gardener, forced to remove drifts of Bavarian snow). Finally, the *pièce de résistance*, the Venus Grotto, completed a Wagnerian trio, with a subterranean setting drawn from of the first act of *Tannhäuser.* It was in the grotto that Ludwig would purportedly drift in a golden boat, listening to Wagner and entertained by illuminations conceived by von Dollman and August Dirigl and inspired, in part, by the Blue Grotto of Capri.

Ludwig spent considerably more time at Linderhof than his other palaces (which were never fully completed). For this reason, it is perhaps the clearest illustration of how the king saw himself, but perhaps more importantly, it is a space to consider his reimagining of the mythical past as an avenue for a more hopeful future that tragically would never come.

Trade card featuring a painting of Linderhof Palace, c 1898.

The Venus Grotto.

The Hall of Mirrors.

Herrenchiemsee Palace

While Ludwig's seemingly limitless imagination had dreamt more castles that were never built (including Falkenstein, which would have been on the ruins of Bavaria's highest elevated castle), Herrenchiemsee was the last to begin construction.[14] Ever motivated by his obsession with absolute power in a monarchical seat with almost none, after visiting Versailles in 1874, the Moon King became obsessed with building a French-style palace on a scale much grander than the diminutive Linderhof.

A picturesque site was chosen in the middle of Lake Chiemsee on the island of Herreninsel. Originally home to an Augustinian monastery, Ludwig sought to exchange the religiosity of the original Baroque design for the secular opulence of the *ancien régime*. Once again, Georg von Dollman headed the enterprise, assisted by Christian Jank and Franz von Seitz, planning a second Versailles with a Hall of Mirrors even wider than the original. Although ground was broken in 1878, Ludwig would only stay in the palace once and for a few days in 1885. The rooms prepared for the king were richly appointed and filled with technological wonders (like a heated bathtub), but the majority of the castle remained an empty shell, covered by painted drops during the king's visit. This contrast was, in part, the product of Ludwig's bankrupt personal finances, caused by his lust for palatial construction.

More than even Neuschwanstein and Linderhof, the incomplete Herrenchiemsee provides the perfect metaphor for the queer, melancholy king: a gorgeous exterior, unadorned and crumbling beneath.

Two-Up, Two-Down

SHEFFIELD, ENGLAND

Helen Smith

Queer history has been dominated by the stories of the middle and upper classes. Privileged people, men in particular, have left more 'evidence' of their lives in archives, in literature, in culture and on the landscape. The power structures of an elitist and patriarchal society in Britain have ensured that it is rare for the historian to be able to access working-class queer voices, which were often silenced, or deemed unimportant. One way to correct this is through the study of criminal records.

Criminal records highlight the government's culpability in the persecution of queer people, but they can also provide the details of working-class people's lives: where they lived, what job they did, where they met sexual partners and their sexual proclivities. Similarly, the newspaper reports written to shame men who had been arrested serve the same purpose, with added details about the day-to-day of men's lives. Therefore, queer historians can subvert this material and use it to fill the silences.[15]

In 1954, a case came to court that gripped South Yorkshire.[16] Seventeen men were prosecuted for 'homosexual offences'. All the men involved were working class, and many of them worked together in local firms and steelworks. They socialised outside of work, and some even had sex on work premises. Perhaps the most unusual aspect of the case was that during a work trip to the Festival of Britain in London in 1951, a number of men had sex on the coach. The newspaper articles about this were meant to shock, but they also reveal a culture where same-sex desire was normalised, and a refusal to be cowed by the authorities.

Newspapers used the tactic of 'naming and shaming' men who had been arrested for homosexual offences, even printing their addresses. One of the men involved in the case, 'G', lived on Midhill Road, Sheffield, which was a typical road of two-up, two-down terraced houses in a working-class area.

In this way, Midhill Road became a queer space and remains so today because of G's history.

Working-class, queer domestic spaces don't carry blue or rainbow plaques.

They hide in plain sight, like many of the men who lived in them. They were ordinary houses, in ordinary streets that were often shared with families, either parents or wives and children. Because G was prosecuted for having sex with men in public spaces (like the works coach, or the local park) we can guess that he, like many working-class people at the time, didn't have much private space of his own. For every man like G who was arrested, countless others lived queer lives in streets like Midhill Road and left no trace in the historical record.

Midhill Road can stand for all the small terraced houses in provincial streets, rooms in city-centre lodging houses, suburban semis or flats that were home to generations of working-class, queer people. In doing so, it reminds us that queer history is all history, and that queer spaces are everywhere.

QUEER SPACES

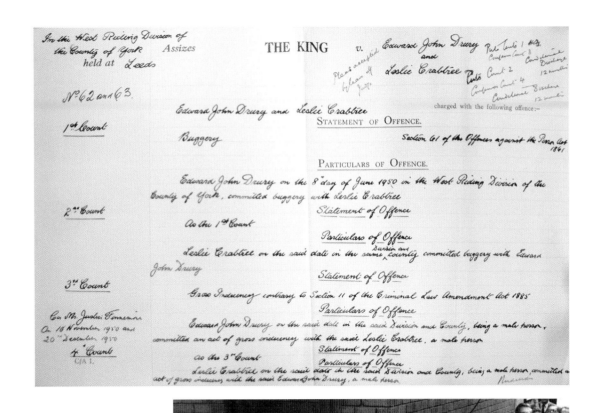

Opposite
Midhill Road, Sheffield, c 1960.

Top
Deposition file for a buggery prosecution held at the National Archives.

Bottom
A fishing trip from Jessop Saville Ltd steelworks in 1961. Note the male-only nature of the trip, which reflects the environment of the works and was the case in the 1951 trip to London.

DOMESTIC

A la Ronde

DEVON, ENGLAND

Freya Gowrley

A la Ronde, now a National Trust property, was home to first cousins Jane and Mary Parminter (1750–1811 and 1767–1849, respectively). The house is a curious, 16-sided building, apparently inspired by the octagonal form of the San Vitale basilica in Ravenna, built c 1796 by an unknown architect. The building features unusual diamond-shaped windows with red borders, and originally it was limewashed and thatched. As such, it would have evoked the fashionable rusticity of the cottage *orné*, or decorative cottage, with its current slated roof one of several major alterations completed at the behest of its only male owner, Oswald Joseph Reichel (1840–1923).[17] Beyond the unusual appearance of its exterior, A la Ronde is perhaps best known for its complex interior schemes, which were designed and executed by Jane and Mary.

The daughters of affluent merchant families, Jane and Mary became independently wealthy upon the death of their respective parents, which facilitated their prolonged period of travel and subsequent cohabitation as unmarried women at A la Ronde. Deriving its name from its 16-sided form, A la Ronde was designed to the Parminters' specifications following their return from their extensive Continental tour undertaken between around 1784 and 1791. During their travels, the Parminters accumulated a diverse collection of souvenirs, including cameos, gemstones, small-scale sculptures and prints, many of which were utilised in the cousins' craft-based projects to embellish their new home.

The cousins lived together at the house from around 1796 until Jane's death in 1811, after which Mary lived alone at the property until her own death in 1849.[18] It was during their period of cohabitation that the women ornamented the house with detailed shell-, feather- and paperwork interiors, and handcrafted furniture. These elements include A la Ronde's famous shell gallery, which comprises an evocative combination of natural found objects, including shells, feathers, lichen, glittering minerals and animal bones, supplemented with mirrored glass, paint, cut paper and pottery sourced from their local environment. Utilising materials collected from the nature that surrounded them, the Parminters transformed the detritus of the beach and countryside, reformulating it to convey their close relationship with the landscape and locale of Devon.

Mary Parminter's will is a vital source for understanding how the Parminters themselves viewed their decoration and cultivation of the homosocial space of A la Ronde.[19] Providing strict instructions for the inheritance of the house, it stipulates that only a female inheritor could claim ownership of the property, although eventually, due to the quirks of the family line, it would come under the ownership of Reichel. Entrance into marriage, making alterations and failure to maintain the house and gardens could all cause disinheritance. These explicit strictures demonstrate that the construction, decoration and projected legacy of A la Ronde was an essential aspect of the Parminters' creation of an explicitly gendered space, providing a home where feminine accomplishment could flourish, sustained and protected throughout the succeeding centuries. While homosocial living in and of itself does not necessarily constitute queer domesticity, the Parminters' self-conscious and highly deliberate rejection of a patriarchal future for their home means that it can be read in this manner. The will, therefore, invites us to consider the inheritance of the house as a form of distinctively female and queer heirlooming, both in the 18th century, and among its subsequent owners.

Above
A la Ronde, Exmouth, Devon.

Opposite, clockwise from top

View of the walls decorated with mosaic in shells, feathers and seaweed.

The drawing room.

Original shell chimneypiece in the drawing room (facing wall).

A Hijra Guru Ma's Rooftop

DHAKA, BANGLADESH

Ruhul Abdin

In South Asia, 'Hijra' is a cultural community beyond gender and sexuality, often referring to an identity category for people assigned male at birth who have a nonconforming gender identity. Hijras are part of South Asian cultural traditions and, during the last decade, they've been granted legal status in Nepal, India, Pakistan, as well as Bangladesh.

In Bangladesh's Hijra community, a Hijra Guru Ma (the mother of the house) takes on children, called 'chela', who do not identify fully as male. Often these chelas, who might be trans, intersex or gender nonconforming, have been ostracised from their biological families, or from society, but they are welcomed into a Hijra family. The Guru Ma becomes responsible for her chela and, in turn, her chela work and share their income with their Guru Ma, eat with her, respect her and follow the house rules. A successful Guru Ma will be able to support her chela, navigate the complex local political dynamics and ensure that her chela can operate in the neighbourhood without backlash. A Guru Ma will allow her chela to have their own chela; however, there is only one 'malik' (leader) of an area. For as long as the main Guru Ma is alive, she will not allow others to profit separately from their locality, even their own chela.

Most often, Hijras live in rented spaces, which may have various conditions and issues regarding accessibility. However, in the Old Town of Dhaka, there is a Hijra family which has been very successful; the Guru Ma has purchased four flats in the building and also owns the rooftops, which the Hijras use as a social and communal cooking space. The space, tiered with two rooftops, embellished and decorated with plants and trees and painted walls, is something that reflects the love and energy that has been poured into it by the Hijras to make it their own. Being safe is such a challenge in the city for the Hijra community, and this place has become a haven for them.

Despite being granted legal status, the Hijras remain a marginalised community and there are limited ways for them to earn money. Traditionally this has included giving blessings at weddings and birth ceremonies in exchange for donations, and by begging or sex work.[20] The Hijra house featured here has a unique location, in an area with a strong convergence of Muslims, Hindus and even a centuries-old Christian cemetery. There are large mosques and temples nearby, and lots of commercial activity and bazaars too, providing ample opportunity for the chelas to make money.

A Hijra home is often perceived to be a sacred space, with rituals and activities that have been associated with centuries-old South Asian Hindu cultural practices, some of which have become limited due to modernity. The kind of space they occupy is dependent on the money raised by the Hijra chela members. Above all, it should feel like it is a safe space.

In a city like Dhaka, for trans bodies and Hijra members, access to a genuine safe place is profoundly important.

Prospect Cottage

KENT, ENGLAND

Chris McCormack

To visit Derek Jarman's Prospect Cottage, along the shingle expanse of Dungeness, is to take a distinctly queer pilgrimage. This architecturally humble home was constructed by a local builder for a fishing family in 1900 before being remade by Jarman (1942–94) as a meditative outpost and, latterly, a testament to his artwork, life-filled collaborations and loves. Spotting the cottage in 1987, while on a bluebell hunt with actress Tilda Swinton, the artist purchased the place from Peggy – a woman with the voice of a male blues singer – using his father's inheritance, soon after learning he was HIV positive. His diagnosis, coming years before the activism-led medical research of the 1980s and 1990s, made long-term survival a possibility beyond hope alone.

Amid the breath-catching weather and harsh landscape of 'the Ness', Jarman's diminutive cottage feels physically overwhelmed. The blackened timber façade, one side emblazoned with John Donne's poem 'The Sun Rising' in woodcut letters, looks onto the hazy expanse of the English Channel. However, any received beatific imaginings are soon dispelled by the hulking nuclear power station which hums distantly at its rear.

Assembled from local materials, the garden brings together stone circular beds of local flora and scrub, knots of pebbles and twisted, metal forms, as if the remains of some inscrutable ritual. These rusting sentinels, swept from the beach and the declining fishing industry in the area, capture the violence of nature but also the toil of lives on the sea. To find oneself walking across these shingle pathways is to enter the place and memory of Jarman's filmmaking and painting, a landscape in which loss and desire's capacity for renewal is overlayed as one. Or, further, to recollect phrases and thoughts from his punctilious diary-keeping, as he states in one entry in *Modern Nature* (1991): 'Before I finish I intend to celebrate our corner of Paradise, the part of the garden the Lord forgot to mention.'[21]

While the sculptural forms impart an undertow of mysticism and danger to this celebration of paradise, Jarman also scanned the horizon for antidote and cure, not least by adapting historical records of healing to cultivate a landscape that is reflective of his defiant repicturing of the signs of death and disease that surrounded him in the late 1980s and early 1990s. He explained, 'I saw it as therapy and pharmacopeia.'[22]

Jarman's visions arrive as ballast against the punitive responses by the state and the media towards queer lives and, at that time, the way in which gay and bi men's lives were inextricably linked with death and disease through HIV. Rather than a retreat from society, the remote location of Prospect Cottage pushes open a space of contemplation outside the grip of oppression, where the nexus of persistent wildflower, lichen and exposed rock forms an unwritten testimony of lives clinging to the edges of the world. The wildness forges an appropriate setting for the all-too-often unspoken memories of lives lost to HIV/AIDS. As Jarman poignantly stated:

'The gardener digs in another time, without past or future, beginning or end. A time that does not cleave the day with rush hours, lunch breaks, the last bus home. As you walk in the garden you pass into this time – the moment of entering can never be remembered. Around you the landscape lies transfigured. Here is the Amen beyond the prayer.'[23]

If the cottage and garden form a signpost or totem against the normative strictures of the surrounding world, they also implicitly question the place of city habitations as the only safe home for queer lives. By uprooting these knotted histories through his life and art, Jarman hands us back a set of possibilities to be tendered, toiled and remade. As he remarked, 'My garden's boundaries are the horizon.'[24]

The securing of the cottage's future by the Art Fund preserves the legacies of Jarman's home – an outpost, a lighthouse, a place of rare lichens and wild moss.

Detail of the cottage, with John Donne's poem 'The Sun Rising' marked out in relief lettering on the timber façade (2012).

Derek Jarman outside his cottage (1988).

A view of Jarman's garden and sculptures, with Dungeness B nuclear power station in the background (2020).

Holy Trinity Church

YORK, ENGLAND

Kit Heyam

The secluded church of Holy Trinity Goodramgate, tucked away behind an easily missed gateway off one of York's busy medieval thoroughfares, witnessed a queer union long before the legalisation of same-sex marriage in the UK. Anne Lister (1791–1840), a lesbian landowner best known today for secretly recording relationships with women in coded diaries, visited Holy Trinity on Easter Sunday 1834 with Ann Walker.

Anne and Ann exchanged rings and vows privately at their home, Shibden Hall near Halifax, before taking the sacrament together at Holy Trinity: in Anne's words, this act 'solemnise[d] our promise of mutual faith.' Anne had attended school in York, and had friends in the area. As she later recorded, this was 'the first time I ever joined Miss W- in my prayers. I had prayed that our union might be happy. She had not thought of doing as much for me.'[25]

The debates over the commemoration of Anne and Ann's commitment at Holy Trinity exemplify the often contested nature of queer spaces.

In July 2018, York Civic Trust – working collaboratively with the Churches Conservation Trust (which cares for Holy Trinity) and two local queer charities, York LGBT Forum and York LGBT History Month – erected the UK's first permanent rainbow plaque at the church. Following consultation with local queer communities, the original plaque described Anne Lister as a 'gender-nonconforming entrepreneur.' This reference to gender reflected the fact that Anne was called 'Fred' by lovers and 'Gentleman Jack' by the local community, dressed in a masculine manner, referred to desire for women as 'manly feelings,' and expressed gendered discomfort when a lover 'touch[ed] my queer' (the word Lister used for genitals): 'This is womanizing me too much… she lets me see too much that she considers me too much as a woman.'[26] However, many lesbians felt that the plaque should refer explicitly to Anne as a 'lesbian,' thereby providing clear evidence of the longevity of lesbian history; while some anti-trans respondents objected to the phrase 'gender-nonconforming,' interpreting it as a marker of trans identity rather than a description of behaviour.

The plaque also described the union between Anne and Ann as 'marital commitment, without legal recognition.' This phrase was similarly controversial. While some appreciated the validation of Anne and Ann's commitment as a marriage, others felt this was inaccurate and presented their relationship as conservative rather than radical, as well as obscuring the fact that the Church of England is still legally unable to register same-sex marriages in the UK. This difference of opinion reflects broader divisions within queer communities today between those who seek to secure queer people's access to existing institutions like marriage and religion – and to celebrate the continuing reclamation of these institutions by queer people throughout history – and those who critique these institutions as inextricably implicated in systems of oppression, such as state surveillance and patriarchy.

The York Civic Trust plaque at Holy Trinity was recast in 2019: the new version describes Anne as a 'Lesbian and Diarist' who 'took sacrament' with Ann Walker.[27]

Holy Trinity remains the first queer space in the UK to be permanently marked as such with a rainbow version of a traditional blue plaque: a commemorative practice which marries assimilation into existing institutions with radical queer visibility.

Opposite, clockwise from top

Interior of Holy Trinity Church, Goodramgate.

Watercolour portrait of Anne Lister, probably by a Mrs Turner of Halifax, 1822.

Replacement rainbow plaque erected at Holy Trinity by York Civic Trust in February 2019.

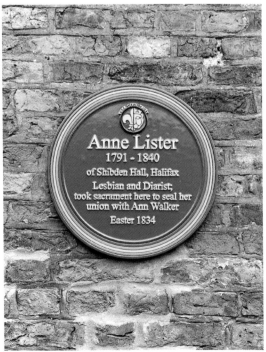

Hotel Gondolín

BUENOS AIRES, ARGENTINA

Facundo Revuelta

Hotel Gondolín is, above all, a home. But it is also a community, a shelter, an emblematic space of self-sufficiency and *travesti*-trans pride.[28] It is an expression of the collective will for a better life, for a different future. It illustrates, with its housing networks, a sum of marginal subjectivities that have been expelled by both state and society.

It is a three-storey, electric-blue building that has housed hundreds of *travestis* and trans people in search of opportunity and a roof over their heads since the early 1990s.

> It is a home that fosters an alternative definition to that which is traditionally understood as a 'family'. Here, family is chosen.

It is one that cares for, accompanies, loves and supports. In its more than two decades of existence, the Hotel Gondolín has also encouraged and supported many in their further education, broadening their possibilities in life beyond that of sex work.

Until 1999, Hotel Gondolín was a family-owned hotel near the *zona roja* (red-light district) on Godoy Cruz Street, in the Buenos Aires neighbourhood of Villa Crespo. The hotel owner saw an opportunity to sublet their rooms to the trans and *travesti* women of the area at double or triple the usual price, as a result of their having been systematically expelled from other hotels. Thus, the overcrowded and unhygienic rooms were the only option remaining for the women, who were not welcome elsewhere. After a series of orders to close down the hotel and attempts to evict the residents, the women managed to peacefully occupy the building and took charge of the space, forming a cooperative to improve living conditions in the hotel that was subsequently transformed into a collective home.

Inside, the residents refer to each other according to a sort of organisational chart with familial names, in which the oldest and most experienced acquire the affectionate titles of Aunt or Grandmother, roles that are assumed and carried out with pride. Thus, the Gondolín is a concrete exemplar in expanding the means of survival for the *travesti* community and others beyond the nuclear family, producing and spreading new social structures, capable of favouring a different and more suitable kinship system.

The Gondolín owes its popularity among the trans and *travesti* community to word of mouth. Women, mostly from the northern provinces of Argentina – which are the most deprived areas of the country, known for their Catholic and conservative mindset – arrive in Buenos Aires asking where Villa Crespo is. They go on to knock on the door of the Gondolín. Aunt Zoe, who has lived there for more than 25 years, says that her ground-floor window is knocked on on a daily basis, by new arrivals asking about available rooms. If they had an eight-storey building like the one around the corner, she says, they would have room for everyone. But for now, they only have 'el Gondo', still standing in a neighbourhood that has gone through intense gentrification over the last 10 years.

Access to housing for the *travesti*-trans community is a utopian dream in Argentina. Faced with this complex situation, and in the absence of public policies to help solve the issue, experiences such as those of the Gondolín have been able to generate housing strategies around a new kind of independent strategy, transcending the false binary of public/private, and forming intergenerational networks and alternative family structures that help deal with the problem and which go beyond traditional, individualistic models of housing. These types of experiences hold a potent and transformative political power that speaks from a perspective of difference.

Above
Cristal, one of Hotel Gondolín's historical residents, posing as the diva she was.

Opposite, clockwise from top-left

The terrace was the only open space in the Gondolín, but as they needed to expand, they had to build rooms in it.

The corridors fulfil a crucial function, not only of passage but of meeting.

Renata getting ready in one of the bedrooms, surrounded by typical teenage drawings on the walls.

The central area on the ground floor is a space of gathering, meals and parties.

The bedrooms fulfilled a meeting space function.

The old hotel office, with the portable pool on the right side and the girls ready to go out.

Villa Lysis

CAPRI, ITALY

Robert Aldrich

Few Mediterranean islands present such an alluring image of idyllic scenery and pleasurable life as Capri, a reputation that goes back to Roman times – when the island also became infamous for the drunken and orgiastic revels of the bisexual Emperor Tiberius in the first century BCE. Those reputations were revived in the early years of the 20th century, as Capri attracted new visitors searching for sun, sea and often sex in the sunny south, which retained ancient legacies, beautiful landscapes and, for those who were interested, potential erotic liaisons.

One of those was Baron Jacques d'Adelswärd-Fersen (1880–1923), a French nobleman with a fortune derived from his family's steelworks. A personality of the Belle Époque elite in Paris, he was a poet and novelist, the author of over a dozen rather overwrought works of decidedly homoerotic sentiment, including a novel about Oscar Wilde, collections of poetry with classical inspiration (*L'Hymnaire d'Adonis [Hymns to Adonis]* and *Ainsi chantait Marsyas... [Thus Sang Marsyas...]*), and ones inspired by Venice and also by Ceylon (now Sri Lanka) and China, where he had travelled. D'Adelswärd-Fersen also published 12 issues of *Akademos*, a journal with regular contributions on homosexual themes, one of the first of such 'gay' periodicals. In 1903, however, he was embroiled in a scandal for 'offences to public decency' and corruption of minors. He decided to leave France for self-exile in Italy.[29]

On Capri, d'Adelswärd-Fersen constructed a grandiose house (designed by an unknown architect) in eclectic Neoclassical, *rocaille* and Art Nouveau style that he named the Villa Lysis and dedicated to 'the youth of love'. Sited on the highest point of the island, with a marble-floored grand hall, colonnaded verandas, terraces and plunging views of the sea, the mansion bore a Latin inscription over the door: 'A shrine to love and sorrow'.

When not travelling, d'Adelswärd-Fersen lived there with his handsome Roman companion Nino Cesarini (1889–1943), a bronze statue of whom graced the garden. Cesarini was a working-class adolescent when d'Adelwärd-Fersen first met him in Rome and described in the dedication of one work as 'more beautiful than the light of Rome'. In principle, he was d'Adelswärd-Fersen's secretary – a not unusual designation at the time for a homosexual partner. They remained together until the baron's death, except during the war years, when Cesarini was a soldier and sustained battle injuries. D'Adelwärd-Fersen indulged in a sybaritic life that combined writing with elegant soirées, sexual frolics with young men and opium-smoking (an addiction picked up in Asia). On d'Adelswärd-Fersen's death, Cesarini inherited, though he later sold, rights to the property, though there are conflicting accounts of his later life. Other homosexuals followed in d'Adelswärd-Fersen's wake to Capri, including Roger Peyrefitte, whose 1959 novel *L'Exilé de Capri* (published in English in 1961 as *The Exile of Capri*) provides an evocative rendition of the baron's life in Italy. Now called the Villa Fersen, the property is open to the public, a memorial to an important but little-known gay author and editor, to a long-lasting intimate friendship between a Frenchman and an Italian, and to an everlasting perception of Mediterranean beauty and eroticism.[30]

'Miss Green', 'Ye Olde Communists' Rest' and 'Riversdale'

DORSET, ENGLAND

Jane Stevenson

After the successful novelist Sylvia Townsend Warner (1893–1978) met fellow novelist Theodore Powys in 1922, she was drawn to the village he lived in, East Chaldon, and through him met an aspirant poet, Valentine Ackland (1906–69). Since her first novel, *Lolly Willowes* (1926), had sold very well, and her second and third had also been quite successful, she decided to buy a house in East Chaldon in 1930, previously owned by a Miss Green, and asked Ackland if she would like to share it. For Warner, the principal charm of 'Miss Green' as she subsequently chose to call it, seems to have been that it was isolated, and cheap.[31] It had four rooms, a tap in the small, dark kitchen which produced a trickle of rainwater from a butt, and a privy in a hut at the end of the garden. Larger amounts of water had to be carried from a well along the street, and there was no electricity; but there were some elegant Regency furnishings: Warner wrote, 'We declared against the grated carrot, folk-pottery way of life.'[32]

Shortly after moving in together, she and Ackland became lovers; in 1930, poor, short-haired, trouser-wearing lesbians may well have felt that their happiness depended on living very discreetly. So, having let 'Miss Green', they moved to an even more isolated cottage on a bare hillside in West Chaldon, in December 1934, which was big enough to entertain in, though their water came from a rat-infested well.[33] While they continued to keep the world in general at bay, they enjoyed receiving guests of their own choosing, and nicknamed the house 'Ye Olde Communists' Rest' because it was so much visited by their London friends.[34] The house was razed to the ground in 1970 and very few photographs survive.

For both women, home-making was, fortunately, immensely important, since the amount of sheer hard work which went into making a cottage habitable in the 1930s was enormous. In 1937, Warner and Ackland left West Chaldon for a house called Riversdale (a name they did not use) in the hamlet of Frome Vauchurch, by the river Frome, on the edge of Maiden Newton. What it offered them, above all, was extreme seclusion. It was separated from town by water meadows, built along the bank of the river, and screened by trees. The approach was also very private: 'Just before the hump bridge over the Frome, the driveway wound into the garden, only later opening out to reveal the house and the view beyond.'[35]

The other great virtue of Riversdale was that it had a quarter-acre of garden, so they could grow their own vegetables. Ackland also shot rabbits and fished for trout. Warner had good years and bad years, economically, while Ackland earned very little, so near-self-sufficiency was an insurance policy against lean times. They eventually bought the house in September 1946, for £2,200.[36] At Riversdale, as at West Chaldon, they were intensely hospitable. Their many guests included composers Paul Nordoff and Benjamin Britten; Bloomsburyite David Garnett; William Maxwell, the editor of the *New Yorker*; Nancy Cunard, most formidable of the Bright Young People; and the artist Joy Finzi.

Riversdale had electricity and mains water, unlike their previous houses, which made a great difference to their quality of life, but it was heated with open fires – they were never able to afford to install central heating. Both women had the urge to accumulate possessions. Their liking for bright, clear colours and 19th-century bric-à-brac was shared by many bohemian contemporaries, such as the artists John and Myfanwy Piper. Individualists themselves, Ackland and Warner chose furniture and furnishings individually, cup by cup and glass by glass.

So, what is distinctively lesbian about this domesticity? Above all, the overriding desire for privacy, for ensuring that anyone who crosses the threshold is an invited guest. Perhaps also, the accumulation of totemic objects, symbols and souvenirs of an intensely shared life, uniquely meaningful to the two of them alone. They exchanged presents on 11 October, the anniversary of their first lovemaking, effectively their wedding, in 1930. Warner wrote in October 1972, 'This anniversary & Jan 13th [also a date associated with the consummation of their love] are unknown. Only her death-day is for the world ... the other two are mine alone.'[37] Thus they made their lives together meaningful by purely private associations, which were commemorated and confirmed by their gifts to one another, encoded representations of a love which had to be discreet, though never disavowed.

Miss Green's Cottage, West Chaldon.

Riversdale at Frome Vauchurch, photographed from the opposite bank of the river and showing corrugated iron cladding. The photograph was made into a Christmas card and inscribed, 'With love and best wishes for Christmas from Sylvia and Pericles [the cat] (who oversaw with guiding Paw)'.

Valentine Ackland with a goat, probably outside 'Ye Olde Communists' Rest' at West Chaldon.

Ackland's writing room at Riversdale.

Sylvia Townsend Warner's writing room at Riversdale, with cat on chair, possibly Pericles.

Photograph of Townsend Warner at Frome Vauchurch, inscribed on the reverse, 'Sylvia and Valentine's poodle Fougere, 1950s–60s'.

Brief

NEAR BENTOTA, SRI LANKA

Robert Aldrich

Brief, near the southern coast of Sri Lanka, was the estate of Bevis Bawa (1909–92).[38] Born into a prosperous family of mixed ethnic background, in what was then the British colony of Ceylon, Bawa, after a time as an officer in the army reserve, became aide-de-camp to several governors, a witty newspaper columnist and an esteemed landscape gardener. A *bon vivant*, he moved among an avant-garde circle of artists, designers and dancers, as well as the great-and-good of colonial and post-colonial society, and also played host and guide to foreign celebrities coming to visit an island with a reputation as a tropical paradise. Though his homosexuality was well known, and freely discussed in his memoirs, status and discretion meant that Bawa avoided censure in a country where homosexual acts remained illegal under the British colonial law code.[39]

Bawa had inherited and landscaped the two-hectare Brief estate, a former rubber plantation, filling it with terraces and stairways, rambling pathways, pools and a profusion of trees, shrubs and flowering plants. So successful was the landscaping that Bawa was commissioned to create other gardens. Some of the decorations in the house, and sculptures in the gardens, were the work of the gay Australian artist Donald Friend (1915–89). Born into a moneyed pastoralist family, Friend at various times lived in Nigeria, Britain, Italy and Bali, and he spent five years in a cottage on Bawa's property in the late 1950s and early 1960s. Handsome young men in exotic settings provided a continuing theme for Friend's work, and his voluminous and lively diaries described his travels, social life and protean sexual encounters. Brief was a meeting place for many in Ceylon's artistic elite and for foreign visitors, among them those of homosexual orientation. Among Friend's other paintings at Brief, a large mural (opposite) in the main house depicts

buildings and landscapes, a bullock-drawn carriage and street scenes, and men working and socialising. For the garden, Friend sculpted imaginative gargoyle-like figures and a life-size statue of a nude young man. Friend's lively memoirs of his stay in Ceylon spoke of his sexual encounters with estate employees and neighbours.[40]

Not far from Brief is the Lunuganga estate that belonged to Bevis Bawa's brother Geoffrey (1919–2003).[41] A Cambridge graduate who also trained as an architect, Geoffrey became an internationally renowned specialist in tropical Modernist architecture, a style he did much to create. His houses and hotels, inspired by traditional Ceylonese constructions, featured open plans, loggias and the incorporation of natural materials including trees and boulders into interior spaces. Geoffrey's gardens at Lunuganga, created in friendly rivalry with his sibling, remain a masterwork of the integration of the natural and built environment. Geoffrey was also homosexual, though more reserved about his private life than his brother.

Brief and Lunuganga bespeak the pleasures of elite life in the tropics during the years before Sri Lanka plunged into a quarter-century of civil war. They testify to the tolerance enjoyed by homosexuals in some parts of the late colonial world, and in later years, despite legal strictures. Brief attracted many in the country's cultural elite and visitors from abroad, including those of homosexual orientation, though homosexual acts were (and remain) formally illegal under the country's law code. Geoffrey's constructions, and his and his brother's gardens, live on as archetypes of innovation and ingenuity in tropical architecture and landscaping. Both are now open to visitors (who can also stay in rooms at the Lunuganga estate and visit Geoffrey Bawa's old office, now a restaurant, and house in Colombo).

Above, left
The main house at Brief, near Bentota, Sri Lanka.

Above, right
The Brief garden.

Opposite, clockwise from top

The Donald Friend mural in the main house at Brief.

The Veranda at Lunuganga, looking towards the lagoon.

Statue by Donald Friend in the grounds of Brief.

Sissinghurst Castle

KENT, ENGLAND

Jane Stevenson

The author and garden designer Vita Sackville-West (1892–1962) and her diplomat husband Harold Nicolson (1886–1968) were a devoted couple, but sex was not at the centre of their marriage, since they were both attracted to people of their own gender. They were also loving parents; and their homes expressed these contradictions. Sissinghurst Castle was a ruinous group of mostly 16th-century buildings when Vita bought it in 1930, and the restoration did not attempt to unite the fragments into a single structure. Their two sons lived in one building, the 'Priest's House', which also contained a bathroom, family dining room and kitchen. Harold and Vita had separate bedrooms in South Cottage, where Harold also had his study. Vita's study was in a different building again, on the first floor of the Tower, so intensely hers that even family members very seldom entered it – if she was needed, they shouted up to her from the bottom of the staircase. The principal Tudor range running north to south contained a 7.5m-long library, and staff quarters. This arrangement required them all to traipse across the garden several times a day, whatever the weather, and there was no family sitting room or guest room: the family was only united at mealtimes. Thus, they did not, in the ordinary sense, have a family life, but lived as individuals.[42] Vita described the ménage in her *Portrait of a Marriage*, published by her son Nigel in 1973. She brought her lovers, who included Virginia Woolf, to Sissinghurst, where she lived full time and worked on the famous garden, while Harold lived in London during the week, and tended to see his men friends there.

It was Vita who furnished the interiors in the early 1930s. The Long Library was the first, and was not a success. Harold described it as having 'the feeling of a hospital ward in some Turkish barracks',[43] and it was rarely used except for formal occasions. Her overall intention was clearly to create a new house which looked like a very old one. The furnishings were rich and eclectic; family portraits and other antiques from Vita's childhood home, Knole, were set off by plain plaster walls. She hung a verdure tapestry behind her writing desk. There were thousands of books, and dozens of old and faded oriental rugs. The furniture was mostly in dark wood, and there was a lot of it. The ensemble, once created, was allowed to age along with its owners: her son Nigel Nicolson observed, 'As the wallpaper peeled and faded and the velvet tassels slowly frayed, she would never allow them to be renewed.'[44]

Above, left
Sissinghurst Castle: the tower and four Irish yews in the courtyard.

Above, right
Harold Nicolson and Vita Sackville-West at Sissinghurst, c 1955.

Opposite
Sackville-West's writing desk, 1962.

Yannis Tsarouchis' Queer Domesticity and an Attempted Exhibition

ATHENS, GREECE

Andreas Angelidakis

I used to jerk off to Tsarouchis' paintings; he captures male beauty and homosexual desire like no other painter I know.

I later appreciated these same paintings with a greater profundity because I read Tsarouchis' biography and his books of poetic aphorisms on beauty and places. He was a kind of horny Kavafis,[45] but one who painted with the trembling hands of somebody who has moved beyond desire.

When I was asked to design the architecture for a Yannis Tsarouchis solo exhibition, I was able to put all that accumulated passion and knowledge on Tsarouchis and his works into a space. It was for me a dream project.

Tsarouchis was born in Athens in 1910, started out as a painter who made his living in theatre, went to Paris in the mid-1930s, came back, served in the military during the war in Albania, went to exile in Paris during the dictatorship in the 1970s, and died in Athens in 1989. Tsarouchis is for me a queer painter, not only because he painted hot men, but because he incorporated a flair and interest in theatricality within his paintings, which ran counter to the prevailing orthodoxy of the period, as well as mixing the contemporary with the ancient, the high with the low, the sacred with the profane, and politics with sex (for example, a painting in which a naked communist is being arrested by a uniformed military policeman, painted during the years of dictatorship in Greece). His studio became a stage where he imagined places and situations for the soldiers and workers who posed for him, mostly naked.

I began to study how to stage a Tsarouchis show by looking at the spaces he created both inside his paintings and out. The house he built for himself –

my main point of reference – and for his works has rooms entirely covered in calico, a type of canvas used by dressmakers and stage designers. With these calico-covered frames, Tsarouchis created new windows and hidden doorways, backstage storage for paintings and an endless off-white soft surface onto which to hang paintings, pin notes and photos, even just to look at how the light falls on the gently receptive surface.

By creating these calico spaces within the actual rooms, Tsarouchis turned the house into one continuous theatrical painting-stage, a salon fermé portal through which to transport his subjects into his signature lyrical reality. One could go as far as suggesting that the canvas-covered rooms in which he staged his works were Tsarouchis' version of the Modernist white exhibition space, his version of white walls, but soft, and tactile.

The first time I visited the upper floor of his house during documenta 14,[46] I wondered if I had ever been there before. I had not, but the spaces seemed familiar. I realised that I knew fragments of this place because I had seen them in so many of Tsarouchis' paintings. Suddenly all those room corners and doorways from his paintings, under which a naked communist got arrested by a fully uniformed military policeman, or a threshold where the naked spirit of Eros arrests a military policeman, came to life, as real moments within his studio, a domestic labyrinth of lustful gazes and existentialist POVs.

I began to imagine fragments of the actual real rooms in the house every time I recognised pieces of Tsarouchis' white calico-formed studio within his paintings. His drawings, scribbles and reference photos would simply be pinned on the bare walls, while his paintings were hung against the backdrop of the calico that covered the walls. Was the calico there so that he might one day completely paint his entire surroundings? Or was the white canvas simply a way to look at life as an empty page, a space of infinite possibilities?

For the exhibition design, I collected the canvas-covered room fragments that he had created and began to form an architectural vocabulary out of them, one consisting of Tsarouchis' spatial favourites: the window, the doorway and the passage, spaces that speak about longing and desire, but also a theatrical arrangement within which we experience the presence and the absence of the other. Tsarouchis worked a lot as a scenographer and costume maker for the theatre, which is a space that depends on queering to exist, and his interior harnessed a flair for the spatial gesture that created maximum poetry and effect with minimal material effort.

The Tsarouchis' fragments I collected were intended to queer the institutional appearance and proportions of standard exhibition rooms. They are designed to expose, to extend the space of experiencing art into something more domestic, coveted, perhaps even erotic, just like Tsarouchis' work and his house. Together they form rooms that are part canvas, part real wall. They form Canvas Rooms inside rooms, and outside of rooms.

Sometimes the back of a Canvas Room fragment is exposed, making a space that feels like an intimate backstage behind something more official and exposed to our gaze: a place to experience a small and lesser-known gouache, or a suite of minor pieces.

Some spaces become narrow passages hosting a series of small drawings, other spaces retain their original scale to welcome singular objects and invite moments of contemplation.

The Canvas Room partitions, when placed in the space of an institution, can negotiate the binary of the institutional vs. the domestic – like a gender that wants to be neither.

To direct my approach, I wrote this text:

A screen
becomes a wall
becomes a window
becomes a door.

At the time, in December of 2020, it seemed perfectly valid to attempt a queering of the corporate exhibition interior through the lens of Tsarouchis and his queer home, work and vision – the calico screens and walls promised a disruption of the normalised exhibition space, its queered domestication. After I handed in my proposal, I was met with almost three months' silence, and the most mysterious cold shoulder I have ever experienced with any institution I have ever worked with.[47]

Finella

CAMBRIDGE, ENGLAND

Elizabeth Darling

In May 1928, Mansfield Duval Forbes, a 39-year-old English Don at Cambridge's Clare College, leased a substantial early Victorian villa called The Yews. Over the next year, working closely with his protégé, the young Australian-born architect Raymond McGrath, the dreary, darkly painted house was transformed into the 'exhibition-piece-cum-arts-centre' that Forbes named Finella.[48] Here, he sought to bring together all those who shared his interest in modern art, architecture and technology, and to thereby promote Modernist culture in Cambridge and beyond.

Finella was also to be Forbes' home, a site where, as a gay man, he could find the freedom of expression he could not enjoy even in as homosocial an environment as Cambridge. Thus, the design drew on a theme based on Forbes' alter ego, the 10th-century Scottish queen, Finella. She, by tradition, was the inventor of glass, and lived in a glass palace topped by a copper thatched roof. She died a heroine's death, escaping capture by her enemies by plunging headlong into a waterfall. Interwoven with this narrative were allusions to Forbes' colonial childhood in Sri Lanka, his fascination with the Pictish culture of his Scottish ancestry, and his identification with Horace Walpole and William Beckford, 18th-century men of taste who were also gay. The result was a set of phantasmagorical interiors designed in the most up-to-date materials and which stood as a blueprint for a new architecture.

Visitors approached the house which, with its new pink paint and trellises, now resembled a Regency villa. Through a pair of gilt-framed glass doors they entered the hallway. At the threshold, in the manner of Sri Lankan *kolam* (decorative drawings in rice flour or powder made at the entrance to a house), Pictish motifs were inlaid into a floor made from Induroleum

(a new floor material formed from wood and asbestos powder). The hall's walls were painted with cellulose paint which dried to an iridescent finish, while the profile of its vaulted ceiling was rendered in wired glass panels backed by silver leaf, and was modelled on Walpole's Strawberry Hill Gothick. By day this was intended to invoke Finella's glass palace; at night, scintillated by the lights at floor level, it became the fatal cataract that caused her death. This led to the staircase hall, which featured a copper Plymax-clad staircase. A figure of an Indian god was placed on a newel, while a Buddha occupied a niche on the halfway landing. The whole was topped by a velarium of yellow silk that filtered a golden light into the interior. As a whole, this admixture of surprising motifs and variegated lighting evoked the atmosphere of Beckford's Fonthill Abbey (see pp 4–5).

The hall was a heady prelude to the Pinks, the main salon space. This large room could be divided by a pair of copper Plymax folding doors set within a decidedly Adam-esque architrave, another nod to the 18th century. From its French windows, visitors looked out at a fountain and statue for which McGrath designed a multicoloured lighting display to animate the water.

In this commission for the house of a queen, in Queen's Road, gathered everyone who went on to be central to avant-garde culture in Britain in the 1930s, including Wells Coates, Serge Chermayeff, Paul Nash and, on one glorious occasion, Charlotte Perriand. Visitors from more mainstream culture came too; the extent to which they understood the signifiers of Forbes' identity is unclear. Thus, Finella might be understood, in Henry Orbach's term, as a closet, in which identity 'is represented through coded gestures that sustain uncertainty'.[49]

Mårbacka

VÄRMLAND, SWEDEN

Katarina Bonnevier

In her Nobel Prize-winning books, author Selma Lagerlöf (1858–1940) created rooms, houses and landscapes; in her life she constructed a home that moved the boundaries of the possible, supporting a queer lifestyle that deviated from the laws and conventions of the time.

In 1908, Lagerlöf bought back her childhood farm Mårbacka, in Värmland, mid-west Sweden, turning the main building from a rugged log parsonage into a fashionable summer villa. She put up barns and staff housing, even a petrol station, and gave everything names from the fictional landscapes of her novels. Then, between 1919 and 1924, Mårbacka was transformed again with the help of the prestigious office of royal architect Isak Gustaf Clason. The resulting yellow-clad country residence became 'the most famous manor in Sweden and of Swedish manors the most famous in the world';[50] not simply a home but a public display. A large house, combined with land ownership, is a historically well-established symbol of power.

The main building was extended seven metres to the east and given a classicist cladding. The new look was materially wrapped around the old timber building, which was plastered in light yellow with classical ornamentation. The Karolingian model Lagerlöf commissioned was strictly symmetrical, so the asymmetry caused by the extension of Mårbacka was a headache for the architects. Eventually, an extravagant porch with five pairs of coupled columns hid the asymmetry in plan and façade. The whole thing was crowned by the emblematic manor roof, with two sloping parts delimited by a vertical waist.

The nationalistic-driven revival of the Karolingian style in early 20th-century architecture alluded to the nation's heroic past; it was the architectural expression of the Swedish warrior kings, a kind of harsh, militant masculinity reminiscent of a time when Sweden was a great power (1654–1718). It was falsely claimed as genuinely Swedish, and gave an air of historic continuity to the newly rich patrons of the middle class who did not have an ancestral history to lean on. Lagerlöf also played her part in this. But something is amiss at Mårbacka; the perfect symmetry of the classical ideal is an illusion. There is a repeated discomfort when the building is described; it is misplaced, a brag piece, even the architect reveals that he was uneasy about the project. In letters to his client, Clason partly withdrew and credited Lagerlöf with the authorship of the transformation. The family portraits in the salon are kitschy copies. It is too much; it plays on but parodies the chosen style. The master of the house does not qualify for hegemonic masculinity, lives beyond the

norms of society, loves other women and stubbornly builds to her own liking. Mårbacka resembles a drag-king, an exaggerated gender parody. Architecturally queer, it conceals its meaning beneath its cladding, passing in plain sight.

The library at Mårbacka is stretched across the upper floor. The adjacent rooms are attributed to the four women of this female-only household: Lagerlöf's bedroom, spaces of her lovers (author Sophie Elkan, and teacher and secretary Valborg Olander) and two rooms for Ellen Lundgren, the house manager. Their relationships are built into the floor plan and inscribed in the décor. The green walls, filled with books, bordered with gold, the four windows draped in jacquard silk and two crystal crowns all add to the pride of the space. The library also performs a parody on the patriarchal idea of the undisturbed space of thought, remote from the everyday of the household; something queer is going on here.

In a time and place where homosexuality was criminalised and counted as a disease, where all women were trapped in a culture of honour (an unmarried woman with her own home bordered on the shameless), these women lived surprisingly openly. With the transformation of Mårbacka, Lagerlöf refused to sit nicely in her allotted place; it is not a humble cottage suitable for a couple of spinsters, in fact she received numerous visitors, and there are plenty of clues there for the queer eye. The master of Mårbacka was a woman who loved women, who made room for a household of women; the agenda was both practical and subversive, projecting a future in Sweden where lesbian relationships no longer need to hide behind straight curtains.

Above
Portrait by pioneering photographer Lina Jonn of Selma Lagerlöf (with short hair, eyes fixing the camera), with the peace activist Matilda Widegren (sitting in front) and two anonymous people, at the time of her debut and bestseller *Gösta Berling's Saga* (1891).

Opposite, clockwise from top-left

The three illustrations here show the different 'outfits' of Mårbacka. First, as here, the old parsonage, painted by Christoffer Wahlroth (1903).

The second 'outfit': the summer villa (c 1909).

The third 'outfit': the Karolingian manor, façade drawing from the office of Isak Gustaf Clason (1924).

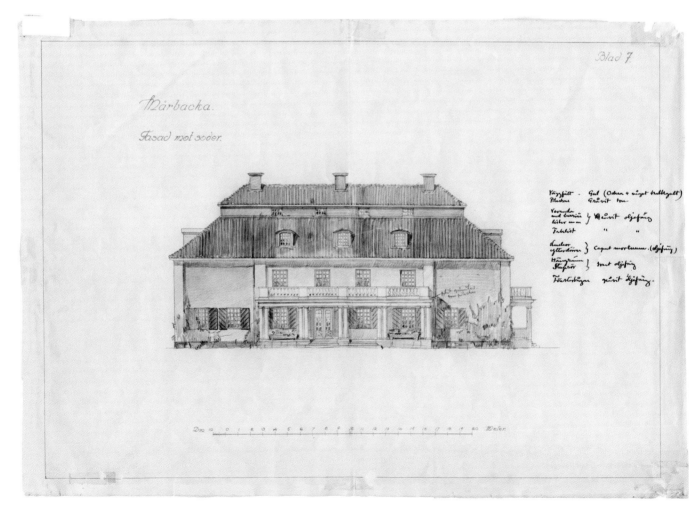

Millthorpe

SHEFFIELD, ENGLAND

Helen Smith

Edward Carpenter (1844–1929) was a pioneer of gay rights, alongside almost every liberal cause imaginable.[51] Alongside his campaigning and writing, he, and his friends and lovers, lived these beliefs and Millthorpe became the focal point of their causes.

Carpenter, who was born in Hove, struggled with his sexuality while at Cambridge, as both a student and an academic (1864–74), and could not find happiness within middle-class, metropolitan society. Instead, he moved north in 1874 with the idea that befriending working-class men and living among them would give him the happiness he craved. Extraordinarily, this gamble paid off, and he settled on Sheffield and the surrounding area as his home. Sheffield was demographically one of the most working-class cities in the country and was known for its independence from elite culture and ideas. As it turned out, this also included a pragmatic and open attitude towards same-sex desire.

Carpenter made countless working-class friends in Sheffield, and many of these also became lovers. Some were casual, but two in particular were the loves of Carpenter's life. George Hukin (1860–1917), a razor grinder in the steel industry, was a socialist who wrote beautiful, thoughtful love letters that give a rare insight into the emotions of a working-class queer man at the time.

After breaking with Hukin, Carpenter moved to Millthorpe, a lovely grey stone, slate-roofed house, just outside the city, in 1883. His goal was to live a simpler life and he shared the space with working-class friends. In 1898, George Merrill (1867–1928), his partner since 1891, moved in and they lived a life of open, queer domesticity. Merrill had been born in a slum and had had few advantages in life, but he was resourceful, charming and sexually exuberant. He took on a domestic role at Millthorpe and was a key part of life there, perhaps most famously inspiring the novelist EM Forster to write his queer classic, *Maurice*, by touching his backside.

Millthorpe became a hub of local queer life, as well as a place of pilgrimage for queer men from across Britain, and the world.

At a time when Oscar Wilde's downfall had created panic and disgust in London, Carpenter, Merrill and their working-class friends and lovers lived an open life, free from persecution.

The location of Millthorpe, and the home that they created there made this possible, as did the distinct 'live and let live' attitude of the local working classes.

Carpenter is famous for his role in queer history, but the two Georges and their counterparts are just as important.[52] While writers and intellectuals from the late 19th and early 20th centuries have left behind their books and ideas on what sexuality meant in the period, many working-class men lived their sexuality free from the angst and self-loathing of the middle classes. The story of Millthorpe and its inhabitants offers an alternative queer history that runs parallel to the more established narrative of prison sentences and oppression. It also foregrounds the experiences and desires of working-class men, and in doing so, illuminates a lost world of desire and experience.

Above
George Merrill and Edward Carpenter, c 1900–14.

Opposite, clockwise from top-left

Pencil drawing of Millthorpe, by G Hammond Steel.

Letter from George Hukin to Carpenter, 1886, reflecting his love for Carpenter and also his insecurities within the relationship.

Hukin and Carpenter, c 1900.

EDWARD CARPENTER'S
COTTAGE MILLTHORPE.

G. HAMMOND STEEL.

55 Alexandra Rd
July 8 1892

Dear Edward

I think you are right. I would rather withdraw from, than approach any nearer to you. I feel so mean and little beside you! altogether unworthy of your friendship. It is not your fault that I feel so, I know. You have always tried to put me at my ease, to make me feel at home with you. Sorry I can not come nearer to you. How I should like! — yet I feel I can't.

Lee Priory

KENT, ENGLAND

Matthew M Reeve

Lee Priory might seem an unlikely queer space. Located in Littlebourne in Kent, the house was a family home acquired by Thomas Barrett Jr (1744–1803) when his father died in 1757 and he inherited the house and its art collection. Barrett spent the years between around 1780 and his own death in 1803 rebuilding his father's home into a remarkable Neo-Gothic villa and expanding its already significant art collection. It would be remodelled by George Gilbert Scott in the 19th century and then destroyed in the middle of the 20th. It is now known principally from the fragment of the house now on display in the Victoria and Albert Museum, 'the Strawberry Room', and from parts of the house now in private collections. Although now lost, the house has been reliably reconstructed from a wealth of fabric remains, drawings and documentary evidence.

The key point of interest in Thomas Barrett and Lee Priory is that both make specific reference to Horace Walpole (1717–97), the art historian, collector, author, politician and medievalist, and to his originary Gothic villa at Strawberry Hill in Twickenham, near London, begun in 1747. During the middle of the 18th century, Walpole's homoerotic circle, which included John Chute of the Vyne, Hampshire, the poet and medievalist Thomas Gray, Dicky Bateman of Old Windsor and others, played an important role in reviving and disseminating the Gothic idiom in England, creating what Walpole, at least, understood as a 'family' of Gothic buildings in the environs of London by Walpole's close friends. In their alternate style and historicism and their fluid materiality, these buildings posed a challenge to the authority of the then-dominant Palladian idiom in 18th-century England. Built by some of the first members of the so-called 'third sex', a term used to describe the new homoerotic subjectivities that emerged in England after around 1700, these buildings were the subjects of the very first critiques in English of what we would now call a 'queer architecture'.

Thomas Barrett and Lee Priory belong to a new generation of Gothic building and patron, albeit one that looked self-consciously to the previous one. Walpole's junior by almost 30 years, Barrett sought Walpole's friendship and access to his senior queer coterie. Walpole would provide introductions to Barrett and his homoerotic circle to his cousin, Sir Horace Mann in Italy, while on the Grand Tour. Mann's home – the Casa Manetti in Florence – has been rightly called 'the nerve centre of the homoerotic Englishman's Italy'.[53] When he returned, Barrett set to redesign his family home. He was likely introduced to the leading architect James Wyatt and antiquary John Carter by Walpole, who had employed both at Strawberry Hill. Barrett would then ask Walpole to review the designs of his home, which self-consciously looked to Strawberry Hill.

The final result was Lee Priory, a remarkable essay in Gothic architecture. It not only had a dedicatory 'Strawberry Room' with a portrait of Horace Walpole above the fireplace, but it also bore metonymic signs on its furniture of strawberry leaves. Understanding these allusions, Walpole considered it 'a child of Strawberry [Hill], prettier than its parent' that was 'so flattering to me'.[54]

> From Walpole's perspective, his own 'queer family' of Barrett and others had created offspring in the built environment, and Strawberry Hill in particular – Walpole's architectural 'spouse' – had created progeny.

From Barrett's perspective, Walpole's home had become historicised – a queer space from a previous generation that connoted literary and antiquarian endeavour, elite homosociality and the projected personality of a famous man. Notably, Barrett's contemporaries connected both the style of his home and his own 'lifestyle' and even manners with that of Walpole and their mutual friend, the poet Thomas Gray. As such, we witness here a complex form of emulation by which a junior man adopts the mores of a senior man of taste. Walpole's queer affect and the style of his home were, by the later 18th century, outmoded and increasingly inconsistent with the conservatism of the years around 1800, which makes Barrett's replication of them all the more exceptional. But Walpole had established something enduring in his creation of a famous home as the simulation, or even avatar, of an alternate self which would have a lasting legacy upon later queer spaces.[55]

From Rehovot

ISRAEL

Doron von Beider

Do you remember seeing Elizabeth Welch in *The Tempest* (Derek Jarman, 1979)? She walks into a grand room singing 'Stormy Weather', wearing an outfit that could only be described as an ensemble of what the sun would look like if it came down from the skies and stepped on the face of the earth. It is the closing sequence, part of Prospero's final magical pageant, and she sings this quite gloomy song while rows of young, handsome sailors fill the air that surrounds her with pink rose petals. Though the room is opulently decorated, Welch's expressions and hand gestures redesign the space with every line from the song she sings.

Well, nothing too exciting ever happened in Rehovot of the 1990s. Not to me in any case, growing up in this safe and privileged suburb, about 20km south of Tel Aviv. The city boundaries became a sort of threshold that had a potential to be crossed in the same way Welch crosses into the pageant. I looked beyond my bedroom window and started to explore and document a comprehensive set of spaces that I could activate on my own or with others, gay spaces, in both senses of the word, that would not normally be described as queer.

The neighbourhood of Neve Sha'anan (meaning 'a peaceful oasis') in Tel Aviv is a major transportation hub, with both the new and old Tel Aviv Central Bus Stations located there. It is named after Isaiah 33:20: 'Your eyes will see Jerusalem, a peaceful abode.' I used to come and visit Leor's studio in Neve Sha'anan in the early hours of the evening. We would talk about art and share memories and stories from times we lived in different places around the world, while gazing out from the square window – this shape was the most commonly used in residential units throughout the country.

We looked towards Tel Aviv's old Central Bus Station, monitoring cars slowing down to check out the transgender girls and people in wigs standing on street corners. This area was very busy in the daytime, though the small craftsmen's studios and miscellaneous stores (that sold trinkets and practical things like springs, locks and bearings) were slowly disappearing. Above them were flats that were mostly occupied by asylum seekers from a few countries in Africa, as well as much older people who had no means of moving to a different place. The mixed-use urban grid, made of different scaled volumes, had been replaced by luxury residential towers which left many spots of dark, protected and empty parking places, away from CCTV, or prying eyes. We watched a car go into one, followed by a blond synthetic wig bought at one of the cheap costume stores in the Dizengoff Center. Later the car drove out, while the wig and lipstick were fixed using a reflection on one of the empty storefront vitrines.

Living outside of Tel Aviv meant that most encounters had to start and end with a car journey. I enjoyed the silence in the car, or enjoyed listening to music; I recorded my favourite creations on a CD and played these on repeat. One evening I had a date. We met outside that weirdly postmodern, Jerusalem stone-covered building of the Tel Aviv Cinematheque. The cinema was completely empty, just the two of us watching Almodóvar's *All About My Mother*. On the way back, while leaving the parking lot, this beautiful guy of Yemenite descent, a heritage that was apparent in his handsome face, came over to the window and asked me for a ride out of town. He said, 'I'll show you the most beautiful synagogue in Bnei Brak.'

Powerful yet functional places, socially formed by their users, can be stripped of their labels and meanings and given new ones, even momentarily. The hand-washing hall in 'the most beautiful synagogue in Bnei Brak', a Haredi city just east of Tel Aviv, was then redefined as a space for a spontaneous and satisfying encounter.

Above
It is a wonder that these rather handsome, precast, engineered, living mechanisms in Mitzpe surrendered themselves to their occupiers, who added a window and closed a balcony.

Opposite
Looking from Leor's window inspired thoughts and ideas that had a tendency to romanticise the violence of the real.

Rather than being vulgar,
the act was layered with
the religious and historical
tension of forbiddances.

Every time I came to visit Efi he would meet me downstairs, holding cups of coffee and biscuits, in the graceful way of a Shah. He lived in Mitzpe Ramon, a local council in the Negev desert. I've always been intrigued by the typical residential blocks that were scattered around there in the desert, as they are almost everywhere around the country; the blocks in Mitzpe were built to house new immigrants from Africa, Europe and India. All received a similar-sized type, no-one had an extra window, a balcony or a better view. Much of what you can define as the Israeli mentality was defined in the constant struggle to thrive in this sort of living mechanism together. Efi lived with his grandmother, mum and three older brothers in a small two-bedroom flat. It was extremely difficult as the boys were all in their 20s, rough, unemployed and bored. We would sit on the pavement in front of the block and speak until it became dark. In the hours that passed by, his brothers, his friends and neighbours, would approach with curiosity, stopping to chat with us, knowing exactly why I had come there.

It was perfectly ok for me not to come to some people's places, the same way I never wanted some people to come to mine. Anyone who lived in Jerusalem had their favourite things to do and buy from within the Old City. When I studied architecture in the Bezalel Academy of Art and Design, I had a small studio, a converted laundry room, surrounded by the huge roof terrace of a building from the 1920s, located in the city centre. I tried to get to know the city better by going for long walks, exploring it intimately.

In one of these wanderings, I became lost in the middle of this labyrinth-style urban fragment of the Old City Souq. A group of guys standing in one of the small streets asked me if I knew my way. One of them, Muhammed, said he would show me the way out and he walked with me explaining the different parts, and the reasoning behind the directions and street names, almost like sawing a path through the memories he carried for generations. As we came to Damascus Gate I was surprised when he continued walking with me, all the way to that studio on the roof, where he stayed for two weeks. I only had one key, but he didn't mind staying in the entire time; he would spend the days on the terrace reading all the books I had there, and we would talk about them in the evening as we cooked and enjoyed fantastic long dinners together. I learned that some special people were self-manifesting infrastructures of queerness; they kept bravely, or stupidly, changing the use and entire meaning of the spaces they occupied, or had access to. One day his father called him and he said he had to leave and that morning was the last time I heard, or saw him.

I've always had a love–hate relationship with any city I've lived in. I've occupied different spaces within them, mostly with no golden curtains, nor any abundance of flowers or marble. In a similar way to Welch and Jarman, I never compromised, and found that we (myself and whomever I chose) enjoyed turning spaces queer, mainly by using expressions and gestures. Thus, for brief but beautiful moments, we were completely absorbed within all of these architectural spaces that we, through our shared existence, completely transformed.

Above, left
These rooftop spaces clearly never reached their intended potential, becoming a laundry area or a solarium; the neglect has left them rather secluded and welcoming to the brave.

Above, right
A journey framed by soundscape and solitude, rephrased silence, created a scale of visuals that shifted from being clear to obscure.

Opposite
A childhood setting: meaningful and profound memories took place within architectural creations that stayed the same while everything around them changed.

COMMU

Spaces of queer community come in many different forms: wherever and whenever a number of queer people, whether multiple individuals or groups, have come together to create spaces of mingling and sharing in defiance of a world that would prefer to keep them closeted in their own private environments. Whether commercial, academic, mobile or stationary, charitable or collectively owned, these are all spaces of commonality and safety, from an artist's studio and architect's office, to a tattoo parlour, bars and nightclubs. This section highlights how queerness has always found ways of coming together and occupying, transforming and creating spaces against the odds – and with undying vim.

Former Guildford Hotel

LEEDS, ENGLAND

Kit Heyam

On the weekend of 15–17 March 1974, Leeds hosted the UK's first ever national conference on trans issues. 'Transvestism and Transsexualism in Modern Society', organised by the trans support and activist group the Beaumont Society, was held at the University of Leeds and Leeds Polytechnic (now Leeds Beckett University), and attracted trans and gender-nonconforming people from across the UK.[56]

Organised by and for trans people who were assigned male at birth (the Beaumont Society at the time excluded other trans people, though this is no longer the case), the conference was an unprecedented opportunity not just to discuss the legal and medical aspects of trans issues from an affirmative and autonomous perspective, but also to socialise. In a period before the internet, many trans people – especially those based outside of major cities – found themselves isolated in their everyday lives, and without opportunities to express their gender freely in public.[57] To that end, on the night before the conference began, the Beaumont Society organised a reception and coffee evening in the first-floor bar of the Guildford Hotel.

The reception, attended by 52 conference delegates and their friends or relatives, temporarily transformed the hotel's first floor into a queer space. Within this self-contained environment, trans women's identities were affirmed through their names and pronouns, and they were able to use the ladies' toilets freely. Even the cisgender journalist Geoffrey Winter, though he 'admitted confusion', recalled instinctively gendering the attendees correctly:

> I had reacted like a man toward women – standing up at their approach and pulling up chairs for them… and then realising and wondering why I was doing it.[58]

Like many spaces, the Guildford Hotel's queerness was ephemeral: following the departure of the Beaumont Society group, it was no longer a trans space, and its norms doubtless reverted to the misgendering and ridicule typical of the treatment of trans people in 1970s Britain (even during the reception, Winter notes that 'the cloakroom girl giggled and said that she thought she was seeing things').[59] Its queer status was also contingent on chance – the assistant manager told the *Yorkshire Post* that 'he had not realised precisely what was involved when he accepted the booking', though he 'added that he would not have turned it down even if he had known'.[60] This is an important reminder of the role of individual gatekeepers in enabling or obstructing the creation of queer spaces. But it was nonetheless crucial to the trans people, for whom it provided safety, community and affirmation in a period when these were difficult to access.

The conference which followed the reception is also a significant milestone in the history of queer people as autonomous subjects, rather than objects, of academic investigation.

'Transvestism and Transsexualism in Modern Society' – the brainchild of University of Leeds trans postgraduate student Caroline Robertson, a self-proclaimed 'radical feminist' – discussed topics including the psychology and causes of trans identities, trans people and the family, trans people's 'legal and social status' and medical transition; and took the form of not only speeches by experts, but working groups made up of the ordinary trans people who attended.[61] Alongside the academic sessions, the conference also included a disco, book stall and sales of large-sized women's shoes. The Guildford Hotel reception was a product of this trans-centred event, and the organisers' recognition that attendees travelling from across the country would both want and need a safe, trans-affirming space to socialise before the conference began.

Opposite, clockwise from top

View of the Headrow, Leeds, with the Guildford Hotel at the bottom left, and the Town Hall on the far right.

The Beaumont Society, 'Conference Report: The First National TV/TS Conference, held at Leeds 15th–17th March 1974', p 34.

Temporary rainbow plaque placed at the University of Leeds in 2018 by Leeds Civic Trust as part of a Rainbow Plaques trail for Leeds Pride, commemorating the 1974 'Transvestism and Transsexualism in Modern Society' conference.

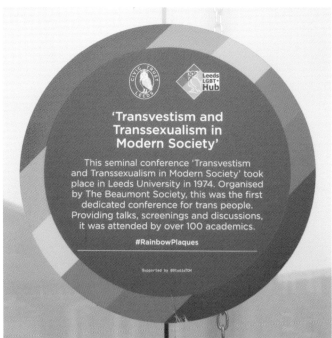

'Transvestism and Transsexualism in Modern Society'

This seminal conference 'Transvestism and Transsexualism in Modern Society' took place in Leeds University in 1974. Organised by The Beaumont Society, this was the first dedicated conference for trans people. Providing talks, screenings and discussions, it was attended by over 100 academics.

#RainbowPlaques

Supported by @StudioTOM

APPENDIX 'D'   Conference Programme (as sent to Delegates)

THE FIRST NATIONAL T.V./T.S. CONFERENCE

AT LEEDS

On 15th, 16th and 17th March, 1974

"TRANSVESTISM AND TRANSSEXUALISM IN MODERN SOCIETY".

Organised by the Leeds University T.V./T.S. Group.

Principal Speakers

Dr. Elizabeth Ferris, MB., BS.,   Mrs. C. F. Cordell,
(Gender Identity Research)   (Social Worker, Founder of ACCESS)

Miss M. E. Williams,   Miss Julia Tonner,
(Public Relations Officer,   (Transsexual Action Organisation
Beaumont Society.)   U.K. Branch.)

Admission to the Conference is FREE, but any Donations towards the costs will be gratefully accepted.

Leeds T.V./T.S. Group,
153 Woodhouse Lane,
Leeds 2.   Tel 39071 Extn. 57

=========

PROGRAMME

All times shown are approximate and may be subject to alteration.

Friday 15th March 7.30 - 10.30pm at the Guildford Hotel, Leeds.
Reception and Coffee Evening for Delegates and Friends. Licensed Bar available.

Saturday 16th March At Leeds University Union Debating Chamber.

10.15 a.m. Opening address: J. B. Willmott (Conference Secretary)
10.30 a.m. Miss Margaret Williams (P.R.O. Beaumont Society)
           "The Psychology of Transvestism and Transsexualism"
11.15 a.m. Miss Julia Tonner (T.A.O., UK Representative)
           "Fit or Misfit?" The position of the Transsexual at work and leisure
           in modern society.
12.00 - 1.00 p.m. Lunch (Available at the University Refectory)
1.00 p.m. Mrs. C. F. Cordell (Social Worker, Founder of ACCESS)
          "Know Thyself"
1.45 p.m. Dr. E. Ferris (Gender Identity Research)
          "Transvestism and Transsexualism: Their Origins and the Problems of
          coping with these conditions".
2.30 p.m. Feature Film: "The Queen"
          Behind the scenes at an American 'Drag Contest' featuring Transvestite
          and Transsexual viewpoints.
4.00 p.m. Conference Workshops
 to   The Conference will divide up into a number of Discussion Groups, each
          of which will be asked to examine some aspect of Transvestism and
5.00 p.m. Transsexualism and its impact on Family and Social life. The results
          will be presented at the Sunday morning Conference Session.
                  -: Tea Break :-
7.30 p.m. Social Evening and Disco Dance for Delegates and Conference Visitors, at
 to   the Lipman Building (adjoining Leeds University Medical School)
          Admission (on production of Conference Programme) 25p.
12.00mdnt. Lounge and Bar (Extension to 11.30 pm) Dancing to Top Discs.
                  ===========
                       34

New Sazae

TOKYO, JAPAN

Takeshi Dylan Sadachi

Established in 1966, New Sazae is a disco-fanatic's paradise in Shinjuku Nichōme, Tokyo's LGBTQ+ neighbourhood. Best described using the old-fashioned term 'gay disco', the venue is one of the oldest queer establishments in the neighbourhood and a pioneer in accepting customers of any sexuality or gender performance.

The disco bar is located discreetly on the second floor in a type of property vernacularly called a *zakkyo* building. Literally meaning 'building of coexisting miscellany', the term describes small-scale multi-tenant buildings, colloquially referring to old and non-gentrified properties that are unfastidious towards the 'quality' of the occupants.[62] *Zakkyo* buildings often attract loanshark businesses, *yakuza* offices and prostitution due to their ability to conceal their activities among more well-received businesses. It is unsurprising, then, that it was an area filled with these buildings that became the queer neighbourhood.

New Sazae was originally located in the basement but moved to the second floor of the same *zakkyo* building in 1978.[63] Despite the inconspicuous location and exterior appearance, Shion, who was the owner until his passing in 2018, has stated he experienced both undercover and open investigations by the police frequently in the 1960s and 1970s.[64]

Shinjuku was the centre of counterculture at the time, and the police were actively searching discos and bars, which were regulated under the infamous postwar 'anti-dancing' law, also known as the Businesses Affecting Public Morals Regulation Law or *fūeihō*. New Sazae often took care of runaway children reported missing, which later helped it to build a special trust with the local police.

The disco established an irreplaceable position in Shinjuku Nichōme, visited by famous figures including Yukio Mishima and Freddie Mercury.

Notwithstanding its fame, the space behind the door is not much larger than a typical Japanese single-person apartment. Nonetheless, the disco is equipped with a bar counter, DJ booth, tables and seats along the wall, with the dancefloor in the middle. The space features a mirror ball, disco lights, string lights and fake plants. On the walls, 70s-era vinyl album covers and sparkly curtains perfectly capture the dawn of freedom on the dancefloor. Mickey Mouse toys and Coca Cola merchandise used as decoration immortalise the influx of American culture during this era, a reminder that disco culture itself was part of that phenomenon.

Queer Black, Hispanic and Latinx communities in the US contributed greatly to the birth of disco, but by the time the sensation had reached Japan, the association with queer people had diminished, allowing the craze to flourish in other areas of Tokyo as well. Today, New Sazae is the last bastion of disco culture in Tokyo, as most disco bars around the city have closed down or changed their aesthetics and playlists. For the queer community in Tokyo, the club continues to hold significance, reclaiming the association of queerness with disco culture.

Above
Coca Cola merchandise and visitors' doodles on the wall at New Sazae.

Opposite, clockwise from top-left

The late owner, behind the bar, surrounded by cassettes and CDs, 2013.

The space in its entirety, with DJ booth and bar in the background.

The exterior of the *zakkyo* building, New Sazae's sign shining through darkened windows.

Mementos on a table.

Overleaf
The seating area and artificial plants.

Taormina

SICILY, ITALY

Robert Aldrich

Overlooking the Mediterranean on the eastern coast of Sicily, and the site of one of the best-preserved ancient theatres, Taormina attracted ever increasing numbers of tourists from the time of the 18th-century Grand Tour, when it drew praise from a travelling Wolfgang von Goethe. One of the most famous expatriate residents was the German homosexual Baron Wilhelm von Gloeden (1856–1931). After a year studying art history and painting (and becoming familiar with the tradition of homoeroticism in Greek art and life), he was advised by doctors to move to a warmer climate than his native Wismar, on the Baltic Sea, because of a chest ailment (likely tuberculosis). Around 1878, von Gloeden settled in Taormina, where he remained until his death, except during the First World War, when he was forced to return to Germany.[65]

Photography was von Gloeden's avocation from the 1890s, and it became his profession; photography and the developing of film provided funds and fame. His many black-and-white pictures of Sicily were widely reproduced in magazines such as *National Geographic* and sold as picture postcards – a new and popular genre in the late 19th century. These images showed a picturesque town with old buildings and 'typical' peasants, conforming to bucolic stereotypes of rural Italy. Von Gloeden is now better known, however, for a large corpus of homoerotic photographs that portray generally nude or semi-nude young men (though sometimes they are posed in mock classical costumes). Some of the views of youths pictured singly or together, their genitalia prominent, insinuate sexual availability or connection; in classical architecture and mythology, this was a coded language, a way for homosexuals to hide in plain sight. The pictures, most of which would have been branded pornographic at the time and for long afterwards, though they now appear rather camp and voyeuristic, accorded with 19th-century Romantic notions of Italian life and the homosexual legacy of Antiquity in the Mediterranean. They both titillated and provided a noble Mediterranean antecedency to still reprobate desires.

Homosexual acts were not criminalised in Italy, and von Gloeden appears to have lived happily in Taormina, recruiting local youths as models. He paid a share of his earnings from photographs to the models and set up several in business, a largesse no doubt welcomed in poverty-stricken Sicily. Though exact details are lacking, he enjoyed sexual relations with some of the models, and he had a long-term relationship with Pancrazio Buciuni ('Il Moro', 1879–1963). Von Gloeden's work – scenic photographs and no doubt erotic ones as well – attracted visitors to Taormina, ranging from Oscar Wilde to members of royal houses and film stars. Around the 1980s, he was rediscovered as a leading early photographer of male nudes, the subject of several exhibitions and catalogues. Reissues of his images were also sold as postcards in the tourist shops of Taormina.

Von Gloeden lived in a house near the church of San Domenico, though the building is no longer standing, and there remain few material traces of him in Taormina other than a simple grave – marked by a cross with a photographic portrait medallion – in the local cemetery, where his faithful companion, Il Moro, is also buried. Casa Cusini, the villa of another homosexual expatriate and a friend of von Gloeden, the British landscape painter Robert Hawthorn Kitson (1873–1947), is a historic house museum in Taormina; von Gloeden's work inspired frescoes in the dining room.[66] Von Gloeden's photographs, with the backdrop of Mount Etna, terraces overlooking the sea and provincial architecture, as well as comely young men, recall the seduction exercised by the classical and modern Mediterranean on generations of homosexuals.

Taormina — Mandorli in fiori   N.º 133

Above, left and opposite:

Wilhelm von Gloeden

'Flowering Almonds',
c 1890–1914.

Greek theatre in Taormina,
1890s.

'Two Male Youths Holding
Palm Fronds', c 1895.

Vespasiana

BARCELONA, CATALONIA, SPAIN

Ailo Ribas

It was eight in the morning. There were around 30 fags under the rising sun. I watched them pass and accompanied them at a distance. I knew my place was in their midst, not because I was one of them, but because their shrill voices, their cries, their exaggerated gestures had no other purpose, in my opinion, than to pierce the thick contempt of the world.

– Author's translation from Jean Genet, *Diari del Lladre* [*The Thief's Journey*] (1993)

In 1933 a ragbag of effeminate queers, *transformistes*, trans people and sex workers – denizens of Barcelona's underbelly, *el barri xino* – led a funeral procession down the wide, tree-lined boulevard La Rambla mourning the death of a public urinal (*vespasiana*) obliterated by an anarchist bomb. This is one of the earliest recorded trans protests. Observing this march, the French writer and activist Jean Genet – who at the time was hustling his way through these very streets – described it as follows: 'The *Carolines* were magnificent: they were the Daughters of Shame. Arriving at the port, they veered right towards the barracks and on the rusted, pungent iron of the public urinal, on the heap of dead metal, they laid their flowers.'[67]

Genet was known for his proclivity for fanciful embellishment. These sentences, being the only known record of the march of the *Carolines*, and the only recorded use of their name, ask us to reassess the fine line between fiction and truth.

On 1 May 1890, almost half a century prior, the first International Workers Day demonstrations in Barcelona took place, in the district that later became known as *el barri xino*. The meeting place for the local demonstration was in a clearing known as *el Camp de les Carolines*. This colloquial name supposedly persisted among locals even after the area's urbanisation in 1894–95, and may explain the attribution of the name 'the *Carolines*' to the queers and sex workers who years later came to frequent it. Curiously, local historians have also postulated that the route taken by the *Carolines* in 1933 roughly followed that of the striking workers in 1890.[68] Irrespective of whether this is true, the parallels between these histories inspire the tracing of connections between two separate yet undeniably overlapping groups vying for survival in a highly contested and rapidly urbanising landscape.

Mounting animosity between revolting workers – aligned in many cases with antimilitary, anarchist and anticolonial revolutionaries – and the Spanish state led to over a hundred bombs being detonated in a 15-year period, culminating with *la setmana tràgica* (the Tragic Week) of 1909. *La setmana tràgica* saw anarchists, republicans and socialists violently clash with the Spanish military all across Catalunya, protesting unfair, classist military conscription.

Vespasianes, at once acutely public and sheltered from the public eye, constituted the ideal site for both the disposal of anarchist explosive devices and the solicitation of homosexual encounters. Renowned for both activities – and thus avoided by many – these public urinals are the physical embodiment of the tensions, commonalities and converging needs of both groups. Despite their common struggle as outsiders who, at different times, had called *el barri xino* home, the fervent homophobia and whorephobia of the anarchists was enough to drive them apart. Using the criminalisation of prostitution as justification, the anarchists, under the leadership of the Federació Anarquista Ibèrica (FAI) in 1936, applauded punitive measures against homosexuals, trans people and sex workers and prohibited performances of *transformistes*, ultimately closing countless venues that such individuals called home.[69]

Whether the ill-fated *vespasiana* was thus merely an easy, accidental or special target for the anarchists during their nationwide insurrection in January 1933 is of little importance. We will never know for sure whether the acrid, piss-corroded and twisted remains of their beloved sanctuary, to which they made their final pilgrimage, were ever more than words on a page. But at the end of the day, whether these histories are true or not is unimportant. What matters is what these stories represent, and how we use them. The *Carolines* – Daughters of Shame, mythical precursors of the queer sex worker revolutionaries to come – serve to illuminate the ephemeral nature of marginalised histories; those that have survived by being swallowed, gestated and coughed up by so many before us; those that bring into question the boundaries between truth and fiction. They serve to remind us that fiction is not truth's opposite, but rather one of the many languages through which we savour, question and communicate our lived realities, and one of the countless threads from which we collectively weave our futures.

Factory Nightclub

ATHENS, GREECE

Andreas Angelidakis

My first ever commission as a young architect was a complete failure because I was fired and never paid, but the space I devised eventually ended up hosting what was, in my opinion, the most fabulous queer club Athens has ever seen.

The club I am talking about is Factory, and the story goes like this: I graduated top of the class in 1992 at the original OTT school of architecture, the deconstructivist Gehry skatepark the Southern California Institute of Architecture (SCI-Arc) in Santa Monica. I arrived back in Athens, and the top PR of the moment, Angelo Droulias, got me the job of designing a club for the local nightclub Mafia. They showed me a kebab shop behind Omonia Square, the city's queerest public space. Omonia has been home to the city's most decadent characters since the 1950s, as famously depicted in the paintings of Yannis Tsarouchis (see pp 38–9).

I treated the kebab place like some kind of urban-forensic drag-queen remake-renovation. I made no drawings and proposed as little architecture as possible, but made sure that everything was very, very fabulous. I had the workers paint the place silver and black, including all the old kebab machinery, benches etc. I added some bubbly furniture from a failed club project by the same owners, and had them upholstered in silver and fluorescent pink leatherette. The club featured an entire basement, which I suggested would make a great space for a sex dungeon. This was 1992, and you could still die of AIDS.

The owner left me in there with a team of builders, and after three weeks I'd transformed the place. Once it was all done, he came back, and he absolutely hated it all.

I tried explaining that the minimal gestures we'd created there, the sporty bondage touches and the silver spray paint everywhere, resulted in a space that spoke about its past, yet looked to the future. It was perfect for an underground gay club. They never contacted me again, or paid me.

A year later, sun-soaked and high on E in Mykonos, I met Gregory Vallianatos, the notorious HIV activist and politician, and the fabulous and hot Alkis Efthimiades, fresh from fashion and Milan, who told me that the Factory club night, the first openly hedonistic gay club night in Athens, was looking for a permanent home. I put Alkis in touch with the Mafia who had hated my project so much, and lo-and-behold Factory found it perfect, moved in, and the space became Athens' coolest gay club for several spectacular months.

It was the ultimate success, a kind of grungy Studio 54 where every walk of life was manifest.

The gays, the socialites, the sex workers, the horny migrants and leftover soldiers who frequented the little streets behind Omonia Square, now all converged on the Factory.

The club only lasted a few months before politicians imposed strict night-time curfews on nightclubs. The Papathemelis (Minister for Public Order, 1993–95) Curfew, aka the law that forced clubs to close by midnight, resulted in perhaps the first of the big street riots in Athens. It was not violent, but it was loud and provocative, with sexy, angry, naked gogo boys dancing on police cars, and powerful mobile sound systems allegedly pumping Snap!'s iconic 'Rhythm is a Dancer' into the side streets of Omonia, while furiously flaming transgender street girls fought imaginary vogue battles with the dumbfounded police, who did not know how to react to this queer riot, because it was actually a party.[70]

Opposite, top
Factory began as the first openly hedonistic club in Athens. Pictured on the left, Gregory Vallianatos (activist and Factory co-founder) prompts the crowd to party with his ubiquitous whistle.

Opposite, bottom
Beyond the gays, Factory drew Athens' motley crew of fashion people, proto-queer club kids and anybody willing to try.

The Black Lesbian and Gay Centre

LONDON, ENGLAND

Veronica McKenzie

The achievement of a physical centre for the Black Lesbian and Gay Centre was not the starting point, but the triumphant culmination of years of activism and community building. The Black Lesbian and Gay group was an important development in the establishment of a black queer community in the UK. The Friday-evening meetings, which started in 1981, provided a safe space, and became a lifeline for myself and many others. I was privileged to learn from this diverse, beautiful and sometimes raucous group of people – a support network who shared my culture and experiences – and to feel part of a movement, empowered to tread my own path in life. A subcommittee set up to find a space which could be used full time had secured funding from the Greater London Council, and in 1985 the Black Lesbian and Gay Centre (BLGC) project moved into an office in Tottenham from which to base their search for a centre.

Hindered by discriminatory landlords, and the loss of funding, the search was long and drawn out. Despite these obstacles, the BLGC's contribution to the fight for LGBTQIA+ equality was notable. They formed coalitions with unions, and community groups, rallying thousands to protest against the rise in anti-gay sentiments, notably on the 'Smash the Backlash' march in Tottenham in 1987 – organised by Positive Images and Haringey Black Action, it was the first demonstration in the UK to highlight the existence of black lesbians and gay men. Some 3,500 people took part.

The BLGC also campaigned against negative portrayals of Black LGBTQIA+ people as part of the Black Lesbians and Gays Against Homophobia in the Media campaign (1990), in conferences such as 'Black Lesbians and Gays in the Community' (1987) and through literature such as 'Shot By Both Sides' (1995), in conjunction with the Lesbian and Gay Employment Rights (LAGER) charity.

These efforts contributed significantly to the empowerment of the Black LGBTQIA+ identity.

In 1992 the centre finally secured a permanent home in a converted railway arch in Peckham Rye, establishing the first black lesbian and gay centre in Europe – possibly the world. However, by then the political climate, and challenges of securing funding, made it difficult to maintain the space. One councillor even stated that he would fund a black lesbian and gay centre 'over his dead body', as Anne Hayfield recalled in my documentary film on the centre, titled *Under Your Nose* (2014).

The centre closed in 1999, moving to a small volunteer-run office. When that closed, a volunteer moved the helpline into their home, where the phone continued to ring for several years afterwards. The BLGC fostered many life-affirming friendships and relationships, underpinned by the belief in a society that could be truly equal for all.

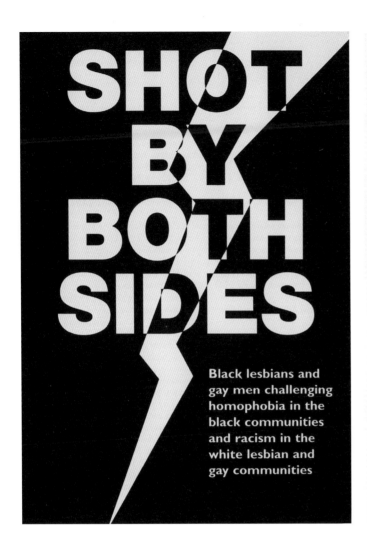

SHOT BY BOTH SIDES

Black lesbians and
gay men challenging
homophobia in the
black communities
and racism in the
white lesbian and
gay communities

**Black Lesbian
& Gay Centre**

BM Box 4390   071-732 3886 (office)
London WC1N 3XX 071-837 5364 (helpline)
Newsletter: August/September 1992

MOVE TO CENTRE

The formerly office-based Black Lesbian and Gay Centre project has moved to a centre in Peckham, South London.

For years BLGC has been searching for a suitable building from which to expand the services it offers. Earlier this year it at last found a centre space - a railway arch in fairly good condition at a reasonable rent. At the time, the project was crammed into two small rooms in Tottenham, North London.

The move took place at the beginning of August. It will now be easier for members to make use of the library and other resources, and for staff and volunteers to get together at the new premises.

The centre, the first of its kind in Britain, still needs more furniture, equipment and building work to make it accessible and welcoming. It is due to open around the end of the year.

The new Black Lesbian and Gay Centre

Clockwise, from top left

'Shot By Both Sides' pamphlet, produced in conjunction with the Lesbian and Gay Employment Rights (LAGER) charity (c 1995), written by Anne Hayfield.

The BLGC project newsletter, August/September 1992.

Staff and volunteers meet at the BLGC in Bellenden Road, Peckham Rye, c 1993.

Alan Buchsbaum's Apartment/Office

NEW YORK, USA

Ivan L Munuera

In 1976, architect Alan Buchsbaum, together with his friends Robert Morris and Rosalind Krauss, whose loft he later designed, purchased an industrial building on 12 Greene Street in New York City's Soho neighbourhood. Morris and Krauss each occupied their respective upper floors, while Buchsbaum occupied the first two levels. The architect used the ground floor as his office space and the first floor as his apartment, which included an open mezzanine overlooking the former. For Buchsbaum, the two floors were a laboratory in which he could experiment with architectural ideas, a repository of his interests – both in design and otherwise. From the very beginning up until his last plans for the space, Buchsbaum used industrial-grade ceramic tiles, soon to become his trademark material, to clad the corridor, bathroom, kitchen and even his bed platform. A variety of tiles was specified in every plan, drawing and draft of this project, in both his apartment and his office space,[71] and in colours ranging from oyster white to olive green, turquoise blue and shiny black.[72]

The central element of Buchsbaum's renovation was the bathtub, which had the shape of a splash and was positioned at the very end of the ground floor, surrounded by the exuberant tropical garden in the loft's greenhouse. In his original plans for the office, he stipulated that the tub be placed in the 'employees' lounge',[73] a space that staff used for lunches and breaks – a communal gathering place that was far from private. As Buchsbaum once pointed out, 'If you're friendly enough to live with somebody, then it's not too far-fetched to bathe in front of them'.[74] The location of the tub, which made it the real protagonist of the office space and was intended to shock clients and visitors, was not only a cocky gesture, but in combination with the tile-cladding, paid homage to the gay bathhouses of New York as social centres.

At the time, men-only spaces for dancing were still illegal, and New York legislation required clubs to have at least one woman for every three men. Bathhouses, guised as health or cultural facilities, provided gay men with an escape from constant police scrutiny and rampant homophobic attacks by serving as a space where they could meet openly. Diverse in their spatial organisations, the city's bathhouses all shared one distinctive architectural element: ceramic tiles. They were commonly employed because they were affordable; easy to find, maintain and replace; and industrially manufactured in a variety of models, which allowed for specific and customised applications. Their clinical and shiny surfaces rejected the past and snubbed the possibility of stains or marks (or at least making them easier to erase), promising another world and another future.

As early as 1901, tiles were used in the city's public restrooms and subway stations, since they could be easily sanitised.[75] Both spaces, especially the restrooms, were known to be areas for cruising and were essential for the configuration of the gay community that was taking shape at the beginning of the 1970s. No other architect used tiles as much as Buchsbaum, who stated: 'Design is coming out of the closet if you like, or rather opening the closet door and revealing the contents'.[76] Upon opening these closet doors, a river of tiles flowed out and connected bathhouses and cruising spaces to the interior renovations Buchsbaum designed with his firm, Design Coalition. Even though tiles were highly used in the decades to come as a 'postmodern' ubiquitous element, Buchsbaum employed them in his designs, acknowledging their queer history.

More than any other of his projects, his own apartment and office explored the many possibilities of the material. The clandestine and hidden atmosphere of cruising spaces was mimicked by the serpentine glass block wall that divided Buchsbaum's bed and bathroom from a service corridor, which was backlit by airport blue-lights recessed into the floor and designed by Paul Marantz.[77] The effect created shadows on the glass divider when people walked by, reminiscent of the sneaky views in saunas. The use of tiles, glass blocks and industrial lighting systems re-signified the materiality of these elements, invoking a complete urbanism, as did other elements included in Buchsbaum's design, like metro shelving, Russell & Stoll lamps, Edison Price voltage tracks and Mercury Circle line fluorescent lights.[78] Buchsbaum employed tiles not only for their evocations of furtive and sexually charged spaces but also as their part of a wider social recomposition through materiality, and to pay homage to the queer New York City urbanism of the 1970s.[79]

Opposite, clockwise from top-left

The clandestine and hidden atmosphere of cruising spaces mimicked by the serpentine glass block wall that divided Buchsbaum's bed and bathroom from a service corridor, flowing into a river of tiles.

Queering the office space: a splash in Buchsbaum's greenhouse.

Buchsbaum conceived his own loft and office space as a laboratory in which he could experiment with architectural ideas.

BUCHSBAUM LOFT 1
THIRD FLOOR

BUCHSBAUM LOFT 2
MEZZANINE, FIRST FLOOR

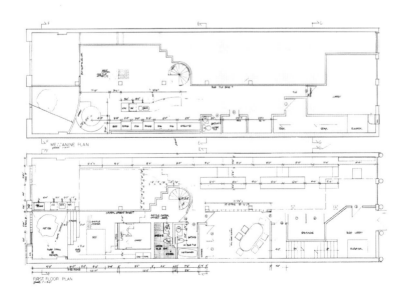

Theatron

BOGOTÁ, COLOMBIA

León Daniel

Up until the 1980s, homosexuality was illegal in Colombia – all gay bars and places for the LGBTQ+ community were informal and clandestine; all users had to adapt and make-do with low security and precarious conditions.

In 2002 Edison Ramirez opened 'Theatron', the most successful nightclub in Colombia's recent years. It was opened with the intention of providing the LGBTQ+ population of Bogotá with a space worthy of diversity, amusement, socialisation and 'rumba' (a popular Colombian term used for 'partying'). Through his own intuition, and ideas he gathered from venues in other countries, Ramirez envisioned a building with its own unique architectural style, conveying a distinct sense of personality to the space. After a long period of location scouting, he found the Teatro Riviera, a 1,000-seat theatre whose golden days had been in the 1960s, and which had functioned in its later years as a porno cinema and then an evangelical church.

Ramirez began by adapting the theatre's lobby into the main venue space, an initial exercise that quickly became a success, and from where parties began incrementally expanding into other areas of the building. Each subsequently transformed space acquired an atmosphere and theme of its own.

All visitors can now freely navigate between the 13 spaces that have been transformed, and which constantly change and adapt depending on the queer public's changing tastes.

Theatron's main space is that of a theatre – this high-volume, free-of-columns area provides perfect acoustic conditions that are ideal for the enjoyment of music. The viewing platforms are vertically stacked, protruding forwards to the stage, and the dancing space is organised on different levels, with the party being visible from all points in the hall. The theatre stage serves its original purpose, hosting some of the best shows at an international level, including drag queen performances, strippers, live music and DJ sets.

Theatron picks up the theme of Mexico City's gay neighbourhood, the 'Zona Rosa' (pink zone), for one of its most iconic and original spaces, the 'Plaza Rosa'. This space is located on the rooftop of the building. It is an open terrace surrounded by themed bar-façades, creating an atmosphere in which the partygoers feel as if they are partying on the street. This can be read as representing the desire to live in and enjoy public spaces in a manner free from aggression and violence, something which is hard to achieve for an LGBTQ+ person in the streets of Bogotá.

Theatron's success has been such that it even began expanding into surrounding buildings, by creating holes in walls between different properties. It now occupies the whole block.

It currently has a capacity of 7,500 people per night, in over 10,000m² of space. Beyond spaces for partying, the complex now houses resting spaces, a sex shop, exclusive clubs for women, and a restaurant.

Theatron also participates in and hosts social events with the ambition of and focus on fighting discrimination towards sexual minorities. It does this by offering its facilities and logistical systems to organisers and groups. The effect of this space on the city area has been such that it has helped in the formation of a gay neighbourhood; apartments for rent in the neighbourhood were not leased to queer people only a few years ago, while nowadays this very area is almost exclusively lived in by people of the LGBTQ+ community.

There are security patrols at night, organised and coordinated by the Theatron's administration, so that local queer residents can live in complete safety.

Theatron is a great example of appropriation, reuse and redefinition of a place by and for the queer community.

Above
Reuse of the Teatro Riviera seats for the first bar, in 2002.

Opposite, clockwise from top

A tunnel that connects two buildings from the inside is made by thousands of tiny mirrors, referencing the texture of a disco ball.

View from the Plaza Rosa – street food is sold in the space and there is even a stage for outdoor shows.

The main room in 2020 – the DJs are located in the former projection booth, from where they control the music, lighting and ambient form.

The main room in 2002 – at this time the area with the seats was used for resting and for some sexual activities.

The Cave of Harmony

LONDON, ENGLAND

Elizabeth Darling

In the late 1910s and 1920s, Fitzrovia became a significant site for the formation of queer identities in London.

Here women and men subverted the conventions and expectations of their Edwardian upbringings to create new ways of living and being.

As they made homes in the bedsitting rooms of Fitzroy Street and Charlotte Street, and socialised in cafés and clubs, they created a community in which they could feel 'at home' in both public and private space.

A defining characteristic of queer space is its deformation, subversion and appropriation of space. In a world hostile both socially and spatially to those who defied norms, adapting existing buildings and interiors (sometimes permanently, more often fleetingly) was a quintessential activity. This can be seen at the Cave of Harmony, which became an important gathering place for the queer community of Fitzrovia (and beyond) in the 1920s. It was founded as a cabaret club by the actress and dancer Elsa Lanchester (1902–86), the actor Harold Scott (1891–1964) and the journalist Matthew Norgate. Its name was suggested by the writer Sylvia Townsend Warner (1893–1978) (see pp 32–3), and it enjoyed a peripatetic existence in its short lifetime, occupying three different sites in about eight years.

The founders of the Cave worked continuously to subvert norms. At 107 Charlotte Street, they turned a military drill hall into the site of their 'select evenings', while at Great Earl Street, Seven Dials, they occupied a former public house. At 84 Chenies Mews, the appropriation was more thoroughgoing. Built within a small studio that occupied the space between the large house on Gower Street and its stable block, Lanchester installed both her club and herself: a balcony-loft was built, reached by a ladder, which served as her home. With pink-painted walls, yellow woodwork, red velvet curtains across a small stage and a refreshment stall (decorated and run by the painter John Armstrong) the Cave was ready to host its guests.

Members, who paid £3 a year (half the cost of the actor Hermione Baddeley's and her aristocrat husband David Tennant's Gargoyle Club in Dean Street), entered a club that, like the spaces that housed it, self consciously contested the conventions of entertainment. Neither formal theatre nor a nightclub, the Cave offered a bohemian hybrid of dancing, music, refreshments and performance. The latter varied between the arch and camp and the avant-garde. A typical evening might comprise Lanchester performing, with immense solemnity, Victorian music hall songs followed by her skit with Angela Baddeley (later Mrs Bridges in the TV series 'Upstairs Downstairs'[80]), of Mrs Brickets and Mrs Du Barry, two charwomen letting off steam after a morning's work. Or Lanchester, drawing on her training in avant-garde dance with Isadora Duncan, might perform a dance based on the casework of the sexologist Krafft-Ebing. The short plays could be amusing (Evelyn Waugh recalled 'a highly indecent but very incoherent 17th-century Italian comedy'[81]) or deeply serious (Pirandello and Chekhov). Performers included the actor Raymond Massey and director James Whale (who later cast Lanchester as the eponymous heroine in his film the *Bride of Frankenstein* (1935). Performances over, dancing to the in-house band then followed; all fuelled by 'Russian Tea' (vodka) dispensed from a samovar.

No wonder, then, that this hybrid liminal space attracted an audience which ranged from an older generation of progressives – the writers HG Wells, Arnold Bennett and the economist Maynard Keynes – to younger radicals: the actor Tallulah Bankhead, the painters Dora Carrington and Robert Medley, the architect Wells Coates, dancers Anton Dolin and Rupert Doone, and writers Aldous Huxley, Osbert Sitwell and the brothers Alec and Evelyn Waugh.

Safe within the Cave, they could find others who shared their desire to challenge convention and to live and create differently.

THE COFFEE - STALL PRESIDED OVER BY AN ARTIST "BARMAN": MISS ELSA LANCHESTER AND MR. JOHN ARMSTRONG AT THE "SELECT EVENINGS" CLUB.

APPEARING AT THE NEW CAVE OF HARMONY CABARET: MISS ELSA LANCHESTER AND HER EXPRESSIVE HANDS.

Miss Elsa Lanchester is one of the cleverest of our revue artists, and much interest was roused by the recent re-opening of the Cave of Harmony Cabaret in the disused Grapes Inn in Seven Dials. The premises have been cleverly arranged, food being served in the old vaults, while a dancing floor is situated above, and a cabaret theatre on the top floor. Miss Elsa Lanchester is associated with

Mr. Harold Scott and Mr. Mathew Norgate, the secretary of the Stage Society, in this venture, and the two former are the principal artists in the entertainment. Miss Lanchester gives a number of songs, including some of Maurice Chevalier's numbers. She sings in French, and gives an admirable rendering of "Savez-vous planter les choux ?" and other songs.

THE PRESIDING GENIUS AT THE NEW SEVEN DIALS CAVE OF HARMONY.

Photographs by Gregory Bernard.

Haven for Artists

BEIRUT, LEBANON

Nour Hamade

The Arab world has in recent years had a reputation for restricting and censoring certain cultural forms. Here the 'repressed sex' (prohibition, censorship and denial exercised through power and legislation within society in which, initially, cisgender homosexual men were described as the third sex) does not officially exist, and the concept of queerness is suppressed. Taboo and silence have contributed to a stifling and restrictive environment which queer people in the Middle East are forced to navigate.

Queer existence in Lebanon is somewhat ambiguous. In Article 534 of the Lebanese Penal Code, a relic of the French Mandate, 'homosexual activity' is included in a list of illegal 'sexual acts that go against nature'. The associated punishment is imprisonment of up to one year. From Lebanon's independence in 1943 all the way through to 2017, the laws around same-sex activity remained highly prohibitive. In 2017, Judge Rabih Maalouf ruled that 'homosexuality is a personal choice and should not be a punishable offence',[82] referencing Article 183 of the nation's criminal code, but the change in legalisation has not yet been enforced in the constitution as the country faces issues that are affecting a larger majority of the population, hence progress for 'minorities' has firmly taken a back seat.

Although the subject of same-sex desire remains a fragile topic in the public sphere, 'underground' queer spaces have been created regardless, and are now scattered around the fragmented city of Beirut. 'Haven for Artists' serves as an example of such a space, a local NGO, created by artists, that acts as a community hub for the arts. It aims to endorse, encourage and celebrate the contemporary 'underground' art scene in Lebanon and the wider region. Haven is the centre of a network that brings together a variety of local and MENA (Middle East and North Africa) artists, with the intention of facilitating creative collaborations and developing a strong community of diverse people and practitioners. The organisation runs a multitude of programmes and activities, including gatherings, exhibitions, events, the Haven House workshops and an innovative artist-in-residency programme.

The residency spaces house four artists at a given time (before the 2020 ammonium nitrate blast and Covid-19); local, regional and international artists apply to pursue specific creative projects that challenge conventional art. There are no taboos, and non-binary modes of creating (methods of making that use atypical points of references, and which eschew traditional rules) are welcomed and supported. A platform has been created where emerging artists can express their artistic beliefs, amplify their activism and cultivate their identities. The physical space, an early 20th-century traditional Beiruti house tucked between the narrow streets of Gemmayze (a place of heritage and migration), enables the community to appear – above ground – and foster a context in which discussions on identity, sexuality, sex, love and being 'other' can take place without risk; discussions that are all too often not possible in the domestic, familial or public sphere for the individual queer body in the region.

Beirut has been destroyed and rebuilt seven times, and since the 2020 explosion the city is in urgent need of new political and social energy; Beirut needs to be rebuilt again.

Spaces like Haven represent what the future of the city and its society could look like – a new paradigm of openness, equal rights and creative freedom.

Ultimately, queer space cannot be created or designed simply as a safe space; to be effective on wider society it must be, like Haven, a space of activism and inclusion; a genuine cultural generator of profound change.

Above
Collective Discussion Zone: debates, conversations and support between queer individuals is empowered at Haven for Artists, an inclusive space for 'others'.

Opposite, top
Mirella Salamé, a performance art piece in the group show 'Radical: Choix et Conséquences' curated by Haven for Artists, French Institute Beirut, 2017.

Opposite, bottom
Explicit Expression: underground art expression is open for the public at Haven for Artists, challenging the notion of what can be expressed in an often conservative cultural context.

XX XX, Elephant Party

MAKATI CITY, PHILIPPINES

Isola Tong

I hold the local club scene and the community that surrounds it very, very close to my heart. It is in the Elephant Party where I was exposed to radical flamboyance – drag and many queer expressions of gender; through fashion, hair and make-up, and most importantly dance. The dancefloor of ambiguous beauty is a passageway of nothing staid, and observing this allows me to realise that my own ambiguous identity and expression is dancing its way to somewhere else. But another thing I found incredibly important on that dancefloor and sharing the club scene will always be the friendships between queer individuals.

– Celeste Lapida

Elephant is an underground queer party in the XX XX club which typically opens every Thursday night. It attracts eccentric personalities from the country's academic, fashion and art worlds. To date, the party has invited dozens of queer international performers and DJs such as Ouissam.jpg of Hanoi, Herrensauna of Berlin, DJ Boring and performance artist Sam Reynolds from London, among many others. It also provides a space for local queer artists to experiment in ways that aren't possible in commercial galleries and other heteronormative spaces. The party's programme goes beyond the bacchanalian hedonism which tends to be reductively tied to gay lifestyles – it has become a collective political act by queer people to fight for better rights. More than just a space and a party, Elephant is a community; a home; a family of the dispossessed who could not find a place elsewhere where they could be themselves.

The tough lockdowns during the Covid-19 pandemic were the nail in the coffin that sadly forced most clubs and bars in Manila to close, but Elephant continued to operate online through a variety of platforms. On 24 October 2020, during the height of the Covid-19 crisis in the Philippines, the founders of Elephant collaborated with Community Bread, a New York-based queer-owned platform that helps queer artists and performers in the midst of the economic difficulty caused by the pandemic. The event featured local queer DJs Karlo, Adrienne, Hideki Ito and Dignos, as well as performances by artists Isola, SSSSTEALTHHHHH, Bohovee and Lady's Joyce. On 13 February 2021, Elephant participated in Oxtravaganza, an international online Chinese Lunar New Year party which included New York's BUBBLE_T, Los Angeles' Send Noodz and QNA, and San Francisco's Rice Rockettes. Despite the shutting down of physical spaces which hosted queer events, parties such as Elephant didn't die. As long as there are queer people, there are queer spaces, in physical or digital space.

Above

Photographers Mav and Cenon in drag inspired by the 17th century and Marie Antoinette, 23 July 2017.

Opposite, clockwise from top

Scenes of queer anarchy and unhinged expressions of individuality are common inside the XX XX club. The artist Jellyfish Kisses and Isola Tong are pictured here dancing in front of the DJ's booth, 11 August 2017.

Transgender artist Isola Tong captured dancing on the ledge by the DJ's booth, 23 July 2017. The costume is inspired by late 1990s Asian futurism and it was designed by Filipino brand Salad Day.

Artists Isola Tong and Anton Belardo manning the DJ booth as a duo. Drag artist Superstarlet XXX is wearing her signature red wig, 1 January 2018.

Architecture Fringe

Andy Summers

Within our queer cultural ecology, nightclubs have long played an important role in the development and protection of queer people and queer culture.

Simultaneously being a place of refuge, release and rejuvenation, the nightclub is where many can go to feel safe, very often for the first time, and to be themselves as they explore not only who they are but also who they could be. A space of personal, social and sexual liberation.

And then there is the music. The creation and emergence of dance music originates with black musicians in the United States, of African and Caribbean descent, many of them gay, lesbian, bisexual or transgender. Nightclubs are therefore also spaces of resistance and protest, where the defiance required to push back against oppression can find early expression and radical voice.

The Architecture Fringe is an activist, volunteer-led organisation based in Scotland which explores the impact of architecture in its social, political and cultural contexts. To explore queer/ed space, the organisation commissioned queer club producers based in Glasgow to imagine their ideal nightclub, to set and design the conditions on their own queer/ed terms. Paired with local architects, the teams were tasked with exploring new iterations of possible queer/ed aesthetics, architectures and occupations of space.

DJ, producer and club promoter Sarra Wild of OH141 collaborated with architect Cécile Ngọc Sương Perdu. The proposed, imagined nightclub is located in the heart of the city centre, camouflaged by unassuming shopfronts, surrounded by many of the city's pre-eminent cultural institutions and production spaces. This location is specifically chosen with access in mind, to counter inequalities in class, ethnicity and ability due to the central city being equidistant from most neighbourhoods, accessible by public transport and unaligned to any particular group or gentrified enclave. The hidden nature of the nightclub, seen but unseen, present but oscillating in visibility, speaks to the lived experience of many within the queer community. For some who are out and more comfortable with themselves, the club is fully visible, with its intentions and promises clear. For others who are perhaps not out yet, in the closet or are exploring who they are, the more hushed but seductive presence gives the confidence to enter without identification or explanation – a place of refuge and inspiration on the journey to self-acceptance.

Once through the level-access door, the intricacies and atmosphere of the nightclub are before you. A series of layered spaces, all on one level, steadily lead to a central cloister. In contrast to the highly urbanised, hard outside, the inside of the nightclub is luscious, soft and colourful. Plants abound, framing and defining space. Water is also ever-present with pools interspersed throughout, offering glimpses of reflection and refraction, but also moments of calm from sensory overload. Surrounding the cloister are smaller spaces where the atmosphere and ambience can be controlled through adjustments in volume, lighting and visibility. Beyond the main dancefloor is an alternative space, with different music and a distinctly different vibe. Spaces throughout are for abilities which are seen and unseen, from physical capacities to spectrum disorders and sensory sensitivities.

In imagining a queer/ed space, where queer people are able to set and design the conditions on our own queer/ed terms, authentic accessibility emerges as the guiding principle throughout. In the choosing of a central location, in being present but disguised within the streetscape, in directing that the nightclub be all on one level with a plurality of interdependent but autonomous spaces within, an electrifying atmosphere is imbued that can therefore be deftly attuned to a plurality of interests, expressions and needs.

Opposite
Queer space imagined by Sarra Wild and Cécile Ngọc Sương Perdu for the Architecture Fringe.

Baños Finisterre

MEXICO CITY, MEXICO

Emiliano Pastrana

Baños Finisterre is one of Mexico City's few surviving bathhouses, located in the city's central historic neighbourhood of San Rafael, not far from the famed Paseo de la Reforma. All of the city's extant bathhouses were constructed during the second half of the 20th century in a style that can be considered Functionalist. They have long been a vital part of daily urban life as places where the general population would have access to showers (something many households in the city once lacked), steam rooms and massages: a whole experience based on hygiene and comfort. The hours of operation of bathhouses in Mexico reflect their functional origin: they are usually from 6am to 8pm, with the exception of Sundays, when closing time is around 6pm.

The physical space of Baños Finisterre consists of a lobby, individual steam rooms and a 'general steam' area, which includes a series of small private rooms, toilets, four separate steam rooms including both wet and dry saunas, collective showers and a recently added whirlpool area.

The traditional Mexican bathhouse is a place patronised by 'traditional family' clientele, which means heterosexual adult males – there is no general section for women. As one might expect, most of these establishments have come to be frequented by gay men, who often connect to each other through discreet looks and gestures in quiet, out-of-the-way spaces. In this sense, one could say that many Mexican bathhouses are queer spaces hidden in plain sight, as it is impossible to know looking from the outside if gay activities are permitted or possible inside.

Most of the time, the only way to find out is by venturing in.

Some bathhouses have taken notice of the appeal that a fundamentally nudist space has for the homosexual community, and tolerate and accept their gay patrons and their activities. In a small selection of bathhouses, this has resulted in a complete shift in clientele, to a mainly gay male population that attends bathhouses not only to cleanse, relax and socialise, but also to flirt and have sex. Baños Finisterre is one of these places, where sexual activities take place in most areas with the full acceptance of staff.

The internal distribution of spaces, as well as their furnishings and use of light, sound and steam, are all factors that come together to influence and foster the queer dynamic of Baños Finisterre. The small hallway that connects the private rooms area and the steam rooms serves as a meeting point, based on its centrality and visual dominance. Both this hallway and the adjacent steam room, on the right, which in turn connects to the dry sauna, have access to the general shower area, creating a circulation pattern that facilitates unexpected encounters.

The determining element of the wet steam room on the left is a continuous bench running along its four walls, allowing the user to easily see in every direction while relaxing, inviting interactions with neighbouring bathers. When the steam is in full force, visibility is reduced, lending a seductive *dark room* atmosphere, which in fact becomes a *white room*, given that the whole bathhouse is brightly illuminated.

The shower area is the biggest room and provides access to the fourth steam room, which in turn leads to more private rooms. With its two massage beds, a cold shower, regular showers, plastic chairs (to rest from the steam) and popular music playing on a speaker, it serves multiple practical and social functions. It is here that patrons gather with old or new friends or hook-ups over drinks, enjoying the company and the ambiance of this very unique place in the Mexican capital.

Above
A place to fully relax and let go of inhibitions.

Opposite, clockwise from top

The main hallway, flanked by small private rooms.

The bathhouse: an ideal space for voyeurism and exhibitionist practices.

The inevitable meeting point.

Dragon Men

TOKYO, JAPAN

Takeshi Dylan Sadachi

With the self-proclaimed achievement of being 'Tokyo's No 1 gay bar and club', Dragon Men is located in Shinjuku Nichōme (literally, District 2 of Shinjuku), an area often regarded as Tokyo's LGBTQ+ neighbourhood. Having opened in 1996, it actually is one of the most known establishments in Nichōme, situated in a multi-tenanted building down an alley just off the busy Tokyo Metropolitan Road Route 305. Looking at the venue's conspicuous façade you are able to grasp the entirety of the interior's street-level floor space, which is an unusual feature for the area. Half of its floor space is occupied by a bar counter and seating area, the other half being the dancefloor and stage.

As the name suggests, Dragon Men generally attracts male customers and the official website states in English, 'We, Dragon Men, strive to inprove [sic] our selves [sic] and serve as many gay customers as we can, regardless of age or race.'[83]

While its target customers are diverse in race and age, they are homogenous in gender and sexuality.

In fact, Dragon Men is known for its Western gay crowd, attracting Japanese gay men seeking Western men, locally called *gaisen*. In Japan, dance clubs are far less common than people might expect, as *izakaya* (casual bars with food) and *karaoke* are the most common places for a night out. Therefore, it could be considered inevitable that Dragon Men attracts Western crowds, as it provides a rather familiar style of night out.

Dragon Men also capitalises on its popularity among foreigners through a grandiloquent use of Japanese elements. For instance, while the venue's official name in Japanese is *doragon men* in phonological katakana characters, the façade features signage including logographic kanji (Chinese characters adopted in Japanese), *ryū* (dragon) and *otoko* (male/man). While the official name is phonetically transcribed, which is a preferred practice in Japanese, the signage is a semantic translation and transliteration to kanji.

This act is reminiscent of *gairaigo kinshi gēmu*, meaning 'no loanword game', a party game where participants are challenged to chat as usual in Japanese without using ever present loanwords – mainly those of Western origins. This requires one to 'kanji-ise' terms such as *kamera* (camera) to *shashin-ki* (photo-machine), an act often inaccurately described as 'pure' Japanese despite most replacements being Sino-Japanese vocabulary. Hence, the full kanji signage can be understood as an attempt to exaggerate the 'Japanese-ness' or at least 'Asian-ness' of the venue.

In addition, the façade features *renji mado*, wooden latticed windows with parallel strips, as well as eaves with crossarms called *udegi hisashi*, both typical of Japanese teahouse architecture known as *sukiya zukuri*. Inside the venue, you will also find Japanese paper lanterns above the bar counter.

These elements of traditional Japanese architecture, both inside and out, create a strong contrast against the modern appearance of the venue, with the frequent use of straight lines and sharp angles, shiny metals and matte black concrete, as well as disco balls and bright coloured lights. Bombastic revivalist elements seen in modern architecture often appear themed, paradoxically marking the space as rather 'foreign.' Dragon Men is no exception, evidenced by a strong presence of international crowds and the locals attracted to them.

Above
The interior of Dragon Men.

Opposite, clockwise from top

The exterior, featuring the kanji sign with a calligraphy-inspired font.

The exterior, featuring Japanese architectural elements.

The bar counter, with Japanese lanterns.

Carolina Youth Action Project

SOUTH CAROLINA, USA

Seb Choe

Down the carpeted hallway of a United Methodist church in North Charleston, one hears the voices of a small group joyfully chanting a call-and-response:

'We have nothing to lose but our chains! WE HAVE NOTHING TO LOSE BUT OUR CHAINS!'

For a period, Carolina Youth Action Project, or CYAP, housed their headquarters in a rented room of this church. As an abolitionist organisation that centres on political education and community organising, a welcoming headquarters is essential to CYAP's mission of building power among girls, trans youth and gender-nonconforming youth in South Carolina.

Though CYAP's campaigns around transformative justice and reproductive justice align in many ways with the legacy of movement-building across Black churches of the Deep South, CYAP's location in a church today feels a bit out of place. Ironically, many of the individuals that find a haven in CYAP's 19m² room may very well have worked to *escape* church environments that were less than nurturing.

But despite the CYAP headquarters' small footprint and location, it is nevertheless a case study of revolutionary queer space (is queer space not *always* about the creative use of constrained territories?). In response to white-painted cinder-block walls and harsh overhead fluorescent lighting, CYAP installs floor lamps that cast a warm glow on walls adorned with LGBTQIA+ flags, bold posters demanding the removal of police from schools and hand-drawn portraits of revolutionary Black women like Septima P Clark and Ella Baker, whose advocacy for popular education during the Civil Rights Movement remains an inspiration for Southern organisers today. And though the view outside the window reveals North Charleston, a Black neighbourhood that suffers the highest eviction rates in the country, the CYAP office feels like a sanctuary in which to imagine better futures.

The central area of the room is multipurpose – folding tables offer a co-working space for CYAP staff as they scheme workshops, retreats and campaigns. On other days, tables are replaced by a ring of folding chairs around a large whiteboard, which facilitates popular education workshops and rich, vulnerable conversations, which occur regularly between youth leaders. The perimeter of the room is activated with spaces that are just as essential. A cosy corner is

littered with fuzzy blankets, pillows, yoga mats and acoustic instruments – reminding occupants that *rest is radical*, especially for the Black and Brown youth that CYAP uplifts. An altar table sports candles, quotes by Assata Shakur (a revolutionary Civil Rights activist) and handwritten names of activists and friends honoured by the CYAP cohort. A floor-to-ceiling floral wallpaper marks the 'warm-and-fuzzy' wall – studded with small envelopes labelled with each CYAP member's name, often stuffed and overflowing with warm, handwritten affirmations. This wall also features a play-shelf, littered with fidget toys and Play-Doh, that benefit neurodiverse individuals as well as anyone requiring a sensory break. A snack table and mini-fridge boast a range of refreshments, all lovingly labelled with allergen information (interrupting a session to grab a snack is encouraged!). The library features a stack of abolition and queer theory books – *Fumbling Towards Repair* by Mariame Kaba is paired with well-used boxes of markers, construction paper and scissors, which elevate the documentation of one's own lived experience as equally valued knowledge. Finally, a body corner offers lotion, tissues, free menstrual products and contraceptives, reminding us to nurture ourselves.

While to an outsider, the CYAP office might seem ordinary, for those who have found community here – unlearning carceral attitudes, exploring one's gender identity or shedding tears from emotional conversations around self-acceptance (in my case) – the room feels queer in the truest sense, a safe chamber to explore our bodies, selves and desires together, towards collective care and liberation.

Above
A poster for CYAP, showing volunteers at a fundraiser party.

Opposite, clockwise from top-left

Youth leaders underneath the CYAP banner in the headquarters.

Staff members in the 'cosy corner'.

Memes from CYAP's Instagram, inviting participation in community programmes.

CAROLINA YOUTH ACTION PROJECT

COME FOR THE DIY STATION

QUEER AF

STAY FOR THE LIBERATION

WANT TO SUPPORT SPACES FOR GIRLS, TRANS YOUTH, AND GENDER NONCONFORMING YOUTH?

APPLY TO BE AN ORGANIZING FELLOW!

The Locker Room Project

CAPE TOWN, SOUTH AFRICA

Jackson Davidow

The crumbling of apartheid coincided with the rise of lesbian and gay political organising and visibility in South Africa. In April 1994, citizens of all racial backgrounds went to the polls in the country's first democratic election, voting in Nelson Mandela as the President of an African National Congress (ANC) led government. Supportive of the lesbian and gay movement, the ANC enshrined a policy that prohibited unfair discrimination on the basis of sexual orientation in the Constitution's Bill of Rights, adopted officially in December 1996. This 'Equality Clause' made South Africa the first country in the world to acknowledge lesbian and gay rights on a constitutional level. Yet despite this remarkable and thrilling legal development, queer people, brutally oppressed during apartheid, lacked vibrant cultural identities, infrastructures and spaces.

Held at Cape Town's River Club on 9 December 1994, the Locker Room Project was one of the earliest attempts to build a queer public culture in the reborn nation. A one-night, extravagantly kitsch *Gesamtkunstwerk*, thought to be the largest work of public art in South African history at the time, it promoted collaborative creative production,

bringing together visual art, architecture, design, fashion, photography and music. Developed by two white gay men, artist Andrew Putter and architect André Vorster, the event popularised the term and notion of 'queer' in Cape Town, at least within the art and architecture worlds. It also served as a memorial to Vorster's lover Craig Darlow, a white man who had recently died from AIDS-related complications.

With the event a month away, Putter and Vorster created an instructional booklet that fleshed out their embrace of the expansive term 'queer' rather than 'gay' or 'lesbian', identifying their target audience:

The word queer has many meanings: playful, productive, pleasure-loving, deviant. It could describe an off-the-wall approach to life. It questions conventions. It always finds creative alternatives to things we usually take for granted. Queerness is not a cut-and-dried definition of one's sexual orientation. People (hetero- and homosexual alike) are waking up to the fact that their sexual identity will always defy neat labelling.

Above, left
Although the Locker Room Project was a one-night event, it helped create a queer arts scene in Cape Town at a pivotal historical juncture.

Above, right
One of the transformed rooms at the River Club featured a luminous locker room – a quintessential space of queer desire.

Opposite
To celebrate and partake in the newly visible queer public culture, partygoers designed and sported elaborate costumes.

The River Club was a 1940s recreation centre for railroad employees on the banks of the Liesbeek River in Observatory, a suburb of Cape Town; the sprawling rooms, grand corridors and copious bars were ideal for the occasion. Following a call for involvement across creative fields, about 50 people showed up to the first planning session, where Putter and Vorster explained their desired dandyish, campy aesthetic, introducing the overarching theme of sport; the locker room was undeniably an archetypal site of queer desire. Teams of artists, designers and students settled on sport-related subthemes, plotting out how they would transform their assigned rooms into wondrous spaces of queer paradise.

As the first edition of what became an annual party called the Mother City Queer Projects, the Locker Room Project created a magical space and transformative experience for its gleefully costumed attendees. Out of the approximately 2,000 participants who came to party, dance and play with sexual identity, nearly everyone was white. Engagement with communities of colour was an afterthought for its organisers – something both Putter and Vorster later lamented. Despite aiming to be a queer space and collaborative artwork for a forward-looking Cape Town, the Locker Room Project reflected the uneven national histories of sexuality and race, epitomising the frenetic sense of excitement, grief and redress that characterised post-apartheid life.

COMMUNAL

89

The Kloset Yuri Book Club

BANGKOK, THAILAND

Nichapat Sanunsilp

The Kloset Yuri Book Club is a space for lesbians, bisexual and pansexual women and non-binary people to meet and socialise in. The club is located in the Saphankwai district of Bangkok, where a lot of fashionable cafés have emerged in recent years. The Kloset is part of two rows of townhouses that face each other back-to-back. Because of this architectural situation, the rear of The Kloset is connected to the rear of a café called Slow Jam, a café for gender-fluid clientele, with only one sliding door and a set of curtains between them. Though The Kloset has its own street frontage, many of its clients prefer to access the book club through the café, and get a drink before they read; coffee during the day and beers at night, meaning the two businesses end up supporting one another.

Clientele tend to initially meet each other through online platforms, and then once they have become acquainted, they come to the club to meet up and hang out in person. In The Kloset they play musical instruments together, board games and video games, as well as meeting other new people in the LGBT+ crowd and forming friendship groups.

Kilin, one of the Kloset Yuri Book Club owners, said she was not able to say that the club was a completely safe space for LGBT+ people as some of them find love in it, but some find love and then leave with broken hearts, a statement that shows the gentle and caring nature of the space and its management.

The whole look, feel and atmosphere of the space is inspired by the film *Carol* (a romantic drama from 2015 starring Cate Blanchett). Kilin explained how completely enraptured she was by Cate Blanchett's character. She wanted to make the space, like the journey of the character in the film, about finding happiness in the present: a place where as an LGBT+ individual one can be unselfconsciously free from having to conform to any kind of gender norms.

Any woman or non-binary person can join the book club by paying 50 THB per day for a pass. There are books from the genre 'Yuri', which is a term from Japanese subculture for lesbian romantic love stories, of which Kilin is a connoisseur. She explains that the main plotline of these publications is not always romantically driven, but can be quotidian dramas or even crime novels, which just so happen to have lesbian lead characters. The club also has a lifestyle YouTube channel about the community. Apart from the broad selection of Yuri books, it also has board games and musical instruments which members are allowed to use and share as and when they please.

The space is often used for events, and sometimes The Kloset also collaborates with Slow Jam café for evening events like Ladies' Night, Gays' Night and many others over the years.

Another of the owners, a lady called Mhee, is a self-proclaimed introvert, and explained that many of the customers are introverts like her as well. For this reason, they have a space specifically dedicated for people who want to use the space quietly and just be by themselves, but in a supportive and friendly environment.

Unlike gay men, the stereotype of lesbians and bisexual or pansexual women in Thailand is that we are not very outgoing and don't like partying, but it is perhaps simply that there are not many places for us to come together in. Unfortunately, the lesbian population of Thailand does not yet have a strongly organised sense of community that is as visible as that for gay men. There are many of us, but we are mostly scattered around as individuals or very small kinship groups, without many clubs or well organised groups to join. It is not easy for the owners of The Kloset to run such a unique space, but The Kloset is precisely what the bisexual and pansexual women and non-binary people of Thailand need, a place for extroverts and introverts, the partygoers and the book-nerds to gather, meet, mix, mingle and form a sense of solidarity and community in a welcoming and inclusive space.

Club Kali

LONDON, ENGLAND

DJ Ritu and Lo Marshall

Club Kali was founded by DJ Ritu and Rita, who at the time were both working in caring professions and saw the need for a safe yet fun space for the South Asian LGBTQIA+ community. The bold and brazen goddess Kali was adopted as the club's icon, reflecting its strong female roots and founders, mirroring Ritu and Rita's desire to present an assertive image that was intersectional in challenging inequalities, while playful and enlightened. Club Kali has always been actively anti-racist and trans-inclusive, resisting oppression by creating a celebratory space where South Asian LGBTQIA+ people and non-Asians could gather as a community passionate about intercultural exchange.

Club Kali attracts people of all faiths, races, genders and cultures seeking an alternative LGBTQIA+ scene. In the 1990s, it generated a pre-social media global reputation by word-of-mouth, with clubbers arriving in coachloads from everywhere! Kali was a magical place; with sarees and incense, dhol drummers, muscle-boys, glamorous Chutney Queens and an eclectic musical blend, with bhangra and Bollywood in the mix with Rai, house, R&B, disco, pop, Turkish, Greek, Arabic, drum'n'bass and reggae. At grassroots music venue The Dome, queues wrapped around the corner and the venue's cavernous interior was packed to the rafters.

Ritu's DJing career began in 1986 at the London Lesbian and Gay Centre (LLGC; see pp 150–1), where she established the Saturday-night women's disco, playing chart hits, soul, Motown and occasional Greek, Turkish, Asian and African tracks. A founding member of Shakti, the first South Asian LGBTQIA+ organisation in the UK, Ritu co-created the ground-breaking Shakti Disco at the LLGC in 1988.

Club Kali encompasses the community-oriented and political potential of nightlife, providing behind-the-scenes support, and collaborating with wellbeing and sexual health organisations. By embracing the cohesive power of dance and music, and a multicultural music policy, it increased the visibility of people of colour and challenged racial inequality in the LGBTQIA+ scene, while becoming a hub for many non-Asians.

In 2021, recognising Club Kali's enormous contribution to LGBTQIA+ life and decolonisation of dancefloors, a heritage plaque was awarded by Islington's Pride, and will adorn the Victorian façade of The Dome in Tufnell Park, Club Kali's spiritual home. The Dome's large wooden-sprung dancefloor was perfect for the big, brash dance moves of Bollywood, bhangra and garba lovers. Club Kali's programming has showcased LGBTQIA+ cabaret and drag artists,

especially queer and trans people of colour. Bolstered by her role in Shakti and international reputation as a DJ and radio presenter, Ritu booked high-profile British Asian musicians to grace The Dome's resplendent stage, including Rishi Rich, Jay Sean and Nitin Sawhney. These performances effectively 'sanctioned' LGBTQIA+ lives and showed LGBTQIA+ South Asians that they deserved the best artists at *their* night.

> Diversity and unity are in Club Kali's DNA, so there's always a festival to celebrate – Christmas, Eid, Diwali, Chanukah, Easter, Navratri and Vaisakhi.

One-off events are also part of Kali's journey and DJ Ritu hosts and curates nights at arts venues and festivals, including BFI Flare (the British Film Institute's LGBTQIA+ film festival), the Victoria and Albert Museum, Wellcome Trust and Institute of Contemporary Art. More recently, Club Kali has appeared in London venues like the Temple Pier Bar&Co boat and Nightclub Kolis.

DJ Ritu reflects that she often felt like 'the only one' – her club work is driven by a desire to bring people together and help them feel 'included'. Club Kali is the UK's longest-running world music club and for many folks, it continues to be the place they feel safest and most at home. The fierce and loving character of goddess Kali is channelled through the passion and dedication shown by Ritu and Rita in creating a safe and joyful LGBTQIA+ space, with South Asian people and culture at its heart.

El Hangar en Santurce

SAN JUAN, PUERTO RICO

Regner Ramos

Picture this. You're in front of a booth with artisanal skincare products at an agro-ecofriendly, queer-run market located on an urban lot in San Juan, adorned with trees and plants. Oh, and there's an aeroplane hangar right there in front of you. You decide to buy the agro-ecofriendly, artisanal sunscreen balm that'll protect you from Puerto Rico's 30-degree summer heat (you hope), from the woman who made it.

And right before she hands it over to you, her hands place the balm over her heart, she closes her eyes, says a prayer and then gives it to you.

That's El Hangar in a nutshell.

Run by a local queer collective led by Carla Torres, El Hangar en Santurce is a space for alternative modes of queer world-making on the island of Puerto Rico, deeply rooted in decolonial practices. When Carla first saw the abandoned space, she saw possibilities: a junkyard that needed a ton of work, but a place to imagine the future (according to an Instagram post's caption).

El Hangar hosts events based on anti-colonial and political resistance, where art, music, dance, performance, agriculture and activism meet, preserving a particular wave of queerness that is inseparable from the island's African legacy. Where other queer spaces in San Juan generally appeal to a more global idea of queerness – or homosexuality – El Hangar feels truly specific to the Caribbean, and to the intercultural exchanges that occurred between the different islands and countries that were exploited by European colonisation. For instance, the *flamboyán* tree – emblematic of the way that the Puerto Rican landscape has been represented in art and culture for ever and ever – growing right in front of the site might be a symbol of it; that species is originally from Madagascar.

The concrete fence that defines its boundaries is painted in swirls of colours, announcing its link to the LGBTQ community, while a Puerto Rican flag made out of wood stands over the entrance. From bonfires to markets, El Hangar uses its exterior space as much as its interior, which, of course, makes sense, considering our hot, humid, tropical weather and the fact that its main building is a small, vaulted aeroplane hangar made out of metal and concrete. Inside it, the collective runs a variety of events, ranging from film screenings to dance workshops. With three meek, little wall fans ventilating the heat coming out of the metal walls, there's humid, balmy air all around you, and when you factor in people dancing on the stage, you can imagine how intensely hot it gets.

But no matter how balmy it gets inside El Hangar, it represents, for Carla and many queer people here, a place to meet, share, let go and breathe. It seems that El Hangar really found its purpose during 2019, when Hurricane María hit. A category 5 hurricane that pummelled the island, María caused billions of dollars in damage, over 4,000 deaths and a near-total devastation of our electrical infrastructure, which resulted in a months-and-months-long blackout (up to a year for some areas of the island). Looking for refuge during the hurricane, Carla and her crew camped at El Hangar for months, and under that new, post-storm Caribbean reality, El Hangar nurtured alternate forms of kinship that continue today, particularly for Puerto Rico's most vulnerable queer populations – the working class, trans people, queer POC (People of Colour) and immigrants – protecting them within its vaulted metal ceiling, under mango trees, behind a rainbow fence.

Opposite, clockwise from top-left

A drawing of El Hangar, by Gabriela Ennich and Regner Ramos.

Mural detail on the fence.

The interior space, as shown in the 2021 music video 'Cuerpa', performed by Ana Macho, directed by Josh Anton and with lighting design by Nos Veran.

Front elevation, July 2021.

Frenz-Frenzy

OSAKA, JAPAN

Isola Tong

Hidden in the northern end of the *shōtengai*, or covered street closed to traffic, in the red-light district Doyamacho, the queer mecca of Osaka City, is a hyperchromatic little bar famous among both local and foreign LGBTQ+ and allies. Frenz-Frenzy has a big reputation that far exceeds its compact floor area. Its notoriety has even reached the ears of Western celebrities who visit the city during tours, some of whom were Lady Gaga, Perez Hilton and Adam Lambert. Lady Gaga, during her 2009 tour, dropped by and sang karaoke with guests. Founded by the jovial Australian drag queen known as Sari-chan, the bar was envisioned to be an unapologetically queer space that welcomes both local and foreign clients.

Dubbed as the 'rainbow haven' by the owner, the interior of the bar is indeed a kaleidoscope of multicoloured neon.

Every nook and cranny is covered with otherworldly colours, from the eye-catchingly dizzying mosaic of colours on the outside wall and main door, to the neon brick tiles on the interior walls. This psychedelic architecture was a backdrop to the many memories of libation and debauchery I have from there with my friends and lovers. It was also a place of comfort where I would go when heartbroken or having troubles at work. Japanese society is still quite conservative compared to other developed nations and these safe spaces provide a home, a community for both local and foreign queers. Sari-chan was always there to listen to my problems and his Japanese bar tender, Taiga, was always there to make me my favourite cocktail – Tequila Sunrise. In the end, it is always among the queer community where we get the necessary support, acceptance and understanding. In every major city on earth, there will always be queer spaces that may be hidden but strive to fight for their own existence, and Japan, despite its samurai-machismo culture, is no exception.

Above

The colourful exterior façade of the Frenz-Frenzy bar greets the patrons, July 2021. The shocking colours are hard to miss and it has become a local landmark.

Opposite, clockwise from top-left

Detail of the multicoloured exterior wall, with a textured surface.

Surreal toilet décor.

Playful and wildly neon decorative moments in the bar.

View of the bar and the karaoke lounge.

The bar awash with neon colours.

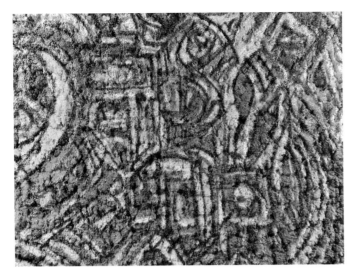

Women's Anarchist Nuisance Café

VARIOUS LOCATIONS, LONDON

Sebastian Buser

The Women's Anarchist Nuisance Café (WANC) was a creative feminist do-it-yourself (DIY) activist space which took place on a biweekly/-monthly basis in squats and semi-autonomous spaces in the London boroughs of Hackney and Tower Hamlets, between 1998 and 2012. It was conceived by Caro Smart and James Rose in a squatted Manor House called Toxic Planet in Stoke Newington, and was later joined by Sal Tomcat at the Radical Dairy, a squatted social centre run by the infamous WOMBLES, which stood for White Overalls Movement Building Libertarian Effective Struggles. The WOMBLES were an anarchist/libertarian communist group who took their inspiration from the Italian social movement *Tute Bianche* (meaning 'white overalls') that sought to support social struggles through direct action. Many more people tirelessly volunteered their time to create WANC, from skipping food (a practice of salvaging food discarded by wholesale markets) to cooking, cleaning and creating flyers for the night's themed events.

Like other queer autonomous spaces of its time, WANC fused culture and politics in a spirit of creative playfulness to create a DIY 'panacea to passive consumerism'[84] of the commercial lesbian and gay scene. The aim was to provide a space for mutual participation. It offered room for political discussions, performances, workshops, was sex positive and centred on the communal eating of vegan food. The category Women was open for anyone who identified as such, celebrating all its possible pluralities, and grew to encompass trans men and non-binary folk who still had links to the women's movement.

Many state that the uniqueness of WANC was its ability to follow the migratory rhythms and cycles of occupation, eviction and re-emergence, while maintaining its identity across 12 different sites over 14 years. As Caro Smart, co-founder and eventual guardian of WANC, stated,

'The fact that we had this constant kind of death and rebirth thing going on each time a building got evicted, gave it a freshness and reanimation. It never got stale or fixed.'[85]

WANC had incarnations at the Cholmeley Old Boys Club, China Man Punk Squat, Women's Spiral Squat, Plusch Zentral Queer Squat and Shacklewell Old Baths in Dalston. The novelist Sarah Waters read from her book *Fingersmith* (2002) at WANC during their two-and-a-half-year stint at the Radical Dairy. RampART squatted social centre, in Whitechapel, was their longest home, for around four years. After this they had stints at Passing Clouds, a community-run music venue, also in Dalston, before going back to the Cholmeley Old Boys Club, which had become a semi-legal space, in which they had their last café. WANC stopped running due to the difficulties of finding adequate venues, which was made harder by the passing of Section 144 of the Legal Aid, Sentencing and Punishment of Offenders Act (LASPO) in 2012 – making squatting in residential properties illegal.

Top
Collections of flyers from 2004 to 2007, and the RampART Social Centre on Rampart Street, which WANC used between 2004 and 2008.

Bottom
Collections of flyers from 2001 to 2002, and the Radical Dairy Social Centre at Kynaston Street, which WANC used between 2001 and 2002.

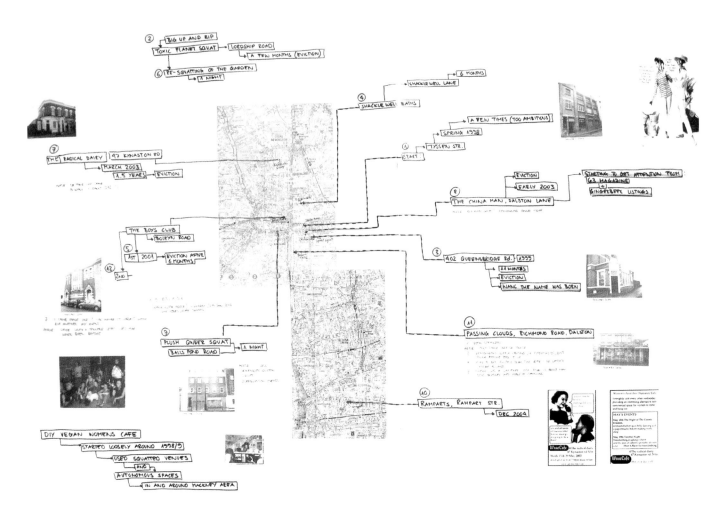

Map showing WANC venues in Hackney and Tower Hamlets (handwritten annotations):

BIG UP AND RIP
TOXIC PLANET SQUAT → LORDSHIP ROAD
↳ A FEW MONTHS (EVICTION)
RE-SQUATTING OF THE GARDEN
↳ A NIGHT
SHACKLEWELL LANE → 6 MONTHS
SHACKLEWELL BATHS
A FEW TIMES (TOO AMBITIOUS)
SPRING 1998
THE RADICAL DAIRY | 47 KYNASTON RD
↳ MARCH 2003
↳ 2.5 YEARS → EVICTION
TYSSEN STR.
START
EVICTION
EARLY 2003
STARTING TO GET ATTENTION FROM G3 MAGAZINE (+) GINGERBEER LISTINGS
THE CHINA HALL, DALSTON LANE
THE BOYS CLUB
↳ BODEYN ROAD
↳ AST 2001 → EVICTION AFTER 6 MONTHS
2ND
402 QUEENSBRIDGE RD. 1999
↳ 11 MONTHS
↳ EVICTION
↳ WANC THE NAME WAS BORN
PLUSH GINGER SQUAT
BALLS POND ROAD → A NIGHT
PASSING CLOUDS, RICHMOND ROAD, DALSTON
RAMPARTS, RAMPART STR.
↳ DEC 2009
DIY VEGAN WOMENS CAFE
↳ STARTED LOOSELY AROUND 1998/9
↳ USED SQUATTED VENUES
(AND)
↳ AUTONOMOUS SPACES
↳ IN AND AROUND HACKNEY AREA

Clockwise from top

Map showing WANC venues in Hackney and Tower Hamlets.

Cholmeley Old Boys Club was home to WANC when it was squatted by co-founder James Rose in 2001, and then rented as a venue from 2010 to 2011. Collection of WANC flyers, including one made by co-founder Caro Smart using an image from a 'Blue Peter' annual depicting Olympic athletes.

WANC café costume, made by Sebastian Buser for the *Fabulous Façades* performance devised by Ben Campkin and Lo Marshall, drawing on evidence collated as part of Urban Lab's research project 'LGBTQ+ Nightlife in London'.[86]

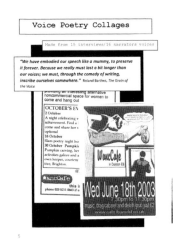

Voice Poetry Collages

Made from 15 interviews/16 narrators voices

"We have embodied our speech like a mummy, to preserve it forever. Because we really must last a bit longer than our voices; we must, through the comedy of writing, inscribe ourselves somewhere." Roland Barthes, The Grain of the Voice

It came out of nowhere

Bachillerato Mocha Celis

BUENOS AIRES, ARGENTINA

Facundo Revuelta

In 2007 the first national census of the *travesti*-trans[87] population was carried out in Argentina. The results showed a life expectancy of 35 years and a common desire: access to education. It was in this context, in 2011, that the Mocha Celis[88] was born; the first school on the continent born from, and aimed at, the LGBTQ+ population.

The school is an example of community education, created and run from the perspective of attaining rights and organising resistance, but it is also an example of a way to think about new directions in public education. 'La Mocha', as it is affectionately called, has more than 100 students each year, between the ages of 16 and 60. As its director Francisco Quiñones recounts, the school functions as a space for support, not in paternalistic, traditional pedagogical terms, but in the complex framework that not having finished high school implies, because this situation means, in many cases, remaining excluded from healthcare, housing, work and all that this implies for a person's prospects and confidence.

Among its objectives is to promote job placement through various types of workshops. Through them, many of the students that make up the school body go through their first formal work experience. They are trained not only in different trades, but also in methods of productive self-expression and the cultivation of pride and self-esteem; that is, it is sought that they become independent producers of knowledge and meaning. The school also has a Student Welfare unit, which assists homeless students in obtaining housing subsidies, or in the processing of an identity card application for those who do not yet have one.

'La Mocha' is also a creative space in which two books were produced (one of which is *The Butterfly Revolution*, an update of the first census from 2007); a documentary titled 'Mocha' was made and commercially released in Latin America and Europe; a photographic exhibition in conjunction with the Trans Memory Archive was put on; as well as plays, documentary shorts, poetry slams and festivals.

During the pandemic, the *travesti*-trans community saw their housing conditions, food, health and economic vulnerability become even more aggravated. In response to this situation, the Mocha Celis launched a campaign called 'Teje Solidario' (Solidarity Weave). It is a self-managed aid network, made up of more than 700 people within Buenos Aires and its surroundings, where volunteers can donate resources, time and/ or money. It is fundamentally a network of affection, support and love.

The school logo is strongly linked to the collective imagery of Argentina. In it appears Domingo Faustino Sarmiento (1811–88), the so-called 'father' of education, with a frown and a severe face, an iconic image engraved in everyone's memory. But this version shows a *travesti* version of Sarmiento, made up, with blushing cheeks, hair dyed blonde and lips painted in an angry red or pink that returns a different and updated vision of the story that was built around this historical and controversial figure.[89]

Above
The pride of students and teachers during the presentation of the documentary 'Mocha', which they produced themselves in 2019.

Clockwise from top

The first graduation in 2014 was special, as it was carried out at the Ministry of Education, with the students carrying the Argentine and LGBTQ+ flags.

The school's logo, Faustino Sarmiento's *travesti* figure.

During the pandemic, the teachers put together and designed some booklets with the face of Mocha Celis to distribute among all the students.

Kitty Su

NEW DELHI, INDIA

Ekam Singh

It's been a remarkable decade since Keshav Suri, of the Lalit Group of Hotels, decided to open the ground-breaking nightclub Kitty Su, which, in his own words, is not just a nightclub anymore, but has since evolved into a huge space for inclusion and diversity for the LGBTQ+ community, acid-attack victims and the differently abled. Amazingly, it has not only survived, but has become a movement of sorts. From its grand space in the basement of a five-star hotel in the heart of New Delhi, the club stands testament to the spirit and perseverance of the resilient LGBTQ+ people in India who have been frequenting the space since before the decriminalisation of homosexuality in 2018.

'There are a few places in a city that become larger than themselves. They take on a persona of their own. Kitty Su is one of those spaces,' says an employee at Kitty Su. 'We are following the inclusive and gender-agnostic policies of the Lalit Group of Hotels.'

With outposts now in Mumbai, Bengaluru, Kolkata and Chandigarh, Kitty Su is both a beacon of hope and a rite of passage for LGBTQ+ people in India, almost the quintessential queer safe space.

Over the years, the clubs and the hotels at large have not only brought the community together but have provided a safe and welcoming place of employment for many LGBTQ+ individuals.

Most prominently, after the Pulse nightclub shooting (in which 49 people were murdered in a mass shooting at a gay nightclub in Orlando, Florida, in 2016), Kitty Su launched its Pure Love campaign and Pure Love nights: dedicated safe nights for LGBTQ+ people. Cutting down entry costs, welcoming patrons of all socio-economic classes, allowed Kitty Su to broaden inclusivity across class and income brackets.

One of Kitty Su's greatest contributions has been to facilitate the rebirth of drag culture in India, bringing established drag performers from around the world – like Milk, Thorgy Thor and Violet Chachki – and giving a platform to desi drag queens Lush Monsoon and Betta Naan Stop,[90] the likes of whom have now graced magazine covers like *Grazia*. Kitty Su has been responsible for bringing drag culture into mainstream pop culture in India. This has enabled performers not only to have a place to show their art but also to earn a living doing what they love.

Before the decriminalisation of LGBTQ+ acts in India, Kitty Su and the Lalit Hotels changed the way queer India saw itself. In many ways, it is the first place where homosexuals saw other homosexuals in a celebratory environment. A safe space for those of non-normative identities to party and be themselves, without judgment from an often-hostile society; somewhere a trans woman could go through her transition while feeling safe within her workspace. Somewhere where philanthropy, care, empathy and outreach were ingrained into the programming itself.

Since the decriminalisation of homosexuality in India, Kitty Su and the Lalit have continued to lead the charge by communicating acceptance and love right at their doorsteps with signs and symbols of the rainbow flag. With a genderless rainbow mascot, 'ELPHIE', and philanthropic work across NGOs and the Keshav Suri foundation, a message of hope and love reverberates from the walls of Kitty Su alongside the customary fun pop music.

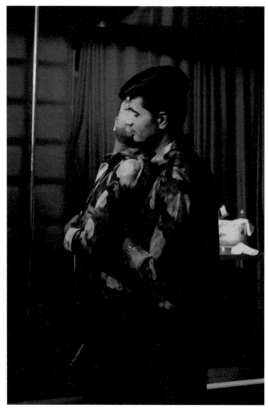

Stalled! Airport Prototype

USA

JSA/MIXdesign

Stalled! is an interdisciplinary design-research project founded in response to national debates surrounding transgender access to public restrooms.

Since its founding in 2015, Stalled! has advocated the need to create safe, sustainable and inclusive public restrooms for everyone, regardless of gender, age, religion and disability.

Initiatives include the creation of design recommendations and prototypes, including the Airport Prototype depicted here, which reconceives the restroom as a semi-open agora-like precinct animated by three parallel activity zones, each dedicated to grooming, washing and eliminating. As a speculative design, the Airport Prototype posits an alternative to the traditionally accepted standard of sex-segregated, multiuser restrooms, and looks beyond the narrow definitions of the gender binary in order to articulate a space that meets the diverse needs of the audience that it serves.

Our scheme takes as its point of departure the standard dimensions of a typical sex-segregated airport restroom.[91] Our goal was to explore different ways that a wide range of differently embodied subjects could mix together in public space, based on the understanding that the seemingly commonplace and universal activities that we perform in restrooms are shaped by the convergence of biological, cultural and psychological factors.

Treating the toilet stall as a privacy unit allows us to take away the barrier that typically divides adjacent men's and women's rooms, as well as the wall that separates them from the concourse.

Immediately adjacent to the concourse, the grooming station features a smart mirror that disseminates digital information (for example, flight departure times) while users groom at a multilevel counter that serves people of different heights and abilities. Those who want privacy can retreat into curtained alcoves for breastfeeding, administering medical procedures such as insulin injections, and engaging in prayer and meditation. Curtains allow for selective privacy as needed without the bulkiness/clearance issues of an actual partition/door.

Washing occurs around a freestanding island inspired by the public fountains that activate Roman piazzas. The communal washing station meets the needs of both adults and children, including people in wheelchairs. Inset floor lights indicate the location of motion-activated taps in the wall that allow water to flow into inclined splash planes placed at different ergonomic heights.

Located at the back of the facility, the eliminating station consolidates rows of bathroom stalls that offer acoustic and visual privacy. They come in three sizes: standard, ambulatory and ADA-compliant (the US standard for wheelchair accessibility). Two large caregiving rooms are equipped with toilet, sink, changing tables and a shower that allows travellers to wash and change clothes, and perform caregiving between people of different ages and genders. They can be used by Muslims and Orthodox Jews whose religious beliefs prohibit them from exposing body parts in public. Muslims can perform bathroom ablutions using the hand shower and flip-down seat in the shower.

Unoccupied stalls are indicated by recessed floor lights; when entered, they turn off and the now-occupied stall glows from within. From the inside of each stall, users can survey their surroundings by looking through a band of blue one-way mirror located at seated eye-level. Stalls contain low-flush composting toilets that treat human waste through aerobic decomposition.

In 2019, Stalled!, in collaboration with the National Center for Transgender Equality and the American Institute of Architects, amended the 2021 International Plumbing Code to allow for the creation of all-gender, multiuser restrooms, paving the way for designs like the Airport Prototype to be realised in the built environment.

Opposite, top
Airport Prototype floor plan.

Opposite, bottom
Aerial view.

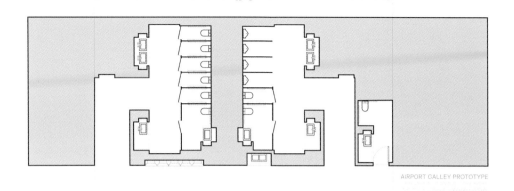

AIRPORT GALLEY PROTOTYPE

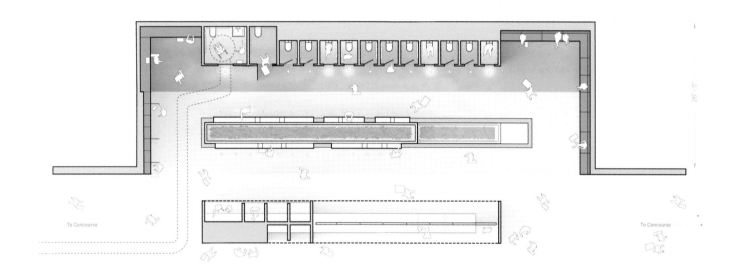

To Concourse

To Concourse

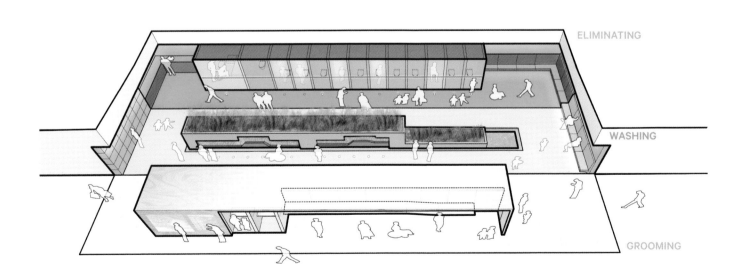

ELIMINATING

WASHING

GROOMING

COMMUNAL

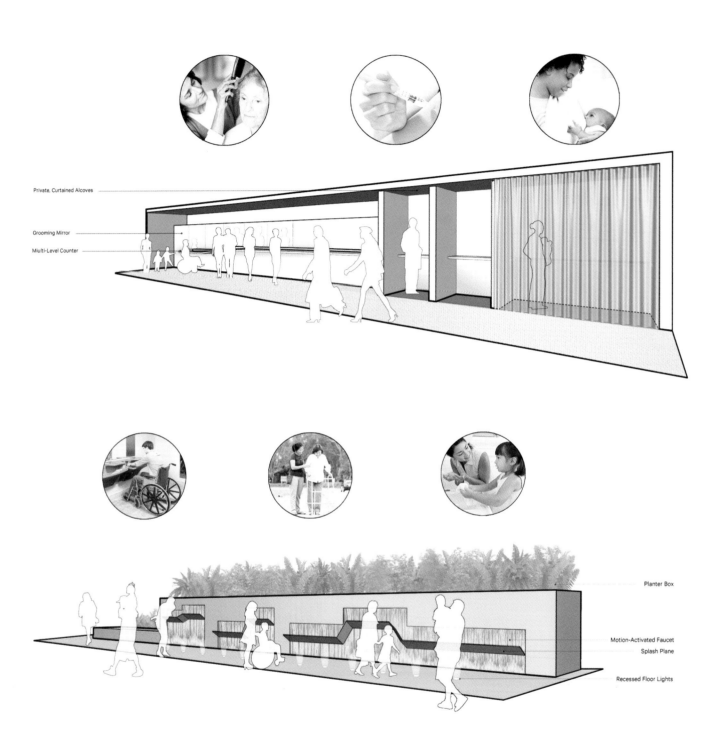

Private, Curtained Alcoves

Grooming Mirror

Miulti-Level Counter

Planter Box

Motion-Activated Faucet

Splash Plane

Recessed Floor Lights

Top
Grooming station.

Bottom
Washing station.

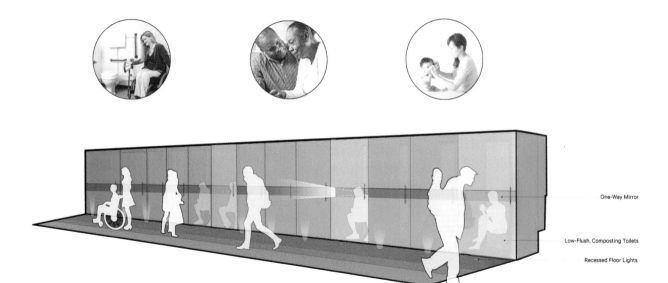

One-Way Mirror

Low-Flush, Composting Toilets

Recessed Floor Lights

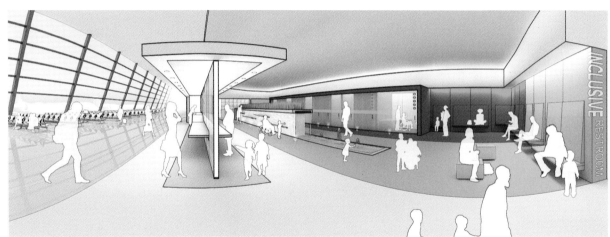

INCLUSIVE RESTROOM

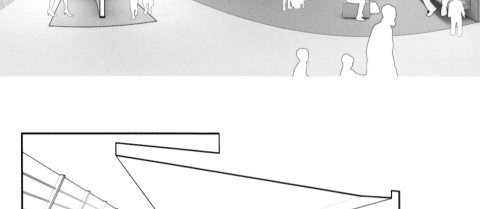

Top to bottom

Eliminating station.

Still from a 360-degree rendering.

Section perspective illustrating a multisensory experience that changes from station to station.

Public
Open
Smooth
Light
Dry
Reverberant

Private
Closed
Coarse
Dark
Wet
Absorptive

GROOMING   WASHING   ELIMINATING

Circo Bar

SAN JUAN, PUERTO RICO

Regner Ramos

'That's the most twisted space of all the twisted spaces!' Master Top (the pseudonym he asked for) told me while I was interviewing queer people in Puerto Rico for my ongoing research. If you ask half the LGBTQ community how they feel about Circo Bar, they'll tell you they love it. And the other half will tell you why they absolutely hate it, arms flailing in the air.

'It doesn't have any solution, it doesn't make any sense! It's a shit show,' Master Top told me. I was enthralled.

'First, there's three spaces; the first one takes you to the second one, and you just don't understand the transition between the two. From the second space to the dancefloor, that doesn't make sense either. And the one on top, let's not even mention it!'

Master Top is right – there is no seeming logic to Circo, but then again, most Puerto Rican LGBTQ venues are an oxymoron. From the outside, Circo, on Calle Condado, looks like any abandoned Puerto Rican building in the Santurce neighbourhood of San Juan. It doesn't have signage, its concrete walls are painted grey, the ground floor has no windows and is entirely closed off from the derelict street it's located in – for privacy and security – and the second floor looks like it's a house that someone may or may not live in. A balcony wraps itself around the corner, overhanging the pavement, adorned with locally made concrete balustrades.

Circo looks like it's two buildings, but really it's one; it's just got a massive gap running down the middle, creating a formal separation on the façade, and then there's the really strange 'second space' Master Top mentioned: a double-height smoking area that feels like you're in an alley, not inside the building. You enter that space from the main bar area, which is what Circo started with, back in 2010, before expanding sideways and vertically. A rubber curtain separates the two spaces, so every time you go in and out you feel like an SUV at a carwash.

High above the interior/exterior smoking area is a mirrorball (Why? And also, who cares?) and two balconies, accessible by way of a metal staircase leading to the upper storey. The second level of the club features billiard tables – which both locals and tourists love – and the interior space keeps the domestic character of the original building, with its balconies, even though they're closed off using iron grids familiar to many Puerto Rican buildings. But the space most Circo-goers love to go to is the main dancefloor below and across from the rubber curtains that assault you each time you go through them.

In this main dancefloor, a blown-glass chandelier hangs over the main bar, which visitors can circle around. Instantly recognisable, the chandelier is what everyone posts on their Instagram story to announce they're at Circo – though some say they do *not* want their Instagram followers to know that they're at Circo, nor want to be associated with it. And if that doesn't do the trick, the loud circuit music playing in the video will do it. One of the walls is covered entirely in mirrors, making the space look larger than it is, while also allowing people to make eye contact despite the strobe lights and low-lit atmosphere.

Frankly, Circo is perfectly designed for cruising. With plenty of nooks and crannies (and restroom stalls) to escape to, visitors constantly move from one space to another, circling around the bar, then going up to the billiard bar, and coming down the stairs again, in an endless procession where every room has its own vibe and music genre. That's what works so well: Circo provides visitors with essentially four different bars located in one building.

Above
View from Circo Bar's elevated DJ booth to the main dancefloor.

Opposite, clockwise from top-left

The smoking area, separating the two main interior spaces.

A drawing of the bar, by Christian González-Román and Regner Ramos.

Calle Condado during an off-night at Circo Bar.

Alyssa Edwards performing on the main stage.

Loverbar

SAN JUAN, PUERTO RICO

Regner Ramos

'It's like being inside a dollhouse,' my assistant Christian told me. Eureka, he was absolutely right, that's exactly what being inside Loverbar feels like – I hadn't quite been able to put my finger on it. Everything inside Loverbar – the newest queer-owned, queer-run club in San Juan – feels plastic and crafted. Loverbar announces itself as *queer,* branded to a particular kind of clientele that might tend to feel out of place in other LGBTQ venues (usually conceived by, and for, cis-gay men). The décor is a celebration of all that is considered femme, with a bit of punk inspired by John Waters; the façade is covered in a colourful mural with curvy shapes and animal print – created by local artist Popa/Paula I Del Toro – almost giving the feel of the building being tattooed rather than painted; and a tilted, heart-shaped window acts as the pick-up area for to-go orders from the kitchen. Inside, the furniture is all repurposed, repainted and reupholstered, and the wooden mezzanine level is barely high enough to be an actual mezzanine (I saw an Instagram story of a drag queen that jumped in high heels from the mezzanine to the ground floor's stage, and survived). Visually, that upper level feels like it abides by building codes through the skin of its teeth, and the stairs that lead up to it are so narrow and tall you need to watch your step or say *adios*.

At its core, Loverbar is a brilliant example of Puerto Rican queerness: resourceful, ad hoc and vibrant.

The Loverbar team work with what they've got and turn it into a spectacle.

From an architectural standpoint, describing a space as 'plastic and crafted' might be considered a no-no. But in Loverbar, it works. It makes it very unpretentious and familiar. The fact that everything inside it is repurposed or donated, and given new life, attests to the Puerto Rican queer community's need to use whatever is at hand, given the economic difficulties of life on the island. This notion of 'a new life' is as much about the *things* inside Loverbar – for example, it has a community closet where people can drop off clothes and take whatever's there for free – as it is about the people who are part of the Loverbar family, the building itself and the site in which it is located.

Loverbar is located in the Paseo de Diego, a pedestrian street in the Río Piedras neighbourhood, which once acted as the economic hub for shopping in Puerto Rico. Today, Paseo de Diego is known for being nearly entirely derelict, abandoned and the total antithesis of what it used to be: thriving. Loverbar's presence shakes things up, though, injecting Río Piedras with energy and urban life, and boosting the local economy, despite the hardships of opening in the middle of the Covid-19 pandemic. It also acts as an example of new, possible queer futures for San Juan, for spaces accessible to all.

Loverbar is described by a lot of people here as a 'safe space', and this definitely has to do with it protecting *and* employing vulnerable populations, especially Black trans folk. It is also *affordable*. In a seemingly unending recession, it creates a much-needed inclusive space, especially for queer students, given that it's located right next to the University of Puerto Rico's main campus. Its very existence marks the very first queer venue by and for LGBTQ people in Río Piedras, where the community has always had a strong presence, but very few proper spaces that cater to them. And given that in Puerto Rico so many queer spaces are ephemeral – borrowing straight venues for particular events on off-peak nights, and where venues close because of the economy – it gives queer people a home base and ownership over our (abandoned and derelict) architectures, in the form of a big, colourful doll's house.

Above
The writing on the garden perimeter reads, 'Your gaze violates us.'

Opposite
Interior details.

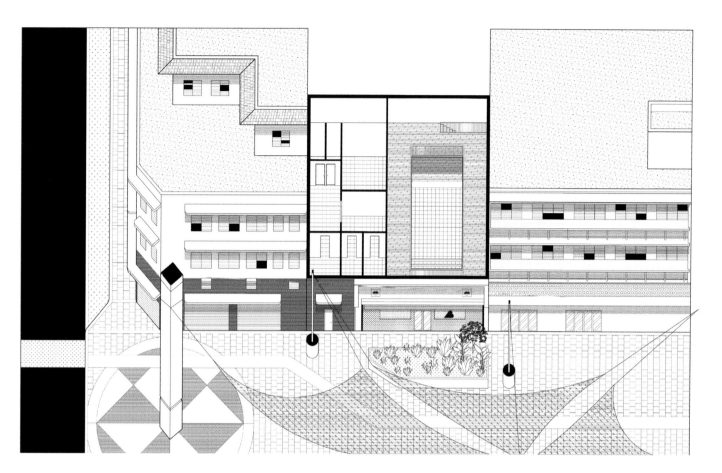

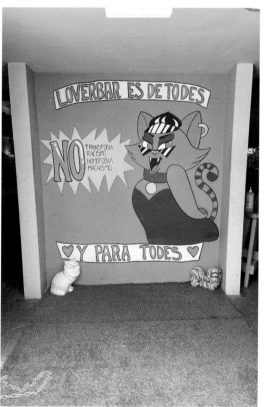

A drawing of Loverbar, by Brian Torres-Negrón and Regner Ramos.

The bar, located below the mezzanine level.

The foyer features a mural by artist Yarantula, with a manifesto: 'Loverbar belongs to everyone and is for everyone. No transphobia, racism, homophobia, misogyny.'

Clockwise from top

Bar detail.

The heart-shaped window that opens to Paseo de Diego. Depending on the day, the window is sometimes used to take orders so people don't need to come inside.

Mezzanine level, overlooking the bar on the ground floor.

Interior view, facing the heart-shaped window.

Interior details.

Temple de l'Amitié

PARIS, FRANCE

Jane Stevenson

If 1920s Paris was, as Natalie Barney claimed, 'the only city where you can live and express yourself as you please', this was because those who sought alternatives there envisioned and lived it as such.[92] Because they could live as they chose, without reference to heterosexual paradigms, an international lesbian community grew up there, connected in complex ways with the demimonde and the arts. The American Natalie Barney was the most famous lesbian hostess in Paris. On Fridays, she entertained writers, artists, bohemians and homosexuals at 20 Rue Jacob. After 1927, she styled her gatherings the 'Académie des Femmes', a challenge to the Académie Française, which admitted its first woman Immortal (i.e. member) only in 1980. Sylvia Beach, also a lesbian, who ran the famous bookshop/meeting place Shakespeare and Company on the Left Bank, said of Natalie's Fridays, 'At Miss Barney's one met lesbians; Paris ones and those only passing through town, ladies with high collars and monocles.'[93] While the heyday of the Fridays was interwar, they were resumed after 1949, and continued to the 1960s.

Barney's salon, dining room leading onto the garden and the high-walled garden itself, shaded by mature trees and enclosing a 'Temple de l'Amitié', or 'Temple of Friendship', were therefore, though in a private house, an important meeting place for the French and expatriate lesbian community. Barney seems to have had little interest in décor; her house was furnished with cast-offs from her mother, sister and friends, and she did not pretend to an interest in modern art. Perhaps the most interesting and suggestive of her decorative choices was her bedroom curtains, lawn embroidered with 'may our drawn curtains shield us from the world.'[94] Barney made no secret of her proclivities, but privacy and domestic space were essential to her way of life, since the French Civil Code enacted on 21 March 1804 decriminalised all sexual activity between consenting adults, provided it was enjoyed in private.

The Temple was built around 1810–20, for a secret society, probably Freemasons, so from the start, it was intended for meetings which could not be held publicly; Barney repurposed it. 'DLV' is inscribed both on the floor and on the façade: 555 in Roman numerals. The number 555 was significant to Freemasons, but for Barney and her friends, this may have been understood as 'Dieu le veult'; 'God wishes it.'[95] It was the most private core of a space which was shielded from the world, by a locked door, a long court, antechamber, salon and garden. Though

it must sometimes have seemed that the whole world came to Natalie Barney on Fridays, she in fact controlled who entered the house and garden; who had privileged access to the bed in the Temple of Friendship, or even the right to know it was there. If there is a principle to be discerned in interwar lesbian spaces, it is resistance to scrutiny.

Lesbians were very important in interwar avant-garde Paris as patrons and enablers. Removing the influence and patronage of Barney, Gertrude Stein, the Princesse de Polignac and Sylvia Beach from the history of Modernism would drastically revise the cultural landscape of the 20th century. Additionally, the expatriates in particular were highly conscious of themselves as a group of women united by a sexual identity, however different they were in other respects. They knew one another socially and sexually; Djuna Barnes represented them as a community in *The Ladies Almanac*, and Romaine Brooks painted many of them: Truman Capote, marvelling at the contents of her studio, described it as 'the all-time ultimate gallery of famous dykes... an international daisy-chain.'[96] More than any other city in the 1920s, Paris facilitated the creation of a community of lesbian women.

Above
Natalie Clifford Barney in front of a wall hanging given by Robert de Montesquiou, c 1925–30.

Opposite
The Temple de l'Amitié, as it was in the 1920s.

Category Is Books

GLASGOW, SCOTLAND

Andy Summers

When thinking about ecologies of queerness, and the infrastructures required to help a queer population adapt, survive and thrive in any particular social, cultural or physical environment, bookshops can be a potent source of individual and collective nourishment. Category Is Books, located in the Govanhill neighbourhood in the southside of Glasgow, is one such source.

Founded by wusband and wusband team Charlotte (they/them) and Fin Duffy-Scott (they/them) in 2018, the bookshop sits on an acute corner beneath a four-storey tenement of red sandstone typical of the neighbourhood. Glazed to three sides as it turns from one street to another, the unit was a former car showroom which, in pure queer fashion, could only ever accommodate two cars at a time. It's not at all big, this space.

On approaching the shop, it is the windows that first speak, applied as they are with a slowly evolving array of beautifully hand-painted signs that billboard the bookshop's support of the trans community and its stance on racism within the neighbourhood.

Above the door, painted onto the glass, it reads ALL WELCOME.

Then, stepping into the bookshop, the atmosphere is immediate, warm and anticipatory, where you already know you're going to discover something, buy it and love it. In the centre of the shop, as a focal point, are some armchairs and a small coffee table on a large rug, set up as an invitation to sit, relax, read and chat. Panning around, the walls – and windows – host bookshelves of varying sizes, heights and styles interspersed by plants, lamps and artworks. The books are sorted into categories, many of which transcend typical retail arrangements to introduce whole worlds of lived experience through the simple stroke of a marker pen: Black Queer Non-Fic; (Gender is a) Drag; Queers with Lots of Feelings; Middle Eastern Queer; Parenting; Poetry is Not a Luxury; Silence = Death; South East Asian Queer; Trans Fiction; all chosen with great care. Completing the layout, a blackboard noticeboard faces the door, the counter and till across to the left.

Category Is Books is first and foremost an independent queer bookshop, stocking a wonderful array of queer local, national and international books, comics, zines, pamphlets and badges. There is a thriving queer publishing scene in Scotland, and the bookshop is a cherished outpost and important resource. The bookshop hosts book launches and readings within its space, as well as open-read nights where queer writers of prose, poetry and anything in between can share their work with an audience.

But it is with the activities beyond those associated with a bookshop that Category Is Books expands exponentially as a queer space, flourishing radially in all directions towards wider queer culture, queer politics, community care and collective action. The blackboard mentioned earlier offers some insight into this wider work, with the activities chalked up weekly. The central space within the bookshop is ephemeral, deftly transforming almost every second day into a space of liberation, action and support. On Mondays and Tuesdays, an inclusive pop-up barber shop materialises, offering queer, butch and femme cuts, alleviating a point of stress and trauma for many who may not feel comfortable or be accepted elsewhere. Wednesdays host Town Meetings, where the local queer community meet to share information on collective action and community care. Sunday mornings are inclusive yoga. And across the week the space hosts queer film nights, clothes swaps, ally workshops, peer-support groups and response nights to government consultations.

The infrastructure of queer life can be fragile and often transitory, and the queer spaces that aid the stability and nourish the growth of a local scene are sadly all too rare. Category Is Books is an inspirational example of one of these rare spaces.

Opposite
Founders of Category
Is Books, Charlotte and
Fin Duffy-Scott.

Top
The windows as evolving
billboards.

Bottom
Interior décor.

Today x Future

QUEZON CITY, PHILIPPINES

Isola Tong

23 AUG - Today x Future
14 SEPT - Futur:st

Today x Future created a beautiful venue that mixed every subculture in one space. It created a safe space where there was no prejudice and pretension. It's important to the community cos it supports creativity and the art.

– Ed Cruz

I became a DJ here, this is so sad. Thank you, guys, for everything; you truly made Manila a better place!!!!!!

– Javier B

For over a decade, this legendary bar, founded by Sharon Atillo and Leah Castañeda in 2008 in Cubao, Quezon City, provided an inclusive space where Filipinos as well as visitors from abroad were welcomed regardless of ethnicity, gender, taste and background. Before closing their doors permanently on 18 June 2020, for 12 years they served as a hub of creatives, both queer and straight. Musicians, writers, intellectuals, artists, architects, filmmakers, photographers and designers who eventually became influential in the local scene called it home. The 'Future', as it is called by its patrons, provided an experimental space where young creatives could perform their music or exhibit their works. In fact, several creatives who made it big in Manila and abroad began their careers at Today x Future. It was

a space like no other in the archipelago, where one could see an underground film showing of queer cinema by Gregg Araki; watch art performances by queer artists; listen to '90s alternative and shoegaze. Many renowned musicians from abroad DJed there: Reuben Wu, from the UK electronica band Ladytron; Erlend Oye and Jens Lenkman, of Kings of Convenience; and The Pains of Being Pure at Heart, from New York City. One event at Future that is of particular interest was Blitz, an underground electronica night that featured queer DJs and artists, which was founded by one of Manila's most prominent queer DJs, Karlo Vicent. The event captured the openness and spontaneity of queer spaces, as he puts it:

I didn't really plan it: there was suddenly a free night at Future, and Sam messaged me like a few days before asking me if I wanted to do a night, I said yes since I've had this idea for a while. I just wanted to do a night where I can play slow-ish electro, organic techno, a bit of Italo and new wave, etc. And no one in Manila was doing it at that time (that I know of).

Indeed, the queering of spaces like Today x Future is all about serendipitous encounters, unplanned eventualities, chance, precarity, the meeting of divergent worlds, danger and the openness to unknown possibilities.

Above
Blitz poster designed by Junie, aka Business Casual. The event platforms queer DJs who play techno, electronic music and house, and is usually attended by Filipinos from the queer subculture.

Opposite, clockwise from top

The façade of Today x Future, juxtaposed with older structures to the right and new mixed-used buildings to the left. The Cubao area has been rapidly gentrifying in recent years.

The crowd goes wild during one of the gay themed parties that heavily features the music of Carly Rae Jepsen (August 2019).

The iconic 'The Future is Now' red neon sign above the bar, illuminating the interior with a warm orange glow.

COMMUNAL

Taprobane

SRI LANKA

Robert Aldrich

Taprobane, the name recalling the ancient Greek word for what was later known as Ceylon and is now Sri Lanka, is a minuscule island off the southern coast of Sri Lanka.[97] The house and garden that cover the islet were the home of Maurice Talvande (1864–1941), a Frenchman who lived in Britain from an early age. There he married Lady Mary Byng, the daughter of an earl and a Danish countess, and dubiously took on the title of Count de Mauny, which had been held by one of his mother's ancestors. The couple had two children, but drifted apart after a few years. De Mauny opened a boarding school for adolescent boys in the Loire Valley, but became embroiled in controversy when he was revealed to be homosexual; he then drifted around France, Italy and Britain. De Mauny first visited Ceylon in 1912, then decided to move there permanently after the First World War, on which he wrote a short volume, *The Peace of Suffering* (1919).

In 1927 he began construction of a villa, with rooms radiating from a large octagonal drawing room. Decorated with wooden panels and *eau de Nil* hangings, a black-and-white marble floor and teak furniture (much of de Mauny's own design, as he became a well-known furniture designer and manufacturer in Ceylon), it was his home for the rest of his life. De Mauny's slightly fey *The Gardens of Taprobane* (1937) describes the building and the lush landscape that surrounded the house.[98] It contains a photograph of his Ceylonese gardener and companion, Raman, and a painting of the count by the local artist David Paynter (1900–75), whose homosexual interests are evident in many of his works.

On Taprobane, de Mauny entertained a succession of celebrity visitors, from the British homosexual novelist Robin Maugham to Lord and Lady Mountbatten.

De Mauny's son Victor inherited Taprobane, and it subsequently passed through various owners. Prominent among them was the bisexual American novelist Paul Bowles (1910–99), more famous for his connections with Morocco. Bowles lived on Taprobane, with his wife Jane and his Moroccan lover, episodically for several years after 1952. The property remains in private hands, now renovated as luxury accommodation for rent to tourists.

Sri Lanka attracted many visitors and expatriates of queer sensibility, from the travelling Victorian social reformer and homosexual emancipationist Edward Carpenter (1844–1929) to the science-fiction writer and long-term resident Sir Arthur C Clarke (1917–2008). The luxuriant tropical setting, the grand archaeological sites of Anuradhapura, Polonnaruwa and Sigiriya, the *perahera* processions at Buddhist temples, the beaches and spicy food, and the perceived tolerant morals and easy-going approach of the local people have continued to beguile foreigners, though the gardens of Taprobane have been overshadowed by more soulless resorts along the seashore.

Above
Portrait of the Count de Mauny, on the veranda of his house on the islet of Taprobane, by the Sri Lankan artist David Paynter, c 1937.

De Mauny's private islet of
Taprobane, viewed from
the shore of the mainland
of Ceylon (now Sri Lanka).
The count's house is almost
hidden by the luxuriant
tropical vegetation.

The interior of de Mauny's
house, overlooking the
Indian Ocean.

Casa Um

SÃO PAULO, BRAZIL

Facundo Revuelta

The name Casa 1 (or Casa Um) means 'first house' or 'home'. The familial home is often understood as a safe and intimate domain, but for LGBTQ+ youth facing violence or expulsion, the concept of home can mean the opposite. Combining housing, social services, mental health care and cultural activities with activism, the Casa 1 complex quickly became an urban landmark not only in São Paulo but for all of Brazil.

The entire complex acts as an infrastructure for support that operates in search of social justice, standing out as an initiative that goes beyond providing shelter, but also provides quality support focused on specific needs. It anchors a network of neighbours, civil society groups, private establishments, public facilities and political leaderships, which converge in an alliance that presents itself to society with diverse performative practices and operating strategies. This young and friendly environment engenders a feeling of belonging, collectivity and ownership of the space, not only by LGBTQ+ people but also by a large part of the surrounding neighbourhoods.

The first activity that Casa 1 embarked upon was the hosting centre, and it is still today one of the central pillars of their activity. It started in 2017, through collective financing, and it has already housed around 380 LGBTQ+ young people expelled from home by their families for their sexual orientation and/or gender identities. There are a total of 20 places for a period of four months. The objective of the project is to be a temporary home, carrying out multidisciplinary work so that young people are helped to develop a level of independence sufficient for establishing their own trajectories after residency in the project. In addition to housing, food and transport, the young people receive all the support and social assistance needed for the organisation of documentation, support in the process of continuity

or resumption of studies, employability, clinical and mental health care, as well as access to the entire programme available at the cultural centre. Many of the young people housed continue to live in the neighbourhood when they leave Casa 1, relying on the centre's infrastructure as a locus for support, identity building and resistance.

Another important piece of the complex is the Casa 1 Cultural Centre, also called Galpão (shed) Casa 1. Its main premises are free and provide universally available services, without any restrictions, strictly following their open-door policies, and like everything else in Casa 1, it is a place of constant experimentation and change. In four years, it has already hosted multiple classes, courses, workshops, lectures, exhibitions, plays, shows and fairs, which focus on promoting cultural diversity, fostering the production of free knowledge and culture, and providing inclusive and quality programmes for its diverse audiences. A fundamental factor for the maintenance of Galpão Casa 1 is the presence of collectives, groups and NGOs that use the space to carry out their activities. It is important to highlight that one of Galpão's founding objectives was exactly this: to have a physical space for projects, especially LGBTQ+ ones, and to be able to carry out activities that they could otherwise not have because of lack of space.

The complex also houses the Caio Fernando Abreu library, which began receiving donations in 2017. Today, four years later, Caio has a collection of 3,879 titles, including books, DVDs and magazines. The collection's acquisition policy aims to give space to, and amplify, voices of representative kinds of literature that create tension in their social, historical, political and economic contexts with regards to identity issues, namely: LGBTQ+, feminist, black and indigenous identities.

Above, left
Renata Carvalho, at the Office Theater of the Italian-Brazilian architect Lina Bo Bardi, presenting 'O Evangelho Segundo Jesus Rainha do Céu' (The Gospel According to Jesus, Queen of Heaven), playing a transvestite Jesus during the Casa 1 2019 Trans Visibility Week.

Above, right
One of the many performances carried out in Galpão Casa 1.

Top
The show 'Seconda Queda'
(Second Fall) in the Casa 1
2020 Trans Visibility Week.

Bottom
Bingo nights are one of
Casa 1's biggest attractions.

Inflation Nightclub

MELBOURNE, AUSTRALIA

Timothy Moore and John Tanner

The interwar Neoclassical façade of 54–60 King Street, completed by architect Marcus Barlow in 1938, has concealed the activities within the 410m² plot: as a butter factory, offices and as an altar to hedonism that has hosted the legendary (Grace Jones, George Michael, David Bowie, INXS, Lady Gaga) and the underground (Barbara Quicksand, Leigh Bowery, Ari Up, Danny Wang, Limpwrist).

Inflation Nightclub opened in 1979 with three levels of entertainment. While its original interior was a facsimile of a New York disco,[99] its 1985 uplift was not typical of any nightlife predecessor due to its youthful designers from Biltmoderne. Their design practice grew out of their early work creating furniture and exhibitions.[100] Their experimental approach to architecture, with a strong attention to materials, collage and set design,[101] was unleashed onto their first major commission.

The 1985 renovation was abrasive: 'Hard surfaces and hard edges define Inflation's style,' wrote Justin Henderson in a 1987 review of the project.[102]

This is evident in the decorative detail, where every element challenges conventions of how one experiences the diurnal world.

At the edge of the first-floor dancefloor are six Riverina granite island tables with 'nibbled' edges, some penetrated with spikes. The 'roughly shaped points on the thick island bar poles are aggressive,' smeared with hammertone paint to give a greasy effect.[103] In the ground-floor café, a clear, curved countertop, with crushed safety glass underneath, is uplit by a sinuous neon light.

Queering can be considered a method to critique and disrupt normative architectural conventions. Despite the idiosyncratic *Mad Max* imagery – of 'axe-heads, spears and contorted steel'[104] – the project quickly entered Melbourne's postmodern canon, with Inflation receiving a 1985 Royal Australian Institute of Architects Victoria Award. A queer methodology may be found, instead, by extending the analysis over time. It is reflected in the accumulation of modifications, from the Biltmoderne fitout, to the later addition of a rooftop deck and the nightly interior modifications for fashion parades, performances, swinger events, stripper revues and parties (including Get Down, Gay Night, Climax, Winterdaze, Beyond, Trough Faggot Party, John, Honcho Disko and Adam).

Nightclubs like Inflation can serve as spaces that actively embrace queer, trans- and gender-nonconforming people, while being spaces of risk.[105] Recent transformations of wealthy urban centres have seen the nightlife that supports the LGBTQ+ community with economic and social capital move on. This is also a condition in Melbourne: the building that houses Inflation was sold in 2018, and the club will close once its lease expires. The building will change uses again after 40 years. This does not come as a shock. It reinforces that the only permanent thing about a city, and its queer spaces, is its temporariness.

Clockwise from top-left

Rippling curved seating with pink tendrils in the Biltmoderne design continued up the wall alongside the first-floor dancefloor.

The basement DJ booth was defended by a rusting steel-plate 'bunker door'.

Since it opened in 1979, Inflation has hosted the legendary and the underground, with a rotating roster of parties, including Berlin Party in 1980.

Royal Vauxhall Tavern

LONDON, ENGLAND

Ben Campkin

There is no clear date at which the Royal Vauxhall Tavern (RVT) became popular with queer communities. Built in 1860–62, it has continuously been identified with sexual and gender diversity and experimentation since the 1940s, and probably earlier. By the mid-1970s, there were regular drag performances using the bar as a makeshift stage. Reconfigured to better suit cabaret in the early 1980s, the venue has become iconic for hosting a lively and international alternative performance and drag scene.

Unusually for Vauxhall's diminishing cluster of LGBTQ+ venues, which are mainly large clubs in railway arches, the RVT is accommodated in a purpose-built public house. It has therefore been vulnerable to the speculative redevelopment that has seen many pubs across the capital, and in the wider UK, close and be converted to residential use. In 2014, it was sold to the Austrian developer Immovate, who were unclear about their intentions. This raised alarm among the venue's diverse clientele, and the performers and promoters in its orbit. Campaign groups Friends of the Royal Vauxhall Tavern and RVT Future formed and acted quickly, using social and traditional media to rally support.[106] They put forward successful applications to list the space as an 'Asset of Community Value' and to have it recognised by Historic England as a listed building; it was listed at Grade II in 2015, the first UK building to be listed for its importance as 'a noted performance space and LGB&T' venue.[107]

The listing application assembled a meticulous architectural and social history from primary and secondary sources. The research developed from the work of performance group Duckie, who had used the venue for many years, and had drawn from its association with the hedonistic and experimental cultures of the Vauxhall Pleasure Gardens, demolished when the RVT was built. The listing recognises the architectural fabric, which dates to an 1863 design by James Edmeston. The building was central to the urban planning that replaced Vauxhall Pleasure Gardens, and which was otherwise demolished in the 1970s.

The application detailed the longer-term legacies of cultural experimentation in the venue and its social significance to the LGBT community.

In the application, the campaigners skilfully wove the history of the building and the urban fabric together, speculating a link between the pleasure gardens and the structural columns in the pub. To emphasise national significance, a comparison was made between New York City's Stonewall Inn (see pp 172–3), listed in 1999 for its significance to the struggle for LGBT rights, and the emblematic role of the RVT, which was subjected to police raids in the 1980s, and has been an important site of protest, social sustenance and creativity for many decades.

The listing application conveys the sense of a building perpetually at risk. Until 2005, it had been owned by the local authority, Lambeth Council. Queer communities had helped to fight off a plan to sell, demolish and redevelop the site as a shopping centre and ski slope in 1999. Lambeth went ahead and auctioned the pub in 2005, at which point it was purchased by the current management, who later sold the freehold to Immovate.[108]

Lambeth now recognises, and is responsible for safeguarding, the venue's legacy. Although today the fabric is protected, the use is still vulnerable to change. In 2016, RVT Future applied for, and won, the designation of Sui Generis (a planning use class meaning 'of its own kind') as a further protection. Yet, with all these protections in place, the freehold and leasehold are currently for sale. The campaigners have set up a Community Benefit Society to raise money towards a community buy-out, but high value makes this a challenging feat.

Above
Royal Vauxhall Tavern, exterior, still from a 3D-scan, UCL Urban Laboratory, 2020.[109]

Drag show, c 1977.

Interior, still from a 3D-scan,
UCL Urban Laboratory, 2020.

True Blue Studio

BANGKOK, THAILAND

Nichapat Sanunsilp

True Blue Studio is owned by Fah Kanyanuts (she/they), a young tattoo artist with a fashion design background. Her tattoo studio is famous for wavy typography, classic fonts and minimal, yet vibrant graphics. Fah didn't think typography was her forte, but somehow, over time and through its popularity, it ended up being part of her personal brand. Her preferred style is realistic depictions, with a few of her favourite projects being the realistic tattooing of characters from famous LGBT+ movies.

The studio was recently relocated from Samyan (a small district in central Bangkok) to the fourth floor of the Tangible Bangkok Building, at Soi Charoenkrung 82. Her first studio was much smaller, with only space for one client at a time. The new studio has several beds, each with its own separate room, and a lounge in which she can chat with her clients and come up with ideas and designs for their tattoos together. The Tangible Bangkok Building also has a café on the first floor and an interior design studio on the third floor. The walls are all bare concrete, and the lights are kept dimmed, giving the space a mysterious, urban vibe. Fah is very happy with how the building is slowly becoming a real community. She is planning to facilitate a workshop teaching people how to make tattoos, and the customers from the coffee shop can now wander around to see some new installation art on the second floor, and have a peek into her studio.

True Blue Studio is LGBT+ run, and LGBT+ friendly, and now has several LGBT+ artists working in the space together.

Fah explained that she has never advertised the place as an LGBT+ space, but regardless, somehow she finds that LGBT+ people always make their way there.

Happily, word gets around. She personally finds it comfortable and enjoyable having LGBT+ clients, and the same goes for her clients, who feel safe with her.

As tattooing is not the most common of subcultures in Thailand, even though it has recently become more popular among young adults, people covered with tattoos are not always welcome in many places, let alone tattoo artists themselves. As many women do not feel comfortable getting tattoos from male tattoo artists, female LGBT+ tattoo artists have become very welcome and popular in the tattoo marketplace. True Blue Studio is always fully booked for months in advance, showing how a friendly and safe LGBT+ space for a small but growing subculture can be both a successful business and an important place of community.

QUEER SPACES

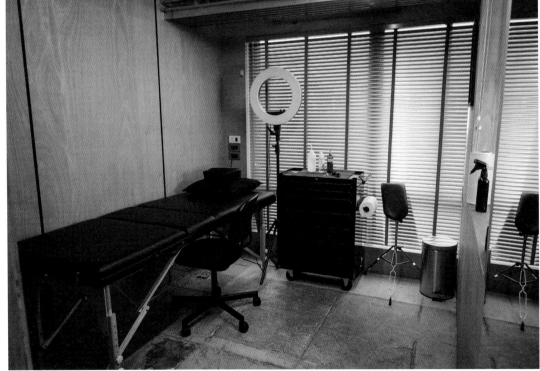

Opposite
A lounge for Fah and other tattoo artists to chat and design the tattoos with their clients.

Top
Installation art on the second floor is part of the café. The work has become a compelling transition for people to walk past before they reach the True Blue Studio on the fourth floor.

Bottom
An individual room for a client.

Milner Park Hotel

JOHANNESBURG, SOUTH AFRICA

Ian Mangenga

Almost 150 years old, the Milner Park Hotel has a complex history; the same roof that paid homage to brutal colonial rulers is now considered a home for radical activists and their intersectional movements.

The Milner Park Hotel, located on the corner of Juta and De Beer streets, is one of the oldest buildings in Braamfontein, Johannesburg. It was built in 1898 and used as a stopover by British troops and the postal services. At the end of the Anglo-Boer War in 1902, the British High Commissioner, Sir Alfred Milner, allegedly had a meeting with General Lord Kitchener of Khartoum in the Milner Park Hotel, hence the name 'Kitchener's Carvery Bar' (KCB) for one of the hotel's clubs today.[110]

As Braamfontein slowly grew into a student town in the late 2000s, attracting young people from all around Johannesburg, the demographic of the hotel changed from old working and retired men to a young, diverse crowd.

In 2016 the FeesMustFall movement broke out across South Africa, following the increase in tuition fees in universities across the country. The renaming of buildings and institutions also became a focal point in the movement, as students started asking questions about access, representation and inclusion.

Colleen Balchin and Phatstoki More were inspired by the movement to address the representation and access of queer people in KCB.[111] Having worked in the bar for five years, Colleen felt that while conversations about change were taking place both outside and inside the bar, this was still not being reflected on the dancefloor.

She believed there was a need for a safe space on the dancefloor, free of misogyny and harassment.

Together they started the Pussy Party. By organising monthly parties which were free for women and queer people, Pussy Party helped bridge the gap between theory, which was prevalent in the student movement, and practice, which served the community at the bar. Although gay men and lesbian women had always frequented the two venues in the hotel (KCB and the Great Dane), Pussy Party created a space on the dancefloor that helped diversify the vocabulary of resistance which had previously been reserved for students involved in politics.

This new movement quickly gained momentum as those who were previously unable to articulate their politics in traditional political spaces, characterised by formal assemblies and meetings, were now able to adopt other forms of expression, which could be seen in their fashion, make-up and choice of music.

Regardless of bearing a colonial ruler's name, Milner Park Hotel today has become a social and cultural landmark as the face of progressive and intersectional politics in Johannesburg. By successfully creating a space with rules that put those at risk first, the hotel put the disco back into discourse.

Above
The Milner Park Hotel, on the corner of Juta and De Beer streets, photographed in 2010, before it underwent renovations. .

Opposite, clockwise from top

The latest additions of a fence outside to control the crowd, 2021.

The two bars, Kitchener's and Great Dane, with graffiti art on the walls, 2021.

The bar and seating area at KCB remains unchanged, with little modifications in the past 30 years.

The KCB dancefloor during the day. Behind the stage is the DJ booth and to the left is a long, padded seat attached to the wall.

Campy! bar

TOKYO, JAPAN

Takeshi Dylan Sadachi

Campy! bar opened in 2013 and is located on Hanazono Road, the main street of Tokyo's LGBTQ+ neighbourhood, Shinjuku Nichōme. The façade is covered with glass windows that leave the interior visible from the street and features a small red bench just outside the door. In a local categorisation of queer establishments, the bar can be classified as both a *mikkusu bā* (mix bar) and a *kankō bā* (sightseeing bar).

Sightseeing bars are primarily gay bars that, partially or mainly, cater to a non-queer audience that want to 'sightsee' and interact with queer staff. Mix bars are queer bars that are inclusive of any gender, sexual orientation and subculture, and although they often centre around gays or lesbians, they stand in contrast to the many gay and lesbian bars in Japan that exclusively target a specific age, body type or gender performance. Both have the overlapping characteristic of being inclusive to non-queer individuals and having gained popularity in the 2000s. Campy! bar still stands out within these categories, however, thanks to its majority workforce of drag queens, who are there to converse and serve drinks rather than to perform.

The glass windows expose these extravagantly dressed 'queens' against interior walls filled with tiles of red, orange, yellow and blue, reminiscent of the 1970s, and despite being a relatively small space with only 27 seats, the bar stands out with bright colours and dazzling lights that spill out into the street.

Campy! bar's space is not so much about shielding queer communities or creating an exclusive space for a sense of bonding but about providing visibility by, to an extent, commodifying queerness.

Previously a heterosexual-owned café, as the area became increasingly queer and nocturnal the establishment closed its doors in the late 1990s and the space was rented and left unused by a senior figure at the publisher of the Japanese gay magazine *Badi*. The current owner, who at the time was an editor at *Badi*, asked to borrow the space for a monthly pop-up café and this became the predecessor of Campy! bar. The café was recognised as the first open-air café of Nichōme in the 1997 edition of *Queer Studies*, a Japanese academic publication, and it stood in contrast to the closed and underground norm of the area.[112] The space's signature open structure was inherited from a non-queer business that had lost popularity due to the dominance of the queer population of the area, signifying that the neighbourhood had in itself become queerer, opportunely reducing the reason for shielding those who came there.

In 2019, Campy! bar opened its first branch outside of Nichōme, in Parco Shibuya, a trendy new shopping mall in the fashionable district of Shibuya, Tokyo. This branch is located on the restaurant floor of the shopping mall, outside of the queer neighbourhood and, contrary to the first location, has chosen a neutral colour scheme. Parco's website explains that 'the white-based retro interior accentuates the presence of cross-dressed staff', implying that the bar is a showcase centred on the staff, rather than a space for customers to socialise.[113] The branch, which equally accommodates non-queer customers, functions as a queer enclave far from the queer district, challenging the geographical boundary of queer space.

Above
By night, the venue's multicoloured interior becomes more prominent.

Opposite, top
The glass-covered façade, with its red bench.

Opposite, bottom
The interior of the bar.

COMMUNAL

Centro Cultural Guanuca

MATAGALPA, NICARAGUA

Sara Yaoska Herrera Dixon and Helen Dixon

Nicaraguan queer history shows how different forms of queerness occupy multiple 'elsewheres.' These can be hidden enclosures, intimate safe spaces, protected public spaces or open sites of visibility and inclusion within street events such as the fiestas populares. These festivals express religious-indigenous syncretism – the layering of precolonial and colonial spiritual and religious beliefs.[114] They are also public spaces for trans people to express themselves and for practices such as cross-dressing, that echo the third gender subjectivities and dissident sexualities originating in precolonial cultures across the Americas.[115]

Queerness has become more visible recently in public places during Pride celebrations, as well as through political protests by the feminist and LGBTQI rights movements.

Situated in a small city in northern Nicaragua, in the market neighbourhood of Guanuca, the Centro Cultural Guanuca acted as an alternative community gathering place where rural and urban queer people could safely congregate. The centre's colonial-style building was first renovated in the late 1980s by the theatre group Cihualtlampa. It has been run since the early 1990s by the feminist collective Grupo Venancia as a site of resistance to the wider context of homophobic machismo. As an important regional 'elsewhere,' this gathering place offered an alternative to metropolitan narratives, which imply that LGBTQI people can only be visible in larger urban environments.

Initially stigmatised in the city as a place run by cochonas (dykes), the Centro Cultural Guanuca was gradually recognised as an inclusive space with free entry, where local families, working people, progressive political activists, feminists, artists and musicians, young LGBTQI people and others could meet in safety and reclaim the deeper egalitarian values of the revolutionary period from contemporary critical perspectives.[116]

As well as housing Grupo Venancia's offices, the building hosted multiple programmes, including a small library, a large workshop space and a central patio with a mango tree and stage. The patio is surrounded by covered archways, where a café-bar and kitchen are located. Upstairs there are two more private meeting rooms and a psychotherapy space, as well as dormitories used by visiting women belonging to rural and national networks.

The cultural centre is approached via a side street. The cream façade of the large house once blended anonymously into the buildings around it.

Later, Grupo Venancia's sign was placed outside, and after that a large mural was painted, portraying the building's inner life. To improve accessibility, a ramp was built from street level to the centre's wooden door, always open to the community until recent events. Through this door, an enclosed entrance area unfolds into the internal patio.

The entranceway marks a transition from the street to a protected open space. This passage was the place of the first publicly announced celebration of Pride in the early 1990s, where an exhibition of images and words by lesbians was consciously situated just inside the door, visible at a glance from the street. Since then, the threshold has been transformed with different interventions and symbolic gestures – from signage about the centre being a 'zone free of discrimination, machismo and homophobia,' to the placement of a 'security detector' with rainbow feather dusters to 'dust off' one's prejudices.

While the early gatherings of lesbians were in the more intimate, enclosed private spaces within the building, these expanded into celebrations, public events and Pride parties occupying the whole building, attracting local young people of different gender identities, expressions and sexualities looking for a safe time out.

Grupo Venancia's work questioning gender norms and heterosexism with local, rural and young feminist networks enabled the Centro Cultural Guanuca to also become a home for these feminists to visit, where they could stay the night for free, and share meals together. The networks' queer-identifying people were thus able to emerge from isolation, connect with each other, empower themselves and participate in the wider feminist and 'sexual diversity' movements.

The Centro Cultural Guanuca was forced to close its doors in 2021 due to the current political climate of state repression against social movements and civil society organisations.

As a sign of continued life and resistance, in May 2021 the mural on the façade was renovated to strengthen its colours and lift morale in the community.

Opposite, clockwise from top-left

Front façade of the Centro Cultural Guanuca, 2008. The signage reads, 'Grupo Venancia: feminist popular education and communication.' The printed sign on the right-hand side of the door says, 'For the right to exist, to organise and to express ourselves.'

View of the lower and upper spaces around the internal patio, as well as part of the structure of the original colonial building.

Stage decoration for LGBTQI Pride, 2014. The empty space anticipates the arrival of participants.

The mural on the front façade portrays the rural and urban communities that mostly use the centre, raising their voices, as well as highlighting cultural and educational activities that link diverse struggles. The ramp lettering reads, 'Neither women, nor the land, are territory for conquest'; the painted banner says, 'For the right to decide'; and the rainbow in front represents sexual and gender rights.

LGBTQI Pride, June 2014. The banner reads, 'For sexual freedom and diversity.' The audience included LGBTQI people, local families, working people, activists, feminists, artists, musicians and others.

Palladium

NEW YORK, USA

Ivan L Munuera

To understand the capacity of queer architecture today, it is necessary to understand how it has been constructed. The 'queer' in 'queer architecture' is not simply an adjective; it is also a verb that performs. Queerness is now often received as a given, as something detached from its historical trajectory. The questions it attempted to address have been lost through a form of collective sublimation.

Queerness can only remain queer if its reactive nature is preserved.

To respond to the question of what queerness inherited, we need a collective endeavour of recollection, an assembly of past examples to create a genealogy, an essential component to build up an emancipatory process. This brings us to New York City, to the early years of the HIV crisis, to a time in which queerness embraced architecture as a means of survival. The history of nightclubs as queer spaces is crucial in constructing a queer genealogy. In that time, nightclubs served as laboratories for sociopolitical experiments; where the definition of and advocation for queerness were approached through experimental ways of understanding architecture. One such 'laboratory' was the Palladium, designed by Arata Isozaki in 1985.

The Palladium in New York was a nightclub that signified the apotheosis of discos as spaces for social experimentation, particularly for the queer community – and the end of an era. Located at 126 East 14th Street, between Irving Place and Third Avenue, the building's history as a cinema, concert hall and club dates back to 1926, when the structure was purposely built as a movie theatre. Its incarnation as a nightclub lasted from 1985 to 1997 and, in little more than a decade, came to define an epoch.[117] It contained, shaped and propagated a very specific architecture, one that I call 'discotecture': the architecture of the disco – that is, an understanding of the architecture of these nightclubs that goes deeper than merely appreciating their spatial configurations, but rather which explores them more as the creation of an event where architecture and urban planning enact the era's politics and social constructions.

The Palladium started life as the Academy of Music, a movie theatre designed by William Fried[118] and located in front of an opera house with the same name. Like many other cinemas at that time, its interior design resembled the Beaux Arts opera houses of the 19th century: frescoes and mouldings decorated the vaults and domes of the main auditorium and were supported by Corinthian columns.[119] From the beginning, the theatre was considered a prime example of New York's cinematic spaces of the 1920s and '30s. This powerful combination of architectural and electronic control over both sound and image represented the culmination of the modern soundscape.

Steve Rubell and Ian Schrager, after their adventure as promoters of Studio 54, purchased the Palladium in the early 1980s with the intention of turning it into a nightclub. The theatrical context suited their belief that nightclubs offered a certain kind of atmosphere, an arena where a new community – the dancers, who came night after night – could perform. In discos and clubs everything becomes a stage: there is no distinction between the DJs and the public; everyone is interacting through their moves and the music, asking for more rhythm and getting it in response, together constructing an agent – the dancer – who has agglutinated the performativity of the building in their bodies.

Isozaki decided to intervene only in the interior. A new, high-tech double staircase, set with 2,400 round lights in glass blocks, was installed to welcome club goers.[120] A silver cubic framework rising 20m was dropped into the crumbling shell of the theatre at the lobby level. The lighting system, integral to the

Above, left
Designed by Arata Isozaki, the Palladium signified the apotheosis of discos as spaces for social experimentation, particularly for the queer community – and the end of an era.

Above, right
The nightclub, an arena where a new community – the dancers – performed their queerness night after night.

architecture, was designed by Fisher Marantz Stone,[121] who also designed the dancefloor: an area framed by two 25-screen video arrays, on which artists showed their works, including Laurie Anderson. The sound system, produced by Richard Long Associates along with EAW,[122] was described as a 'unique beast'. In addition to this, Schrager and Rubell hired Henry Geldzahler, formerly curator of 20th-century art at the Metropolitan Museum, to curate artwork for the space: Keith Haring painted a mural for the dancefloor; Jean-Michel Basquiat also installed some of his artworks; Kenny Scharf decorated the bathrooms; Francesco Clemente designed frescoes; and Andy Warhol the complimentary drink tickets.

Isozaki was not the only designer of the Palladium. The project was incomplete without its inhabitants: a community of cyborg-dancers where the architecture, lighting and sound systems, and the exhibited art, were an extension of their bodies. Even though the Palladium was far from being radical in the politics of its inhabitants or investors, the community of dancers that populated discotectures in New York promoted a kind of activism embodied in their own performativities. The main inhabitants were mostly LGBTQIA+ communities, and African Americans, Latinos and women. These communities were developing forms of resistance and empowerment to make themselves visible during the Nixon and Reagan administrations. As a result of this process, a collective political intelligence was developed, one that would later be momentous in generating the coalitions by which these communities responded to the emergence of the HIV/AIDS crisis in the mid-1980s. The queering element of the Palladium itself was based on creating a space where marginalised people became the epicentre of an architectural design.[123]

Café 't Mandje

AMSTERDAM, THE NETHERLANDS

Jeroen van Dijk

A candid salute from the bar attendant, the old Persian carpets firmly lining the tables, beer accompanied with a shot of spicy gin, and the walls and ceiling filled with memorabilia are just a few peculiarities with which Café 't Mandje welcomes the regular local or the international visitor arriving for the first time. Centrally situated on the Zeedijk or 'sea dyke', a main street now in the city's red-light district, the café's exterior only gives a taster of the riches inside. Its façade is typical of Amsterdam, with its narrow shopfront situated between two doors. The window proudly presents the name of the café, fashioned in a curly typeface used by many old Amsterdam bars and cafés. The window houses a display that almost functions as a shrine to the mid-20th century, when the café thrived under its illustrious owner Bet van Beeren, formerly known as the Queen of the Zeedijk.

It has always attracted newcomers to the city. Established by the openly lesbian Bet in 1927, it became a safe space for those who didn't fit the norm, welcoming lesbian women, sex workers, seamen, artists and homosexuals into the confines of its queer space. Aged 25, Bet acquired the café from her uncle, and named it 't Mandje ('The Little Basket'), as her mother would bring her food in a basket. Many deem her one of the icons of 20th-century Amsterdam and of Dutch gay liberation.

She often caused scuffles in the city and its surrounding villages, crossing through the streets on her motorbike, often with a female lover on the back.

Anyone walking into the café immediately notices the memorabilia and ephemera that line the walls and ceiling of the relatively small space. Bet liked to collect ties from her male visitors and attach them to the ceiling beams, on which some bras and other clothing items can also be found. Although homosexuality has not been illegal in the Netherlands since the 19th century, in light of rigid moral laws (in place until 1971) Bet could not allow same-sex customers to kiss, be intimate or dance with one another. Only on the birthday of the monarch, the Dutch national holiday, would the billiard table be removed to make place for a dancefloor, where men were allowed to dance with men, and women with women.

It was especially in the years after the Second World War, when the café was one of the few meeting places for queer people in the tumults of the red-light district, that it was at the height of its fame. It played a central role in the local area, organising charity events for the youth and the elderly and connecting the sex industry to the local population. Bet died in 1967, after which her sister managed the café until it closed in 1983 due to rising criminal activity in the area. The café's original interior has been preserved in the Amsterdam Museum and the City Archives since 1999, but was meticulously recreated when Bet's family reopened the café on the Dutch national holiday in 2008, keeping Bet's memory alive and welcoming everyone into their treasure trove of queer memory and the amiability of old Amsterdam.

Above, left
Exterior of Café 't Mandje, showing the old signboard in the shape of a basket with flowers, c 1953–1995.

Above, right
Window display showing a portrait of Bet van Beeren and the many ephemera she collected, 2007. (The café was renovated in 2007 and reopened in 2008.)

Opposite, top
The main space in 2007. After Bet van Beeren's death, she was laid on the café's billiard table for several days to be visited and celebrated by the café's visitors and loved ones.

Opposite, bottom
Ephemera hanging from the café's ceiling, 2007. The lace curtain is typical for old Amsterdam cafés.

Futur:st

MAKATI CITY, PHILIPPINES

Isola Tong

Futur:st and Today x Future for me is all about the people and the friendships. I feel very lucky to find a space with all these supportive, nonjudgmental people, where you can just be yourself.

– Micaela Benedicto

I don't feel like this is an original thought, but right now, it shows that there still is a bit of hope for the community and nightlife in general, as Futur:st is the last spot standing – well, a spot that I myself go to, at least. It is something from the past that exists in the present, and it is most probably also very much part of the future.

– Karlo Vicente

Located in the richest city in the Philippines, Futur:st (Futurist) was intended to be the more sophisticated satellite of Today x Future (see pp 118–19), at the heart of the Makati business district. During the onslaught of the Covid-19 pandemic, Futur:st miraculously survived its predecessor and is still in operation at the time of writing. Unlike 'Future', Futur:st has a dedicated space on the second floor to exhibit small works by some of the more established artists in the Philippines. The first floor contains the bar and the architectonic DJ's booth, clad in reflective metal sheets designed by a female Filipina architect, Micaela Benedicto, who also designed the architecture of the entire space. Expats, bankers, artists, celebrities, musicians, the queers, the straights, Gen Xers, Millennials and Gen Z-ers all gather here to wind-down and mingle. Being closer to the expat community of Manila, the bar is frequented by the AFAM (A Foreigner Assigned in Manila), producing a diverse and vibrant atmosphere that far exceeds its modest floor area.

Futur:st had been platforming queer artists and their works since its conception. It is notable that the space had hosted many female, trans and non-binary Filipinx artists such as Cru Camara, Tokwa Peñaflorida, AK Ocol, Anton Belardo and myself. This is true to its core value as an affirmative space, and an ally that supports people of marginalised identities who otherwise wouldn't be given a place to exhibit in heteronormative spaces. One notable queer event, Cherish, was organised by Ed Croix, a non-binary DJ and local legend on the Manila party scene. Cherish MNL is a concept of on-the-go club nights/events for the dancing queens of Manila. Mainly underground dance music and art, it was a nod and tribute to Ed's dear departed friend Jac, who was behind Australia's RAT Parties in the 1980s. Here we see that queer spaces are also intergenerational and transcend barriers of geography and time. They become an axis of multiple subjectivities united by the singular cause of looking for queer kinship and mingling, which are otherwise unavailable in other normative settings within the surrounding city.

Above
Isola Tong in the exhibition space on Futur:st's second floor, where typically small works are hung for display.

Opposite
The façade featuring the iconic arched window and neon pink door.

Oddbird Theatre

NEW DELHI, INDIA

Ekam Singh

When a couple of school friends in New Delhi thought of creating a performing arts venue which they hoped could become a vessel for intimately experiencing non-mainstream, alternative art and artists, they found a former warehouse in a run-down mill compound. A young architecture studio was hired. The brief was simple – an 'open space', a minimal vessel for uncelebrated artists. This was the birth of the Oddbird Theatre.

'Open', as the architects from Studio Juggernaut describe it, was not merely the brief but the philosophy with which Oddbird Theatre was conceived, and the eventual mantra with which it was run. An open space. A space for everyone. In the years it was running, it was an active magnet for queer artists and performers from around India and the world, including the likes of Alok V Menon and plays like *Contempt*.[124] As founders Akhil and Shambhavi would describe their vision, they never set out to make Oddbird a refuge of queer art or a safe space for queer artists, but their outlook and openness enabled the theatre to become one. Their sincerity as allies facilitated conversations with their colleagues and artists about queerness and the issues facing LGBTQ+ people. In contrast to tokenism, the space took it upon itself to give a sense of comfort and security to everyone who came in to experience it, regardless of their gender, caste, colour or sexual orientation. It empowered an intern to cross-dress at their place of work, in contrast to the city outside its walls that would outlaw it. It endorsed people of all kinds, in any combination, mingling on a Friday with other like-minded folk and even the artists performing that night, without judgment or restriction. This was best manifested in the team's decision to add a third bathroom to accommodate transgender, intersex or gender-nonconforming folk. It did this to make its patrons feel acknowledged. By simply being accepting, open and accommodating, Oddbird was able to validate and facilitate queer life.

When you entered Oddbird, you certainly felt different from most performing arts venues. For one, the floor-to-ceiling glass at the front allowed the visitor a tiny peek in. As an audience member, the black-box theatre, or the stripped-down aesthetic of the warehouse, felt approachable. Accessibility for anyone who visited was brilliant. A space encouraging the free-flow of movement. A pre-show area almost as big as the performance area, which encouraged mixing and mingling. You might go in for the artist or the performance but you came out having engaged in enthralling conversations and having made new friends. If one thinks of it, the only physical barrier in the entire area was a curtain between the performance and the pre-show areas.

This open curtain, in many ways, was both a metaphor and a physical manifestation of Oddbird's ideology. There are no walls, just a curtain. You can close the curtain, or open it and let people in. No boundaries. Just come and see. Unfortunately, like so many public establishments, Oddbird Theatre had to close its doors due to the Covid-19 pandemic in 2020. While the team still hopes to operate virtually, the 'open' warehouse is no longer operational. The city of Delhi lost one of its most unique spaces. Its spareness and openness – both physically and metaphysically – stood in contrast to a city of exaggeration and thresholds. Perhaps that is why it was an odd bird.

Above, left
A performance of the play *Queen Size*, with performers Lalit Khatana and Parinay Mehra, discussing queer love and expression in a society that condemns it. The informal, open nature of Oddbird allowed audiences to experience such performances with an intimacy that was both unnerving and moving.

Above, right
Alok, an internationally renowned performance artist and gender-nonconforming media personality, performing a monologue at Oddbird. Their use of mixed media and narrative resonated particularly with a predominantly South Asian audience of queer folk and allies.

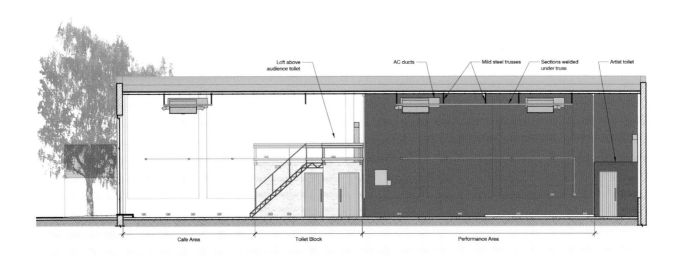

Loft above audience toilet   AC ducts   Mild steel trusses   Sections welded under truss   Artist toilet

Cafe Area   Toilet Block   Performance Area

Top to bottom

Section of the theatre. The team at architects Studio Juggernaut intervened in a way that allowed for flexibility and multiplicity for the artists and the event organisers to shape and form the interior space in accordance with the performance or the event. This minimal approach to materials, finishes and fittings constituted a space akin to a blank canvas for an artist to paint over.

Reception and café area. The café formed the public front of the theatre – allowing for larger gatherings, spill-overs and intermingling. One could grab a drink and strike up a conversation with a stranger before or after a performance – only to realise that the stranger was, in fact, the performing artist themselves.

One of the hallmarks of the Oddbird Theatre was the flexibility and openness. The open curtain, the flexible floor layout, the bare-essential setup within a warehouse and the muted colours created a welcoming atmosphere for the artists and patrons alike.

'Queer Space' course

CALIFORNIA, USA

David Eskenazi

It's 1992. Feminist and queer studies are moving into the arts, from places like Berkeley, California (think Judith Butler's 1989 *Gender Trouble*[125]) and landing in places like the University of California, Los Angeles (UCLA), where we find a group of five undergraduate architecture students initiating a course titled 'Queer Space'.[126] They prepare a course syllabus, where they write that their aim is to bring formulations of queer theory that were present in literary theory, film criticism and history into the fields of architecture and planning. Their aim is to discuss how space is sexualised and how sexuality is spatialised, whether urban communities and enclaves might change understandings of urbanisation, and how social conventions and media shape disciplines. They bring in graduate teaching assistants and a faculty advisor, and invite the wider queer architecture community into the class.

A student-led queer space, about queer space, is formed in an architecture school.

It's no accident that architecture students would enter a discussion about queerness through the topic of space. Space is the site of architecture's impact on the everyday, the real and the politics of bodies. The term *queer space* recurs in architecture: a brief, recent history of the term might pause in the American architectural discourse of the 1990s. It's a term we find as the course title, imported into architectural discourse. It's found again two years later in the 'Queer Space' exhibition at the Storefront for Art and Architecture in New York,[127] and three years later in the seminal book by Aaron Betsky, also titled *Queer Space*, written while teaching in Los Angeles.[128] In all three instances, we see architects, theorists, artists and academics looking for spaces and histories that point towards a definition of the term. At the Storefront exhibition, bodies and cities are examined, while in Betsky's book, it's historical spaces. In the UCLA class, the topics form along similar themes, including 'The domestic interior', 'The media', 'The city' and 'Theory'. These familiar topics can be found in a number of other architectural courses, and the aim of the syllabus was to address them through a queer lens.

Class topics were about things outside the classroom: the city, how disciplines are formed, domestic life. But in a follow-up to the course, the students wrote a frank assessment that reads much like a first theorising of queer space in the context of a classroom.[129] The assessment emphasised how the classroom has long been a contested site of education, a kind of heterotopic space outside of everyday life that constructs values, worldviews and methodologies that students carry with them for the rest of their lives. The angle of its critique is best theorised by writing like Paolo Freire's *Pedagogy of the Oppressed*,[130] which suggests that the learner should be an active participant in creating knowledge, in a kind of nonhierarchical staging of the classroom. To form queerness itself into the classroom is a difficult and paradoxical endeavour – as queerness questions all forms of normative and essentialising truths, and therefore also the traditional role of teacher transferring knowledge to a student seen as an empty vessel.

In the follow-up, the students suggested that the course too often relied on 'binary, polar paradigms' for framing discussions. They explained that this emphasised a totalising gay experience that didn't allow for a more inclusive, queer theory. Further, the space of the classroom itself became a site of problematic patterns: men spoke more than women, people of whiteness dominated discussions and 'the voice of academic erudition enjoyed authority against the testimony of more concrete language.'

In other words, familiar forms of power and authority crept into the space of the queer classroom.

We learn from the assessment that these issues, 30 years later, are still a part of the queer struggle. The struggle between erudition and concrete language, inclusivity and clarity, power and authority are still at the centre of the queer community's self-conception and work against heteronormative forms. The students remind us that if the classroom is the closest physical instantiation of a pedagogy, then it must also be examined as a queer space itself before a queer space can be theorised.

Opposite
Cover of the syllabus from the 'Queer Space' course at the University of California, Los Angeles, 1992.

IF YOU'RE IN A
BUILDING
YOU'RE
IN DRAG
QUEER SPACE

AUP 219.4
SPECIAL TOPICS IN THE BUILT ENVIRONMENT
[4 CREDITS]   ADVISOR: ED SOJA

QUEER SPACE

SPRING 1992

Pop-Up Queer Spaces

DHAKA, BANGLADESH

Ruhul Abdin

In Dhaka it's very difficult for young queers to find a space to call their own, and to find or date other queers without making themselves too visible and risking persecution. Pop-up events provide temporary safe spaces and a window of freedom – for a night of *adda* (hangouts) or dancing without worrying about what heteronormative people will think or do. Over the years there have been many cultural pop-up queer events, including dances, plays, readings, performances, etc.

They are not just entertainment for young queers, but a chance to meet others and find community.

These events usually take place in venues that are supportive of the queer community. There are many challenges to where club nights or events can be held safely. They can take place in restaurants, cafés, cultural centres and, more often, in homes owned by the affluent classes. Sometimes they can be held in diplomatic clubs, with foreign-national queers who have become part of the small community for the time they are in Bangladesh.

The difficulty of holding such events, especially in making sure they are secure for the community, has often meant invitations are offered only to people who are already known by the organisers. As many events are organised by, and for, the same groups of people, they inevitably exclude those who are outside of the circle. There is also a class barrier as events are sometimes priced beyond affordability, where there may be a charge for entry (for organising and providing drinks in a country that is not alcohol friendly), which limits attendees to the affluent LGBTQIA+ community. The potential to diversify these events is limited due to the resource requirements needed to host safe pop-ups. There is an issue of 'visibility' for the people organising, and being too visible, or being known to be an organiser of queer events, has led to fatal consequences in the past. It is not that there are not cheap venues available, it is the issue of risks for those that may be visibly queer, how they leave or enter the venue, and whether the venue is sensitive to the community.

The celebratory nature of the events, and the build-up over the years towards more and more of them, led to the murder of Xulhaz Mannan and Tonoy, both prominent activists in the queer community and involved in the LGBTQIA+ *Roopbaan* magazine. This was a targeted attack by religious fundamentalists who hacked both to death in Xulhaz's home in 2016. At the time, it left the affluent queer gay community in total shock, with fellow activists and organisers seeking refuge in other countries. Since then, organising pop-ups has been reduced and even halted entirely for a period.

Despite this, the middle-class queer community navigates and uses their privilege to continue hosting events that operate within tight and often changing constraints, while others with less financial capacity struggle to do so. With more and more social media exposure on the risks of being openly queer in the country, and with neighbouring India repealing its draconian Section 377 Sodomy Act, there is some hope among Dhaka's young that something similar may happen in Bangladesh. The existence of these ever-shifting and relocating events shows the incredible adaptability of the community in Dhaka, and how, no matter the circumstances, a shared joy in life, socialising and celebration in safe spaces is something that continues to happen all over the city, in all times and under all circumstances, no matter the external threats.

Above, top
A dance-off to Momtaz's 'Local Bus'.

Above, bottom
A bit of fun in dancing with the host!

Opposite, clockwise from top

In a state of joy, dancing under the lights.

Safely dancing under the disco lights.

Posing for the gala event.

Museo Experimental El Eco

MEXICO CITY, MEXICO

León Daniel

Mathias Goeritz, who was born in Germany in 1915, moved to Mexico in 1949, where he produced most of his sculptural work. He was one of the biggest figures of the Modern Movement, and one of the most recognised sculptors of the 20th century in the country.

In 1952, Goeritz met the entrepreneur Daniel Mont, who would later become his great friend and patron. Mont, who was gay, founded a few art galleries and owned Los Eloines, a cabaret considered to be one of the first popular nightclubs, as well as a rare semi-public space in which homosexual relationships did not need to be clandestine, breaching the usual standards of decorum in public life of the time, even if still only in a highly cautious manner.

It cannot, however, be defined as a 'gay' place, as such a term did not exist at the time. Above all, it wasn't an exclusively homosexual place, until when, by organic means – and its owners' overt publicity – the place started being populated by explicitly queer identities, artists and intellectuals with liberal ideas and visions on sexuality and sexual identity.

Although Goeritz wasn't an architect, Daniel Mont commissioned him to create the design of a 'gallery, restaurant and bar', and even though he was given total freedom throughout the design process, Mont did specifically request a bar counter, which – as in Los Eloines' counter – would have been backed by a mural by Carlos Mérida. A Guatemalan artist who migrated to Mexico in 1919, Mérida developed a pictorial language based on geometric abstraction and was one of the most important figures in plastic integration in architecture in Mexico.

With El Eco, conceived as an experimental museum, Goeritz put together his manifesto of an 'Emotional Architecture', which, in his words, is 'an architecture whose principal function is emotion'.[131] The space quite literally avoids the 'straight':

'There are almost no 90-degree angles in the building's plan, some walls begin thin and end thick.'[132]

Another of the many ideas behind El Eco's design was that of 'the penetrable sculpture', which is the idea of making one actively perceive a sexual sense in the architecture.

In reaction to the *Manifesto of Emotional Architecture*, Goeritz was accused of homosexuality by the muralists Diego Rivera and David Alfaro Siquerios (two of the most regarded figures in the art scene at the time), who saw these artistic expressions as counter-revolutionary, and attacking the country's nationalistic principles.

Even though Daniel Mont died in 1953, after the inauguration of El Eco, the place served as a gallery and bar up to 1955, and exclusively as a gay nightclub until 1959, when it was closed following an infamous murder. The main suspect of the crime was forced to reveal as his alibi that on the night of the homicide he was meeting his homosexual lover at El Eco, which caused a long police investigation, resulting in the venue closing permanently.

Later on, after a variety of different uses, the building was abandoned for many years, following which it functioned for a period as a theatre and as a meeting place for political activities.

In a gay magazine from 1985, the anthropologist José Ignacio Lanzagorta found in a Zona Rosa (pink zone) map an advertisement for a club which went by the name of Fiesta San Luis, a place that does not appear on any written or photographic records, unlike some other known gay clubs from that time. Despite not appearing in any of the many official building registers (as a gallery, bar, theatre, etc), Fiesta San Luis had the same address as El Eco, leading one to imagine that the venue was still functioning as a gay hangout.

In 2005 El Eco was refurbished by the Universidad Nacional Autónoma de México (UNAM), restoring and respecting its purpose as an experimental museum, in which, among other events, new architectural interventions were based on Goeritz's ideas and principles.

Currently, even though most publications avoid talking about the past of the building, the museum recognises the queer nature of its home, including a programme that revives the bar in memory of the social spirit of Daniel Mont.

Above
The architecture practice APRDELESP turns El Eco's patio into a park in 2016.

Opposite, clockwise from top-left

Main entrance to the building. There is a forced perspective generated by the position of the walls and the lines of the tiles in the floor.

Floor plan of the museum.

Map of the gay neighbourhood in Mexico City (called the Zona Rosa), with an advertisement for Fiesta San Luis, in 1985.

Art installation in El Eco's yard, 2019.

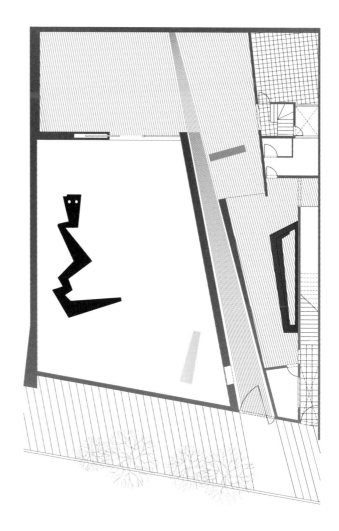

London Lesbian and Gay Centre

LONDON, ENGLAND

Ben Campkin

A note from 1982 sets out the vision for the London Lesbian and Gay Centre (LLGC): 'a central community-based centre run by lesbians and gay men for lesbians and gay men, providing a relaxed alternative to the commercial "scene", which often excludes women, older and younger people, and those without much money.'[133] First imagined by campaigners, the plans were developed through public meetings under the auspices of the radical New Left Greater London Council (GLC), led by Ken Livingstone, and its Gay Working Party.

The centre was located at 67–69 Cowcross Street, a building purchased for this purpose in 1983. Comprising five storeys, it had been a poultry-packing facility. The conversion was to a design by architect Fiona McLean. It incorporated a disco, bars, café, shop, bookshop, a women-only floor and coffee bar, a crèche, meeting rooms, darkroom, workshop spaces and an archive. Accessibility provisions in the redesign encapsulated the GLC's radical equalities policies, as did the cultural and community initiatives that were co-located here. It was envisaged as a central facility that would connect with a network of centres in other boroughs and cities, and that would become an international beacon of lesbian and gay rights.

Formed at a time when the community was battling AIDS and extreme homophobia, the centre became an important site of identification and social life. It was a space of activism, education, publication, archiving, debate, performance, artistic production, dancing, mourning, exercise, sex and much more.

It became a platform for intra-community politics, and debates revolved around the possibilities and pitfalls of coalitions across interconnecting feminist, lesbian and gay, and anti-racist social movements, between different political agendas and identities.

Specific points of contestation included the kinds of activities and groups that would be welcome, such as the accommodation of sadomasochistic groups; whether or not – in the terminology of the day – transvestites, transexuals or bisexuals were welcome; and the male and white dominance of the venue and its programme.

High-profile attacks on the GLC by the homophobic Conservative government (led by Margaret Thatcher in her second term as Prime Minister), the withdrawal of funding, and the GLC's abolition in 1986, were the overriding factors that determined the centre's rapid demise.[134]

As it reconfigured its operational model, from workers' cooperative to social enterprise, it accrued high debts, there were controversies over financial mismanagement and theft, and the costs of purchasing the building were prohibitively high. Remarkably, it remained open until 1992, hosting a wide range of political and activist organisations, services and cultural events, many of which continue to play an important role today.

Above
LLGC leaflet, 1985.

Opposite, clockwise from top-left

LLGC newsletter, November 1988, cover with cartoon section by graphic artist NINE, who worked on various publications linked to the centre.

The exterior, 1985.

Ground-floor and basement plans.

Concept drawing of the basement disco.

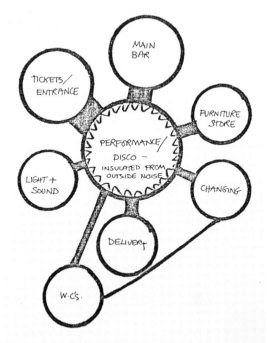

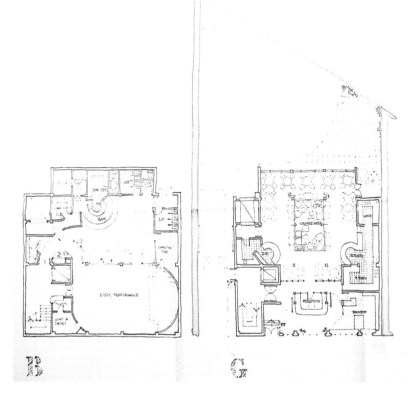

Sagitario

LIMA, PERU

Alexander Auris

Lima does not have a gay street. However, there are areas where there is a concentration of queer amenities which are mostly interior spaces that do not reveal themselves as queer-friendly on their façades. Among these are two poles of queerness, located at either end of Arequipa Avenue, one of the city's main thoroughfares. These areas belong to two different districts, Miraflores and the historic centre of Lima, both with different policies regarding their opening hours. In most districts of Lima, clubs have to close at 3am, but the informality and abandonment that surround the historic centre of Lima allow the party to continue beyond that, sometimes even for 24 hours. This condition of informality has become an opportunity for alternative urban subcultures, or communities that need space, to appropriate the night, and some of the city centre's buildings.

Sagitario is one of these spaces. It is located on the ground floor of the Edificio Wilson, an iconic Modernist building designed as a housing project by the architect Enrique Seoane and built in 1945–46. Designed as a residential structure with commercial space on the ground floor, it has since been converted into a queer club, a gay sauna and a gay hotel. The Edificio Wilson has become Sagitario.

Although it all began with a queer dance club on the ground floor of the building, Sagitario incrementally occupied the higher levels, transforming housing units first into a gay sauna, and later also a hotel. Today, it occupies approximately 40 per cent of the total space of the building, turning it into a factory of queer experiences. It operates like queer clockwork: the club opens at 9pm, at 6am the smell of eucalyptus wafts onto the dancefloor. The DJ announces that the sauna is now open. If you want to go, you have to go out of the building and use a different door. The hotel is 24/7, so either between dancing sessions or after using the sauna, you can take a nap[135] there whenever. You can stay for over 24 hours, moving around the building. You will be ok.

This iconic Modernist building has been queered. Edificio Wilson expresses the different layers of occupation of Peruvian history. It is divided into three parts: the ground floor, with its marble façade that is reminiscent of Neo-Colonial architecture, the intermediate body, with a clear Modernist architectural language, and the top level, with some pre-Hispanic iconography.

This building, a symbol of Latin American Modernism, is unanimously praised by architects. There is a fetish for modern architecture in Latin American architecture schools, and the iconic buildings from this period are studied as if they were perfect objects frozen in time. This traditional form of historical analysis forces a certain distance from the object of its study, and this distance precludes any discussion of the contemporary use of these iconic buildings. Most architects who teach or study this building sadly have no clue about Sagitario.

This iconic Modernist building has been queered, and only queer experience allows us to understand and appreciate it, and by extension this entire layer of the city.

The building has been modified in recent years. Many of the marble pieces that covered the ground-floor façade have been removed or painted over. The original doors and windows have been replaced and the interior of the ground floor has completely changed. The owners of Sagitario have managed to keep the entrance to their businesses separate from the housing units, which is probably one of the reasons for its longevity. The building looks abandoned and has no signs or symbols of anything queer happening inside (no rainbows or flags).

The façade of an apartment building and the language of a Modernist 'masterpiece' disguise a queer performance. Only queer experiences reveal this layer, a language that is shared among us, and that allows us to keep our spaces safe and subversive.

Above
External view of Edificio Wilson – Sagitario.

Opposite, clockwise from top
Dance club, sauna, and the Hotel Sagitario (interior, and two facades).

For those unable to mingle, love and connect with the people they desire in private spaces, often the public sphere – in the interstices and gaps of cities, and at times of day when the rest of the population might be absent – is the place where their queer lives can be lived most freely. In a beautiful and recent evolution of our urban environments, more and more instances of overt public expression have been manifested, where queerness has been able to flourish in full public view. Unabashedly taking over spaces where once shame and violence would have greeted any queer body brave enough to proudly exist in the open, archives have been created that are uplifting queer visibility in history, and in our collective memory. Similarly, new institutions with budgets and a degree of permanence are beginning to emerge, which for the first time provide queer communities with officially recognised anchors in cities that had heretofore contained queerness in a perpetual state of precarity.

MASTERplano

BELO HORIZONTE, BRAZIL

Vítor Lagoeiro

MASTERplano was created by eight artists from Belo Horizonte – the third-largest metropolitan area in Brazil – who got together to promote and use queer raves as a resource for rediscovering and occupying the city and its spaces. Expressing itself through music, art and architecture, the group invites the public to experiment and collectively build hybrid spaces that blur conventional boundaries, like those between institutional spaces and the public realm, or between entertainment and activism.

Such was the case when the headquarters of the city council was dramatically taken over by MASTERplano and transformed into an accessible, queer-friendly temporary nightclub during protests against the rise of public transport fares in Belo Horizonte in 2015. It was during that period when Brazil began to see the rise of the extreme right as a successful political force, one that would profoundly and terribly mark the following years. The coup against president Dilma Roussef in 2016 would initiate a political process that seemed to have reached its climax in 2018 with the election of Jair Bolsonaro, a right-wing extremist who openly attacked human rights, who frequently used hate speech and who enacted policies that undermined whole marginalised segments of the population, including women and the LGBTQ+ community.

One of the consequences of this political change was that life became rather unstable and threatening for many members of the LGBTQ+ community, which made the creation of occasions and spaces that would celebrate and protect queer existence an urgent need across all of Brazil. For MASTERplano, partying and clubbing was perceived as a platform through which such important action could be made possible. The events held by MASTERplano have always worked on strategies that would make the dancefloor a place where dissident bodies would be welcomed, celebrated and respected. The line-ups are always predominantly formed by LGBTQ+ people and women to create more opportunity for such artists, who are always underrepresented in the DJ booths of clubs and festivals in Brazil. Members of the trans community are given free admission to all MASTERplano's events, as they experience the lowest employment rates of any group in Brazil, and

therefore have the least access to entertainment. And finally, the security staff are almost entirely composed of women, as a way of making it safer and easier for other women and queer people to report any violence and abuse.

Before the collective was founded, clubbing in Belo Horizonte was inaccessible to most of its population; events were expensive to attend and generally unwelcoming to LGBTQ+ people and women. As a direct response to that context, the group of people who would later become members of the collective decided to experiment with another way of partying and socialising in the city. On a chilly winter night in 2015, they hired a sound system and set it up on a public sidewalk, right in front of an affordable downtown bar. The deal that was struck between the bar and the collective-to-be was a simple one: the latter needed a power source for their sound equipment, and the former needed to sell more drinks.

Neither hesitated to help each other and, before they knew it, an unexpected and colourful crowd of hundreds were dancing together in the street – and for free, too – until dawn.

Although this is only one example out of countless nights and days, its format reveals another important aspect of MASTERplano's state of mind: finding a way of unfolding clubbing into an urban experience that connects people and their desires with untapped possibilities the city has to offer. After the first trial, MASTERplano continued to experiment with raving in all types of spaces. Flyovers, abandoned warehouses, waterfalls, parks, garages, football fields, skate parks, museums and even bakeries are among the many types of venue that have been used to bring the clubbing scene in Belo Horizonte out into the streets and into much more of an accessible, open and level playing field.

As the project travelled around the city, each subsequent new space would bring together bigger and bigger crowds, and the cumulative experience ended up teaching the collective that unique spatial solutions were required for each of the newly occupied spaces to ensure the party was comfortable, visually stimulating and safe for those attending. The solutions that the collective found to achieve this in a diverse array of spaces are not kept secret because, ultimately, MASTERplano was never intended to be the only stakeholder in Belo Horizonte's queer clubbing scene. It was intended as a catalyst to inspire and open doors for other artists and collectives, for others to pick up the spirit and experiment with their own way of reshaping the dynamics of sociability in the city. The knowledge of how to create and run these raves safely was passed on.

The collective realised that the only way to achieve this aim was to recognise club culture not only as a form of entertainment, but also as a learning opportunity in which stakeholders can share knowledge and experiences, a way of nurturing a brighter future for the queer club scene. That is why, over the years, MASTERplano has also started to offer educational activities open to the general public: workshops, debates, masterclasses and film screenings followed by group discussions. The purpose of these activities goes beyond sharing technical and practical knowledge, as they also aspire to encourage critical thinking within the wider community in Belo Horizonte. Through these activities and consequent discussions, MASTERplano hopes it might assist in the queer community's continuing creative transformation of the city, injecting colour and imagination into its streets, warehouses, parks and many other spaces yet to be explored for years to come.

Above
One of the warmest moments of MASTERplano's dancefloor: when the sun comes up and becomes part of the misty rave atmosphere, 2017.

Top
Belo Horizonte dances
under the sun over the last
minutes of the 12-hour rave
for MASTERplano's fourth
anniversary, 2019.

Bottom
The former pottery factory
occupied by MASTERplano in
downtown Belo Horizonte for
their first anniversary in 2016.

All of MASTERplano's resident
DJs get together on stage on
the morning of their fourth
anniversary party, 2019.

One of the raucous
performances of the band Teto
Preto for the colourful crowd
of MASTERplano, 2016.

Bishopsgate Institute

LONDON, ENGLAND

Stefan Dickers

Bishopsgate Institute was founded 'for the benefit of the public' in 1894, and has been a home for ideas and debate, learning and enquiry ever since, with a busy programme of adult courses and cultural events. Our special collections and archives document the individuals and organisations who have strived for social, political and cultural change.

But they also preserve and celebrate the lives of everyday people – often telling the stories which are neglected by the mainstream.

The Institute has increasingly offered a space for LGBTQIA+ people to come together and learn about their history. Alongside same-sex dance events and courses on LGBTQIA+ literature, our special collections and archives hold one of the most extensive and accessible collections on LGBTQIA+ history, politics and culture in the UK. Covering the late 19th century onwards, collecting started in 2011. Anyone can explore the collections for free, supported by our team of experts.

The collections include archives from the campaign charity Stonewall; Switchboard, the LGBT+ Helpline; the gay men's health charity, GMFA; the Museum of Transology, a collection of artefacts donated by the community and curated by historian E-J Scott (see pp 190–1); queer performance collectives such as Duckie and Bloolips; and material relating to the HIV/AIDS charity the Terrence Higgins Trust, as well as archives of lifestyle magazines such as *Boyz* and *QX*. We hold the archives of individuals, including journalist Paris Lees, LGBT History Month founder Sue Sanders, campaigner Peter Tatchell and many others. We also welcome archives from anybody wanting to document their own personal queer history, such as documents, photographs, diaries, letters or artefacts.

We're proud to be custodians of the Lesbian and Gay Newsmedia Archive (LAGNA) that includes over 350,000 press cuttings from the straight press regarding LGBTQIA+ history from the 1890s to today. The cuttings are organised by subject matter, biographical content and location and often paint a stark picture of the vilification and homophobia LGBTQIA+ people have experienced from society and the press – as well as capturing moments of protest and celebration.

We hold a library of around 15,000 LGBTQIA+ titles, from academic works, biographies, fiction and poetry to pulp fiction, along with journals from around the world. The LGBTQIA+ Pamphlet Collection contains around 2,500 items, including programmes for festivals and events, material from campaigning organisations and catalogues, alongside extensive ephemera such as club flyers, T-shirts, banners and badges.

We also host the UK Leather and Fetish Archive, a national collection documenting the history and heritage of fetish, kink and BDSM in the UK. This archive holds organisational papers, flyers, journals, pamphlets, books and artefacts.

Our collection is growing all the time, and we are always striving to capture the full diversity of LGBTQIA+ life today, as well as the vital histories that brought us here.

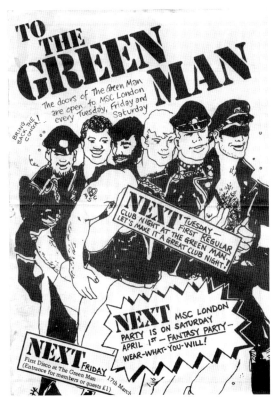

Top
The 'canonisation' of film
director Derek Jarman by
charity, protest and street
performance organisation
the Sisters of Perpetual
Indulgence at Dungeness,
Kent, 22 September 1991.

Bottom
LGBTQIA+ badges.
The Institute holds a growing
collection of over 500 badges
from various Pride marches,
campaigns and groups.
These items, many now
iconic, provided a sense
of pride, community and
identity when worn.

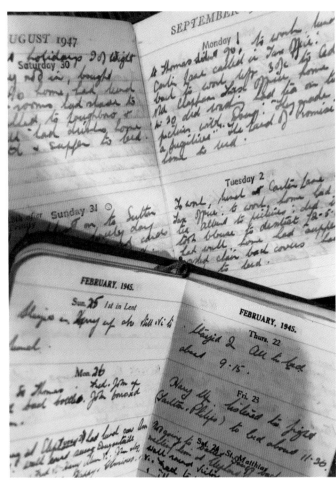

Bloolips

Diaries of William 'Bill'
Mahoney (pictured here)
documenting his life and
relationship living with
partner Doug in Brixton,
London, from 1945 to 1978.
A fascinating and rare insight
into a loving relationship
prior to and after the
partial decriminalisation of
male homosexuality with
the passing of the Sexual
Offences Act of 1967.

Promotional photograph for
queer performance collective
Bloolips, c 1980.

El Último Vagón

MEXICO CITY, MEXICO

León Daniel

Given Mexico City's sprawling nature and its urban infrastructural condition, most people spend between two and four hours a day on public transport. The Metro (underground) is the second most used means of public transportation. Mexico City's underground network was launched in 1969 by the local government. It currently includes 195 stations divided into 12 underground lines, covering a length of 200km beneath the city (some of them extending to areas of the State of Mexico) and carrying 4.5 million passengers a day.[136]

The Metro is not simply and only a transport system, it houses a number of businesses, services and activities, among which can be found a museum, eating places, a cinema, medical clinics, gallery spaces and even pre-Hispanic ruins.

The Metro has become a de facto underground city, in which human interactions often break from the pre-established and imposed order of the city above.

Even though homosexuality was never explicitly regarded as a crime, homophobia and machismo have always been strongly embedded in Mexico's culture. It is common to find public spaces, where there is safety in anonymity, used as arenas for flirting and the initiation of sexual relationships between sexually diverse people.

The writer and photographer Eriko Stark places the first written record of flirting in the Metro in the book *El Vampiro de la Colonia Roma*, by Luis Zapata, published in 1979.[137] However, Zapata himself recognises the existence of such activities since at least the beginning of the 1970s, and although no one knows how this was established as a custom, it is a well-known fact by most everyday Metro users that the last carriage of the train (El Último Vagón) has long since been appropriated by the LGBTQ+ community. This happens for the full working hours of the Metro, and is above all for sexually oriented encounters, either erotic or simply those involving the explicit display of affection between men. This custom is known as '*metrear*'.

The last train carriage functions as a safe space for the queer community; for instance, transgender people who are not able to 'pass' as cis people are discriminated against in other carriages, especially in peak hours, during which time overcrowding often leads to aggression and conflict.

Cruising and the social activities of LGBTQ+ people spread towards the areas of the boarding platform that are closer to the last carriage. In this area that serves as a waiting space and for flirting and showing off, many people leave written sexual and love messages on the Metro walls.

In 2011, in an attempt to terminate these sexual activities taking place on the last carriage of the train, the Metro administration decided to shut the last three carriages during night hours.

Although there was never a formal declaration by the authorities that this action had anything to do with the LGBTQ+ communities, it resulted, either intentionally or unintentionally, in promoting discrimination and homophobia, and generating an unhealthy and dirty image around homosexuals, fostering, among other things, police extortion (demanding bribes from users).

In 2012, those very same carriages were reopened after multiple complaints by the LGBTQ+ community to the local human rights commission, in which the negative consequences of the measure were detailed.

Currently these spaces, also known as 'the happy box', represent a test case of resistance, and despite the multiple measures which have been taken in the past to eliminate their appropriation by the queer community, the necessity and existence of these spaces continues unabated.

Above
The last train carriage
(El Último Vagón).

Opposite, clockwise from top

Showing affection between gay and straight couples in public places is very common in Mexico City.

A photo of 'Huilos' inside the last train carriage.

Couples at the boarding platform.

A message written on the wall of the boarding platform: 'Carlos: I know that you will read this someday. I want you to know that despite the distance, you will always be in my mind and in my heart. Sincerely, Edgar.'

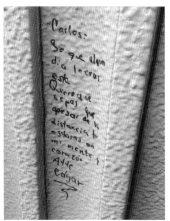

Queer House Party

ZOOM/LONDON, ENGLAND

Lo Marshall

Queer House Party (QHP) forms part of an enduring and essential aspect of queer community organising; making spaces for LGBTQIA+ communities to come together and find joy in adverse circumstances. As the Covid-19 pandemic took hold in Britain, and London went into lockdown for the first time, venues lay dormant, leaving LGBTQIA+ communities without spaces to gather, and performers, promoters and DJs – the cultural heartbeat of many queer spaces – without their regular bookings. In response, housemates, activists, DJs and community organisers Harry Gay, Wacha (Seren Notsarah) and Passer (Nik Erz) used the online platform Zoom to throw a party on the first Friday night of the first UK lockdown in March 2020, with the aim of giving queers a sense of release and community in the face of isolation and anxiety. Since that first Friday, when thousands of participants logged in, Queer House Party has become an award-winning party with a global audience, and a touchstone for LGBTQIA+ folks seeking queer community and culture, often as respite from cis-hetero norms that dominate many LGBTQIA+ people's domestic circumstances and bio-family relationships.

At the core of Queer House Party is an ethos of collaboration, solidarity and accessibility, with the politics of the collective at the fore and often in the backdrop; a beautifully crafted fabric banner reading 'Fuck the Tories' adorns the wall behind in-house DJs. The banner typically hangs alongside camp party paraphernalia (balloons, fringing and buntings), everyday domestic décor (pot plants, mirrors, vases) and functional domestic fittings (radiators, curtains, a fridge).

While online spaces cannot replicate the sensory atmosphere created by sharing physical spaces together, Queer House Party shows the possibilities for online parties in offering a level and breadth of accessibility that is rarely, if ever, realised in LGBTQIA+ spaces, and puts QHP's maxim 'If I can't dance, it's not my revolution' into practice. Geographically speaking, the internet allows the living room that hosts QHP to transcend many territorial borders. The barriers to participation in physical spaces that impact LGBTQIA+ people whose inclusion is disabled by architecture and the built environment (steps and staircases, inaccessible bathrooms) dissolve in virtual space. Tickets are available on a sliding scale, from £15 to £0, ensuring no-one is priced out of participating, and QHP's accessibility team provide British Sign Language, audio description and closed captions to break down obstacles to communication.

A crucial aspect of QHP is its capacity to provide income for DJs and performers, and fundraise in solidarity with a range of organisations and causes whose work addresses social justice issues and social vulnerabilities that have emerged or intensified during the pandemic. This includes Black Lives Matter, Sisters Uncut and United Strippers of the World. This is not the first time house parties have functioned as a way of creating spaces for socially marginalised and oppressed communities, while creating income for the hosts, and raising funds for organisations and campaigns. Delving into queer archives like Rukus! (a black LGBT cultural archive held at London Metropolitan Archives) and those at the Bishopsgate Institute in London (see pp 160–63), you'll find home-made flyers for 'rent parties' and 'benefits' for lesbian and gay organisations, with hand-drawn maps, residential addresses, phone numbers and travel information. QHP continues this legacy of house parties and praxis – where queer community organising and activism manifest as throwing parties in our domestic abodes. Assisted by the internet and adapting to the times we are living through, house parties have extended into online spaces. As lockdown ended in the UK in spring 2021, QHP began venturing into hybrid events held simultaneously online and in venues.[138]

Clockwise from top

Queer House Party DJs Harry Gay, Wacha and Passer, photographed in a residential London backstreet.

Flyer for Friday 27 March 2020, designed by Fredde Lanka.

SolidariTease collaboration between Queer House Party and Cybertease.

An illustration of Passer, Wacha and Harry Gay, by Fredde Lanka (used in a social media post to promote a party).

Caminito Verde

MEXICO CITY, MEXICO

Sergio Galaz García

At the southern edge of Mexico City is a *pedregal*: a unique landscape of endemic vegetation and volcanic rocks chiselled by eruptions, temperate weather and the pouring of summer rains. Sitting over the *pedregal* is an architectural tour de force: Ciudad Universitaria (CU). At the end of the 1950s, the headquarters of UNAM – Mexico's flagship public university – was moved from its old premises in the city centre to a massive Modernist project built atop a lava-bed zone that had until then managed to escape being swallowed by the city. Across CU, hundreds of acres of tended garden spaces fill the vast interstices between its many buildings, creating a unique green area covering much of the university's new campus.

Inside this scenery is a garden of earthly delights, a place made partly out of the *pedregal*, the university and its landscaping, but brought to life through a union of lust and nature. This is the *Caminito Verde* – the Little Green Road – an area enabled, provoked and inspired by CU's unique spatial quality, and used by both students and visitors to gaze at others, and if so preferred, engage in bodily intercourse with one another.

The *Caminito Verde* is as public as it is private. It is secluded, hidden from those for whom it should remain invisible, but also porous for those looking to enter it, accessible to those who *know*. Having evolved within a cocoon of lush greenery, it looks like just another piece of forest from the outside. Its presence is only betrayed by pedestrians casually and strangely walking across one of CU's wide pathways, to then suddenly disappear into the vegetation in the blink of an eye. Once inside, the *Caminito Verde* becomes unavoidably legible as a gay cruising circuit.

While the *Caminito Verde* is programmatically specific as a sexual playground, it is also spatially itinerant, a moving fair of charms. When its existence has in the past come to be known, just like the Romans did with Carthage, the authorities have invaded it, razed it to the ground and made it (temporarily) disappear. Nature, however, has its ways. Over time, institutional efforts to eliminate it have proven futile. In alliance with CU's forests, the Little Green Road always eventually regrows somewhere within that vast green territory which was originally merely intended to have an atmospheric, aesthetic presence in the nominally scholastic environment of Ciudad Universitaria.

The *Caminito Verde* is a multifaceted oxymoron. A nomadic site. A public place of intimacy. A space whose flourishing leads to its inevitable demise and yet whose downfall always leads to its re-emergence in a perpetual and seamless loop of use, discovery, institutional annihilation and pleasurable regrowth.

Navigating this cycle of survival, the *Caminito* stands as a testimony to the creative and resilient quality of queer subjectivity, and the alliance it can forge with public urban natural areas.

Above
Access is through hidden in-between zones of vegetation.

Opposite, top
The *Caminito Verde* is a unique landscape housing hidden activities of same-sex intercourse.

Opposite, bottom
Traces and artefacts of trysts, relationships and encounters can be found within the *Caminito*.

Overleaf
Queer bodies circulate in an unexpected site for pleasurable activities.

Christopher Street

NEW YORK, USA

Sean F Edgecomb

Not far from the intersection of Christopher and Gay streets in Greenwich Village, New York City, sits the nondescript Stonewall Inn, the site of the Stonewall Riots (1969), an event that helped to set in motion Gay Liberation and the LGBTQIA+ Pride Movement. While this site is best remembered for this particular incident, its neighbourhood, 'the Village' (in local parlance), had been the site of a thriving community of Bohemian artists and creatives, including an enclave of highly visible queer individuals, since the 1920s. It was in the post Second World War era, however, that the combination of growing American subcultures (including the Beat Generation, hippies/anti-Vietnam War protestors and the queer coffeehouse set, including writers James Baldwin and Truman Capote and playwright Edward Albee) and a turn towards social justice and Civil Rights, set the stage for dramatic social progress in the LGBTQ+ community in the United States and beyond.

The Stonewall Inn (which first opened in 1967–1969, before reopening in 2006) was a Mafia-run establishment located at 51–53 Christopher Street. A dive bar populated primarily by gay men and trans women, Stonewall was routinely raided by corrupt NYC police officers, when monetary pay-offs were not delivered in a timely fashion by the proprietors. Because homosexuality was illegal in New York state until 1980, these late-night raids often ended with the arrest of its gay patrons, who were rounded up into vans, fearful for their jobs and their reputations in the largely intolerant, homophobic society of mid-century America.

In the humid early morning hours of 28 June 1969, such a raid would take place, but the end result was radically different. While the police sweep started as usual – lining up patrons for arrest, demeaningly forcing assumed trans women into the bathroom to check their genitals against their visible genders and seizing crates of liquor and beer – the situation shifted when the diverse patrons began to fight back. One individual, a Black, self-identified 'drag queen' named Marcia P Johnson, apocryphally threw a shot glass, shattering a mirror. Subsequently, the riot devolved into fisticuffs; police and patrons ripping the bar apart and then taking to Christopher Street as a united front, where glass bottles and pennies were hurled, cars were overturned and an impromptu Rockettes-style kick line was formed as a kind of campy phalanx, with the queers electrically singing:

'We are the Stonewall Girls,
we wear our hair in curls,
We don't wear underwear,
we show our pubic hair,
We wear our dungarees,
above our nelly knees.'

Although met with police batons and tear gas, the rioters were ignited by a sense of solidarity and propelled by a new visibility. They would return the following night to continue this form of radical queer protest as performance. Although several events of LGBTQIA+ protest predated the Stonewall Riots, this event would mark Christopher Street as the genesis location of modern LGBTQIA+ culture.

Today in Christopher Park, directly in front of the reopened Stonewall Inn, stands the Gay Liberation Monument by George Segal. Dedicated in 1992, it features bronze statues of gay and lesbian couples, a hallmark of queer affection and a symbol for LGBTQIA+ community building that started with the riots. The Stonewall Inn, a National Historic Landmark since 2000, and Christopher Street remain pilgrimage sites for queer visitors from around the globe.

Coppelia

HAVANA, CUBA

Ivan L Munuera

One of the best-known images of Fidel Castro's 1959 visit to New York shows him eating ice cream at the Bronx Zoo.[139] This was more than a simple snapshot. Ice cream was part of a revolutionary social recomposition: luxury for the masses at affordable prices. Immediately after the revolution, Castro ordered his ambassador to Canada to ship him 28 containers of ice cream that could compete with Howard Johnson, the most famous United States-based ice cream producer at the time. Upon tasting, Castro decided that Cuba needed to respond on a revolutionary scale by creating something bigger and better, yet priced low enough for everyone to enjoy.[140]

To this day, both Cubans and visitors can, for significantly different prices (cheaper for the Cubans, more expensive for the foreigners), enjoy subsidised ice cream at Coppelia. Located in the Vedado neighbourhood on a site that was previously occupied by a children's hospital, its location showed the new face of Castro's government. Just a few metres away from the former Havana Hilton (now the Hotel Habana Libre, designed by Walton Beckett, Arroyo and Menéndez), the Edificio Radiocentro CMQ (responsible for the regime's radio communication), the Cines Yara, the university and the Rampa (a street rising up from the Malecón and which is the site of most governmental and institutional offices), Coppelia became the intersection of Cuba's possible futures. It was named after Léo Delibes' ballet, one of the signature pieces of the Ballet Nacional de Cuba directed by Alicia Alonso (and the favourite ballet of Celia Sánchez, Coppelia's promoter).

The circular structure opened to the public on 4 June 1966, and its long queues rapidly became famous. Coppelia serves 26 flavours – presumably a homage to the failed rebel attack on the Moncada army barracks on 26 July 1953, an event that inspired the Cuban Revolution. Occupying an entire block situated between Calles K and L and Calles 21 and 23, its grandiose structure – along with the lush vegetation and tables that surround it – can host almost 1,000 people. Reminding one of a spider stretching its legs, and influenced by the concrete structures of Pier Luigi Nervi, the building rapidly became a symbol of the Revolution's social programme. If the mammoth structure could be seen as a macho gesture, the legislations prosecuting the queer community at the time could be seen as a prolongation, both physically and metaphorically, of Coppelia itself, epitomising a new regime that condemned queering practices. In 1965 the UMAP (Unidades Militares de Ayuda a la Produccion) camps were introduced in the country. These detention camps particularly targeted gay men, along with other groups seen as deviants of the revolutionary corpus (from Jehovah's Witnesses to political objectors) – bourgeois degenerates.

Yet Coppelia saw an increasing queering process.

In a time of state-sanctioned persecution of gays, Coppelia became a cruising spot where flavours were symbols of sexual orientation.

In a well-known scene from the film *Fresa y Chocolate* (Strawberry and Chocolate, 1993),[141] the two protagonists meet at Coppelia. One of the protagonists, Diego (a gay man), orders a strawberry ice cream (chocolate being the most popular flavour), indicating that this choice was a coded way of communicating his sexuality. This scene tried to pay homage to the essential role of Coppelia as a spot for social contact, a queer encountering space, that remained coded for decades. Nowadays, its role as a space for interaction has been redefined by the emergence of free Wi-Fi zones throughout the city, of which Coppelia is one. Different social media allow dissident bodies to get in contact with each other, continuing Coppelia's queering history into present times.

After its construction, Coppelia became the intersection of Cuba's possible futures.

Climbing the spiral staircase.

With a structure reminding one of a spider stretching its legs, the building rapidly became a symbol of the revolution's social programme.

The Norfolk Arms

SHEFFIELD, ENGLAND

Helen Smith

The Norfolk Arms pub was situated in Attercliffe in the East End of Sheffield, at the heart of the steel-working district, and it had been a busy pub since the 19th century. At the height of the steel industry, in the 1950s and early 1960s, tens of thousands of men worked in the 'works' in this area. Beer formed part of men's wages (to help keep them hydrated and nourished in the hot working conditions) and many pubs like The Norfolk provided this, alongside a place to socialise with mates.

The dangerous, demanding nature of working in the steel industry created a specific, masculine culture where, as long as men were good, reliable workers, there was little scrutiny on their private lives. Many working-class men had sex with other men without it altering their masculine identity or their status, and some did this while having a wife or girlfriend.[142] They met and socialised in pubs like The Norfolk, or at work, and then used a variety of spaces to have sex, including the more private areas of pubs and workplaces, toilets, parks and each other's homes if they had enough private space.

This seemingly unlikely culture is evidenced by the fact that the nearest Sheffield has come to having a gay scene was the 'mixed' venues of the East End, including The Norfolk. In an oral history interview conducted in 2013, 'R' remembered that during the 1950s and 1960s he would go to pubs like The Norfolk with his friends and would socialise with the steelworkers, resulting in everything from one-off sexual encounters to long relationships.[143] Into the 1980s, as identity politics, gay liberation and the AIDS crisis fundamentally changed the ways in which men experienced their sexuality, pubs tended to become 'gay' or 'straight', rather than mixed. The Norfolk became a gay bar, and then in the 1990s it became The Bronx.

The Bronx was the city's first gay sauna, and the biggest in the north at that time. It survives today as The Boiler Room and has achieved an established position in the UK queer scene. The transformation of this space tells the story of queer history in the city. As a traditional pub, The Norfolk served the working classes and the men of the steelworks but it also provided a space for men who desired other men to meet and find partners.

Same-sex desire was a part of 'normal' working-class life, rather than an aberration or abnormality.

When industry was decimated under Margaret Thatcher, and identity politics changed the way that men experienced their sexuality, the culture of Attercliffe changed, and The Norfolk became a specifically queer space, first as a bar, and then as a sauna. Where same-sex desire had once been hidden, it, rather than the steelworks, now dominates the landscape of the old steel quarter.

Opposite
Arc furnace, steelworks,
Sheffield, 1949.

Top
The Bronx sauna, formerly The
Norfolk Arms, in 2005. Note
the steelworks on the left of
the picture. Compare to the
image below to see how it was
surrounded by the steelworks.

Bottom
The Norfolk Arms as it came
to the end of its life as a
traditional pub, c 1980; note
the steelworks on the right
of the shot.

Homomonument

AMSTERDAM, THE NETHERLANDS

Jeroen van Dijk

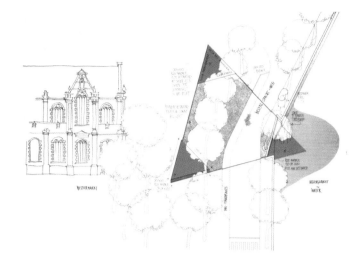

Following German occupation of the Netherlands in 1945, many memorials were built in the city. The National Monument on Dam Square, Amsterdam, became the centre of remembrance in Holland, and many of the old buildings that survived bear new layers of trauma and memory, like the Portuguese Synagogue, one of the only remaining buildings in the city's Jewish neighbourhood, or the Anne Frank House. Not far from the latter, on a small square, lies the Homomonument.

Unusually for Amsterdam memorials, people have been bringing flowers to it every day since it was erected in 1987.

A tangible space for memory, the monument consists of three pink granite triangles, which together form a larger triangle, connected by granite lines cutting through the streets and pavement, making the monument a part of the city's very fabric and identity. It memorialises homosexual victims who were persecuted during Nazi occupation because of their sexuality, making it the first queer memorial of its kind in the world.

The monument was designed by Karin Daan, who won a competition organised by the city government in 1980, after the queer community convinced the city of the need for a gay and lesbian memorial. The monument's triangles resemble the pink fabric triangles used by the Nazis during the Second World War to publicly mark homosexuals, reclaiming the shape as an international queer symbol.

Each triangle symbolises a different aspect of queer memory. The triangle extending over one of the city's canals symbolises the present. It points to the National Monument on Dam Square, and functions as a place for present-day remembrance, therefore activating the past in order to spur social change. The triangle on street level symbolises the oppression and homophobic violence queer people faced in the past. It points towards the Anne Frank House on the Prinsengracht and contains verse by gay Jewish poet Jacob Israël de Haan: *Naar vriendschap zulk een mateloos verlangen* ('Such an Endless Longing for Friendship'). The triangle that rises from street level symbolises the future, and serves as a meeting place for people to come together. It can be used as a podium for public speaking or a social meeting place. It points to the former office of the Dutch LGBTQIA+ interest organisation, the Cultuur en Ontspanningcentrum (COC) (Centre for Culture and Leisure), whose name functioned as a cover, to hide its real purpose.

Since its erection, the monument has been actively used by the queer community, and in 2017 it achieved 'monumental status' from the city government, protecting it from destruction or future alterations.

Above
A poster to attract crowdfunding to build the monument by Karin Daan, 1980. The annotations highlight elements of the monument's design, for instance designating that a line of poetry will be carved in bas relief. Next to the commemorative triangle that extends into the canal can be seen an 'existing urinal', in the shape of a curl, which can still be found next to the monument today. Colloquially known as 'piss curls', these remain popular cruising spots across the city.

Bottom
Flowers on the monument's
'triangle of remembrance',
1997.

Archivo de la Memoria Trans

ARGENTINA

Facundo Revuelta

The Trans Memory Archive is a family reunion. It arises from the need to embrace each other again, to look at each other again, to meet again after more than 15 years with the friends we thought were dead, with whom we distanced ourselves due to differences or exile; and with the memories of those who, indeed, are no longer there.[144]

The Archivo de la Memoria Trans is a collaborative and interdisciplinary project whose mission is to create a documentary collection on the history of the Argentine *travesti*-trans[145] community. The objective behind the project is the construction of an archive that foregrounds stories about lives lived by those in the trans community. It is a way to make the issues pertaining to gender identity in Argentina open, visible and accessible to the entire community through a range of different platforms. It is also a place of work, gathering, discussion and action, where educational training as well as occupational and social classes for trans people are organised. Also initiated and coordinated through the archive are access to and dissemination of documentary collections, through exhibitions, online and printed publications, and denouncing institutional and societal transphobia and campaigning for a more diverse, egalitarian and plural society.

The project began with Claudia Pía Baudracco and María Belén Correa, two activists who were instrumental in creating Argentina's first trans organisation (ATA) and in passing the country's first trans rights bill in 2012 (the Gender Identity Law). Pía and María Belén had always imagined having a space to reunite surviving *compañeras* (companions/partners/friends) and their memories. After Pía died in 2012, María Belén started the archive from a box of Pía's old photos. In 2014, with the help of photographer Cecilia Estalles, they began collecting and digitally preserving Pía's photographs, as well as others from the community. Seven years later, the archive houses a collection of more than 10,000 documents, with material dating back to the early 20th century, up until today.

The drive behind the archive is to make visible these 'invisible bodies', to bring back forgotten – often ignored – testimonies. The fundamental materials of the Memory Archive are the photo albums of a large and extended kinship family. Lots of bags and boxes of classic photo albums from the 1980s and 1990s, as well as letters and postcards, treasured by their owners, who not only kept their own photos, but have often held on to photos of those who passed. Interrupted by exclusion and violence, many things from the past were lost as documenting life was so difficult when existence itself took up all of one's energy. The archive is an opposite gesture. It's a room full of bags with photos and letters waiting to be digitised: photographs, stories, newspapers, magazines and objects that give an account of a type of activism before organised activism, and of why today there are less than 100 trans women over 55 years of age in Argentina,

... essential traces of our past that would be lost without our intimate and subjective acts of remembering. Individual memories that through this process become collective. Being together has always been our way of resisting the multiple forms of violence enacted on us by society and the State. Staying united is how we reinforce, through the construction of this archive, the power of our connection. This is the closest and truest story that can exist about our family, because we wrote it ourselves: the survivors.[146]

Above
'La Cacho', Tamara, Debora and Cinthia smiling and sharing a moment in their room.

Opposite, clockwise from top

The mirrors in Flavia's room, as she prepares to go to work.

Homes were one of the few spaces where the *travesti*-trans community could meet and be in groups, especially during the last dictatorship of Argentina (1976–83), when this photo was taken (1980).

Sandra, Patricia, Claudia, Laura, Marcela and Jessica during the carnival of Villa Martelli in 1984.

Can Sanpere

PREMIÀ DE MAR, CATALONIA, SPAIN

Ailo Ribas

Can Sanpere no és una fàbrica, no és un
edifici, no és un espai; és un ambient, és
un catalizador d'accions, emocions i gent.
Nosaltres en diem la fàbrica dels somnis.

Can Sanpere is not a factory, it is not a
building, it is not a space; it is an atmosphere,
it is a catalyst for action, emotions and people.
We call it the dream factory.

– Can Sanpere Autonomous Social Centre (CSA)[147]

Barcelona and anarchism share a long history,
inextricable from Catalunya's struggles to
remain autonomous under the control of a
centralising Spanish state. From the 1970s, fits
of deindustrialisation spread across Catalunya
(and much of Europe) as the collateral damage of
globalisation and subsequent waves of neoliberal
urbanism left an increasingly precarious working
class in its wake. This opened up a devastated urban
landscape to speculative development interests, as
well as to disenfranchised groups, anarchists and
young activists looking to fight austerity politics and
engage in alternative modes of social organisation.

Emerging around this time, Okupa is a
decentralised, anti-capitalist, anti-tourist and anti-
globalist movement in Catalunya seeking to reclaim
autonomy from the state through squatting buildings
in order to create autonomous social centres (Centres
Socials Autogestionats). The term okupa was coined
to describe the occupation of buildings for political
and subcultural reasons, and is used across the
Iberian Peninsula, across multiple languages. Rooted
in Catalunya's proletarian history and identity, the
Okupa movement claims to be 'defending liberated
spaces for an anti-capitalist popular culture.'[148]

Can Sanpere was a textile factory in Premià de
Mar, my hometown, that operated from the early 20th
century until 1999. Seeking to save it from the fate
of other former industrial sites, neighbours began
campaigning for its expropriation (i.e. the act of a
state or local authority reclaiming privately owned
property for public use and benefit). Despite this,
in 2013, the speculative property developers Nuñez
y Navarro acquired Can Sanpere. This sparked a
fresh wave of meetings, protests and direct action
energised by a young generation of activists
politicised by the 15-M movement. Starting two years

earlier in 2011, the 15-M, or Indignados, movement
was an anti-austerity movement in Spain consisting
of protests, occupations and demonstrations –
largely driven by a galvanised and disenfranchised
younger generation – against neoliberal politics,
unemployment, welfare cuts and political corruption.
The new wave of action against the redevelopment
of Can Sanpere ultimately led to the occupation of its
9,000m^2 compound in April of that year.

Since then, the site has grown into a hive
of communal activities, potlucks, outdoor film
screenings, symposiums, workshops, gigs,
exhibitions, afterschool clubs, allotments and open
meetings where the future of the space – which has
come to symbolise so much more than itself – is
regularly debated fervently into the night. Reclaiming
this space and opening it up to the public has enabled
some of the town's marginalised and disenfranchised
groups – migrants, queers, youths, the working class
– to meet, share resources, organise and support
one another. A plethora of collectives have emerged
from the abundant and fertile ground of Can Sanpere,
including a public education programme (with
support for migrant families), the Xarxe d'Habitatge
(a housing network), Queers Tropicals, a women's
network, migrant networks and an afterschool club
for children.

Queers Tropicals[149] is an LGBTQIA+ collective
that emerged as a direct response to the inadequate
support services for queer people provided by the local
council. Since their first open meeting at Can Sanpere
in November 2018, they have: organised Premià
de Mar's first Pride celebration; held a trans day of
remembrance vigil in front of the town hall; and hosted
a drag show in Can Sanpere that saw local queers
perform in public for the first time, alongside more
seasoned drag performers from neighbouring cities.

At each scale – the Okupa movement, Can
Sanpere and Queers Tropicals – space is not viewed
as a commodity, as an end in itself, but as a human
right, as an indispensable tool in the struggle for
self-determination. There is no such thing as a queer
space. Rather there are ways of organising, using and
inhabiting space that – in a given moment – transform
it from an empty container into an endless world of
possibilities.

To queer is to transform and be transformed.

Opposite, clockwise from top

Can Sanpere, 9 April 2013. The
graffiti reads, 'Can Sanpere
belongs to the town/speople.'

7 April 2013, day five of the
occupation. On the first day,
the occupied factory opened
its doors to the public,
including local giants Ester
and Omar (typical in Catalan
folk tradition).

Queers Tropicals drag show,
10 December 2019.

Queers Tropicals Pride
celebration, 29 June 2019.

9 April 2013. The banner
reads, 'We continue to weave
the alternative.'

South City Beach Kiosk

PERTH, AUSTRALIA

Timothy Moore and John Tanner

Perth is a city that operates on its relationship to the Indian Ocean through the celebration of a coastal zone that is literally liquid and fluid. To provide amenity and points of orientation to the dunescape of City and Floreat beaches on the traditional lands of the Whadjuk people, a masterplan was drawn in 1967 that included three kiosks along with a new surf life-saving club and car park, as part of the upgrade.

The South City Beach Kiosk was built in 1970 as part of this redevelopment. Designed by architect Tony Brand for Forbes & Fitzhardinge, the kiosk includes a commercial food operator alongside public toilets and changing rooms elevated on a plinth. These amenities are positioned radially around the services core, and wrapped by a curved wall that defines binary gendered space.

The kiosk is constructed with off-form concrete; the corrugated and curved wall that wraps the programme acts in compression, which means that the concrete would be less likely to crack. Unlike its contemporaries of block Brutalism, it domesticates the heroic civic scale of *béton brut* with a regional, wavy twist. This demonstrates the yearning of architects in Perth to seek a new identity for expressed concrete by the beach,[150] and appears here, states architect Geoffrey London, 'like an inverted seashell'.[151] This expression continues to change over time, with the original raw concrete finish having been covered up many times over with colourful rendering, 'food and bev' signs, and drying beach bums.

The kiosk has provided a space for a variety of unsanctioned identities that do not conform to the prescribed binary delineated by the two changing rooms. The kiosk has hosted many uses, from skaters grinding on its inverted roof, to illegal New Year's Day dance parties that began happening from the early 2000s.

These parties challenged the normative uses of the kiosk, and rehabilitated its meaning, especially after it had fallen into disrepair from the ocean spray that had corroded the steel reinforcement in the concrete slab soffit over time.

With the kiosk, toilets and changing rooms now closed,[152] the infrastructure of the kiosk has become an intimate container for unregulated bodies. It is liberated from gender segregation through new layers of use and meaning.

Above
The corrugated concrete wall wrapped around a programme that defined binary gendered spaces.

Top
The South City Beach Kiosk provides amenity and points of orientation on the dunescape.

Bottom
The kiosk has supported unregulated uses, including a dance party at sunrise on New Year's Day in 2015.

Santiago Apóstol Cathedral

MANAGUA, NICARAGUA

Aparecida Arguello

From its origins as a colonial-era replica of European architectural prototypes, to its decline following the 1972 earthquake[153] which tore the city apart, the Santiago Apóstol Cathedral has been at the centre of the urban history of Managua. It has also been at the core of the queer history of Nicaraguans, becoming an 'underground' home for queer communities from 1972 to 1990.

Being queer in Nicaragua is not the same as in an Anglo-Saxon or Northern Global context. Until 1972, the city did not have a space built for or by the queer community, as gender subversion and feminised bodies, like trans women or gay men, were criminalised and persecuted by the National Guard.[154] From 1960 to 1979, homosexuality was criminalised[155] by the Somosista dictatorship[156] and *cuirs* (queers) had to camouflage themselves for survival. Following the earthquake, and with the end of the dictatorship as a result of the Sandinista revolution, the Santiago Apóstol Cathedral, which was the centre of religious practice in the city, was deemed unsafe for 'normal' use, and after being abandoned by the church, became a safe space for homosocialisation and cruising, occupied by homosexuals, trans people, prostitutes and lesbians who had nowhere else to go and mingle.

While the city turned its back on its ruined centre, the cathedral, its old heart, became the new communal core, and central place of refuge for the persecuted queer community.

As David Rocha puts it in his book *Crónicas de la Ciudad*: 'The homosexual passer-by transforms these abandoned spaces into geographical points for their pleasures.'[157] The old centre was deserted by the cis-heterosexual population, who moved en masse to the outskirts of the city.

Meanwhile, as Ru, a homosexual man of 75 years explains in *Crónicas de la Ciudad*, the cathedral was used by *cuirs* for their social and sexual relationships, and also for sex work: 'Oh, yes! I worked there in the cathedral. Before they built the government house, all that was desolate. One client entered from one side and another from the other side. You went downstairs where some priests were buried, and you could find women with men, men with men, women with women.'[158]

The cathedral was not just a place of pleasure, but also one of revolution – the Nicaraguan Revolution, the last Latin American battle of the 20th century, celebrated its victory on 19 July 1979 in the plaza in front of the cathedral. Countless members of the LGBTQ+ community participated, fighting against a nepotistic dictatorship, against militarism, social control and the persecution they suffered under the Somoza regime. Despite their contribution, however, they also had to fight against their constant invisibility within the revolutionary struggle, against the machismo at the core of a revolution led by cis-heterosexual men.

Years later, in 1990, Violeta Barrios[159] became the first female president of Nicaragua, and it was sadly her who enacted harsh policies of moral 'cleansing', which involved defining the presence of gender-nonconforming people in the cathedral as corrupt, and the spaces occupied by them as the equivalent of 'Sodom and Gomorrah.'

Today, the cathedral is still in ruins, covered in political propaganda and kitsch decoration portraying the current 'President' of Nicaragua. It is now closed to the public and the queer community has not been able to enter since the police 'cleansed' them in the 1990s. There are currently no plans for restoration, and its clock still marks the hour of the earthquake: 00:35. The scars of the uprising and the Sandinista[160] victory are still visible as bullet holes riddle the building's surface. The abandonment of the cathedral also serves as a metaphor for the marginal realities of *cuir* bodies, which are excluded, abandoned and harmed in this chaotic city designed for and by cis-men, heterosexuality and toxic masculinity.

XXX Park

DHAKA, BANGLADESH

Ruhul Abdin

XXX Park illuminates the unexpected and fascinating coexistence between quotidian urban life and explicit outdoor gay sex in the patriarchal and often homophobic, transphobic and misogynist city of Dhaka. It is still not safe to be openly queer in Bangladesh and, unless you know where to look, the LGBTQIA+ community here is all but invisible, for their own safety. For this reason, an exact location will not be included for this space.

Dhaka has a very limited provision of public parks and open places for a city of its size, and those that do exist are progressively being lost through ongoing rapid urbanisation and densification in the city. The idea of cruising in a city like Dhaka may seem absurd, considering the risk of violence, but it has been happening in XXX, one of the most beautiful public parks. The park's regular visitors, who use it throughout the day for leisure and exercise, mostly do not know that it is used also for cruising by men at night. The fact that this occurs in Dhaka is perhaps testament to the universality of the desire to cruise for gay or bisexual (or closeted) curious men, anywhere in the world, and from all walks of life. How is it possible that it can take place, with limited reports of abuse or violence, in such a central place? This particular park has a very comprehensive system of surveillance, and navigating it requires a lot of courage.

It's perhaps best to narrate the cruising experience from an interview with someone who uses the park regularly at night, and here recalls their first nocturnal encounter:

> I had waited till early evening. I made eyes with a man with a cape; he was also walking slowly, groping his crotch, whilst making eye contact with passers-by, to see if they would react. He made eye contact with me. Then went to pee by a tree. I watched, mesmerised by his courage. He then approached me, with his cock still exposed. I suggested we go for a walk, I was nervous.

> As we walked and talked, he became rather blunt, asking if I wanted to be fucked. I mentioned I was not looking for that. He talked briefly about his wife who lives in the Old Town, she'd gone away to her parents for the weekend. He doesn't come to the park so often. I walked on. He then approached another young man. I was curious to see what would happen. I went back to where the action was, near the rows of the Bokultola (Spanish cherry trees). There were more men gathering. I was even more anxious. I'd found a place to sit. Amongst me were other men, talking away, smoking. It felt like a gay space. A policeman approached me, asked if I was a regular; I'd nodded no. He went on to cuddle between two men, came back to me and said, 'We're all buddies here, don't worry,' and then asked for 20 takas (20p). I sat in disbelief and also wonderment, that this is possible here.

XXX offers the possibility of a queered public space right in the very heart of Dhaka, even one that exists precariously and always with the spectre of extreme risk to those who inhabit it.

There are some spaces in the public realm in the city where queerness can flourish in the semi-dark, such as those areas occupied by sex workers, but most of them are now beginning to be lost. As the city's hidden queer geography is changing, and shrinking, XXX stands as testament to the enduring capacity of alternative sexualities being able to coexist, and even thrive, in the most unexpected of urban situations.

The Museum of Transology

LONDON, ENGLAND

E-J Scott

The Museum of Transology (MoT)[161] is the UK's most significant collection of material culture surrounding trans, non-binary and intersex lives. It was founded in 2014, and now holds more than 400 objects and thousands of written contributions.

It continues to grow, with 95 protest signs saved from the Black Trans Lives Matter march in London on 27 June 2020.

All the artefacts in the collection are chosen by the donors themselves, making them the curators of their own stories. The collection is as diverse as the trans experience itself. It includes fashion, hormones, self-defence weapons, make-up and accessories, art and craft, prosthetics and even post-operative human remains.

There are also contributions that are connected to the lineage of lesbian and gay collections that have preceded it, including badges, political T-shirts and zines.

The magic of the MoT is that the everyday objects in it are familiar to most viewers. The handwritten stories attached to them explain their significance to the donor. There's an affordable, well-loved lipstick that was probably bought down at the local pharmacy, a present from a sister who was the first family member to accept her sibling's gender transition. It's not an expensive lipstick, it's not brandished with a designer logo, but it is precious beyond words. There's a 'My Little Pony' plush toy that offers comfort in dark moments. A baseball cap that reminds one young man of his grandfather who, like himself, always wore hats. It's a story of inheriting nontoxic masculinity from a much-admired male role model.

Above
'The Museum of Transology', exhibition at Brighton Museum & Art Gallery, East Sussex, 2017–19.

Opposite, clockwise from top-left

Object Numbers MOT/254, MOT/238, MOT/231, MOT/304, MOT/223: Black Trans Lives Matter protest signs, London, 27 June 2020.

A 'first' pair of boxer shorts bought by a well-intentioned mum are described as a 'stripey monstrosity' with typical teenage irreverence. They're about being a regular adolescent growing up, more than they're about being trans.

Collectively, these everyday objects afford some humanity to the trans community whose members are so frequently and cruelly dehumanised. They pull us closer to the lives lived behind them. Their familiarity builds an involuntary, knee-jerk kind of connection: the recognition of a shared experience, a mutual understanding. It's this instant recognition that breaks through and combats the widespread *mis*understanding of the trans community that's regularly perpetuated by the UK media (widely considered the most transphobic in the world). These magical museum moments provide us with a precious, sacred queer space in which we can quietly learn more about each other and take the time to understand each other better, drawing our communities closer together, making us stronger.

While historically, museums may not have been saving and displaying trans stories, trans people have been saving their transcestry, nonetheless. Given the opportunity, they haven't hesitated to donate them to the Museum of Transology for safekeeping in order that their stories can be shared with the wider world for generations to come. To not be included on the walls of a museum is to be told that your people haven't contributed to society in a meaningful way. It is to be rendered historically homeless. The Museum of Transology's collection halts the erasure of trans lives from history, tackles the misrepresentation of trans people in the political sphere, and combats the spectacularisation of trans bodies and experiences by the mainstream media. It's about the trans community, by the trans community. Never again can it be said that trans people didn't exist in the past. We're here, we're trans *and* we're queer, and we're going... to the museum.

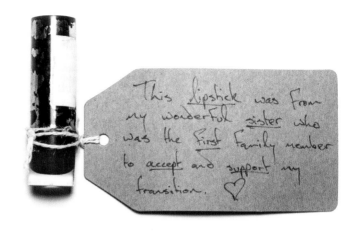

Clockwise from top-left

Object Number MOT/186: Testosterone: 'Sustanon 250 is the best thing that has happened to me apart from my wife and son! It's made me the husband and father I always wanted to be.'

Object Number MOT/161: Red Lipstick: 'This lipstick was from my wonderful sister, who was the first family member to accept and support my transition.'

Object Number MOT/33: 'Stripey monstrosity' boxer shorts: 'At the start of my transition, I asked my mum for boxers. And she came back with this! As lovely as she is, I couldn't wait to pluck up the courage to buy something less tragic!'

Object Number MOT/203: 'Gender Roles are Dead' T-shirt, with hand-drawn lettering by @thefoxfisher.

Object Number MOT/95: Black cap: 'My favourite hat... As a child I would watch my granddad with pure adoration. He was always stylishly dressed in a suit and his best church hat... He had many beautiful qualities which I admire, best of all he was a gentleman. He passed away before I could explain to him how much he shaped me as a person. He taught me kindness and I would like to think many great, great qualities. He also is the reason I love hats.'

Object Number MOT/102: My Little Pony plush toy: 'Immersing myself in My Little Pony is how I manage dysphoria.'

Above
The Museum of Transology
collection on display at
Brighton Museum & Art
Gallery, 2017–19.

The Shophouses of British Malaya

MALAYSIA AND SINGAPORE

Soon-Tzu Speechley

Criminalised by the colonial Penal Code, homosexuality was largely hidden from view in British Malaya. When homosexuality appeared in the public record, it was through sordid headlines. This has made historical experiences of queerness – and of queer spaces – in Malaya difficult to access.

Yet the same press which vilified homosexuals provides clues about where queer people congregated. This offers fleeting glimpses into the queer history of two modern nations, Malaysia and Singapore, which continue to criminalise homosexuality to the present day. In the shophouses of 'a lowdown quarter' such as Singapore's Chinatown, men found others 'of the same ilk', were caught and prosecuted.[162]

Built en masse from the 19th to the mid-20th century, terraced shophouses mirrored Malaya's booms and busts. Rich from rubber, tin and spices, Malaya's towns and cities grew in size and grandeur. Speculators built terraces to varying degrees of architectural pretension, façades enriched with plaster capitals and glazed tiles. People lived above shops, hanging washing on bamboo poles from their windows, while rickshaws parked in shaded five-foot-ways.

Over time, many were subdivided to house a growing population. Some came to be viewed as slums. As the bulk of Malaya's urban environment, the wooden screens and shadowy verandas of shophouses offered privacy to queer Malayans – though not always enough.

The buildings themselves were regarded as somewhat queer by British commentators, who remarked on the hybrid style developed by Malaya's architects and builders. In thousands of shophouses across Malaya, Corinthian pilasters frame Chinese motifs modelled in plaster and porcelain. Visiting Singapore in the 1860s, John Cameron, a Fellow of the Royal Geographic Society, wrote that these shophouses were 'a sort of compromise between English and Chinese'.[163]

Such hybridity was worrisome in colonial society. In his study of Lahore's residential architecture, William J Glover argues that British commentators emphasised the differences between British and Indian buildings because they 'marked the contours of a widely shared anxiety about the implications of cultural hybridity'.[164] Such anxieties were also evident in British Malaya, whose cosmopolitan community appropriated and translated imperial classicism into a syncretic architectural creole. In the words of Chris KK Tan, 'Chinatown was already always queered'.[165]

Above
The five-foot-way of a shophouse terrace in Penang, Malaysia.

194

QUEER SPACES

Many shophouses were brothels, with some catering to a gay male clientele. William Pickering, who oversaw the Protectorate of Chinese in Singapore, estimated that Singapore had half a dozen male brothels in 1899.[166] These venues were tolerated, so long as racial boundaries were not transgressed.

Sex between British and Asian men was a particular source of anxiety for colonial authorities. Herbert Gerhold, Assistant Commissioner of the Federated Malay States Police, was among the British men caught with Asian lovers. Gerhold admitted to being 'tempted to experiment' with a Javanese man named Jusari while stationed in Kuala Selangor in 1937.[167] In Kuala Lumpur a year later, Gerhold took a Malay man he met on Batu Road back to his house.

Despite a string of liaisons, Gerhold argued that these encounters were a 'transitory indiscretion rather than a permanent vice', and that 'in this country, as a result perhaps of the climate… this vice is peculiarly prevalent amongst both Europeans and Asiatics and… is not regarded with the disapproval recorded in western countries'.[168]

In response, Malaya's colonial administration decided 'to send Mr Gerhold to Palestine in spite of his lapses… [and] not to inform the Palestine authorities about his Malayan "past"'.[169]

Cases like Gerhold's may have led to tighter laws against homosexuality. As noted by JY Chua, sex scandals 'threatened the legitimacy and authority of the British colonial administration', and the use of Section 377A targeted 'Asian "catamites" who might imperil the sexual purity and self-control of European men'.§[170] Authorities also feared blackmail.[171]

The first men punished under Section 377A were two 'well-known Chinese' men in Penang named Lim Eng Kooi and Lim Eng Kok.[172] Three years later, one Tan Ah Yiow was sentenced to nine months' 'rigorous imprisonment' for 'a disgusting and revolting practice' performed on an unidentified European client in Singapore.[173]

Anti-sodomy laws became a tool to reinforce the boundaries between coloniser and colonised. Newspapers assiduously chronicled both the lovemaking and assaults which occurred in Malaya's innumerable shophouses.[174]

Despite increasing regulation, shophouses continued to provide spaces for queer Malayans and Singaporeans through independence. From the 1950s to the 1980s, Bugis Street was famous for the trans women who worked in the sex industry there.[175] This reputation made Bugis Street the focus of intense urban renewal. Shophouses were razed and rebuilt; sex workers dispersed.

Yet urban renewal has also created new queer spaces. Following the restoration of Singapore's Chinatown in the 1980s and 1990s, gay entrepreneurs opened a number of venues along Neil Road.[176]

From bathhouses to karaoke bars, renovated shophouses were reborn as queer spaces.

Behind ornate façades, gay bars ply patrons with drinks, providing a backdrop for revelry and romance between hawker centres and temples.

Queer spaces in both Malaysia and Singapore today are by nature contingent and ephemeral. In both nations, Section 377A remains in force. Despite this, the ubiquitous shophouse retains its queer appeal.

Above
The ornate Chinese-style doorway of a Penang shophouse.

QUEER SPACES

Above
A row of shophouses in
rural Malaysia.

Opposite, Top
Postcard of Neil Road in
Singapore, c 1930. Urban
renewal in the 1980s led to a
proliferation of queer venues
in Singapore's Chinatown.

Opposite, Bottom
Postcard of Batu Road in
Kuala Lumpur, Malaysia,
in 1928, a place where gay
men congregated.

Jinriksha Station, Singapore.

T. HOPE & CO

N.S.A.W. Co.

HOCK HOE C

BATU ROAD K.L.

K. Lumpur 12/4/28

Museo Q

BOGOTÁ, COLOMBIA

Michael Andrés Forero Parra

Museo Q is a museological initiative conceived in 2012 by a group of queer individuals who felt there was a lack of space within museums in Colombia for their lives and histories. This need for space did not, however, crystallise in the construction of a physical gallery or in the design of a virtual platform. Rather, the queer space of Museo Q became an ever-shifting assemblage of bodies, buildings, spaces and actions.

The queer space of Museo Q is an example of 'minor architecture' because it operates within major or established structures.[177] The minor is not the opposite of the major; but they are bound together. In relation to the major, the minor holds a revolutionary potential to blur boundaries (interior/exterior, public/private, real/metaphorical), break disciplinary confinements (the aesthetic and technological pursuit of making edifices) and redefine what is considered established (e.g. the meaning and mission of museums).

The queer space of Museo Q, therefore, does not correspond to a static, built object. It comprises domestic environments that stimulate queer friendship, public spaces where queer bodies interact with others, and display cases where queer memories are preserved and shared. Taken together, the living room, the garden and the vitrine co-constitute the minor architecture of Museo Q.

On Saturdays, from 2012 to 2014, often at sunset, the group would gather in one of two living rooms to discuss what Museo Q wanted to be. One of those living rooms belonged to Javier, who lived with his boyfriend and two cats on the eighth floor of a building in Teusaquillo (one of the central districts of Bogotá), and the other to Hunza, who shared an apartment on the first floor of a house in Chapinero (a district in the north of the city) with a friend and two cats. Between these two environments, profound friendships developed. The museum was not an individual endeavour, but a collective effort. The two apartments not only sheltered a group of humans and cats; with their red sofas, warm light, casual conversations, unexpected guests, drinks and music, they also set the stage for envisioning a subversive and affective *museum without walls*.

Without the barriers of walls, the destiny of Museo Q was to evolve into a state of perpetual transit. Whether in the Pride march, at a museum, in a classroom or a bookstore, Museo Q moves and transforms itself in every space it happens to occupy. In 2018, after having developed four art exhibitions, the museum created a booklet on the sexuality of plants for the Bogotá Botanical Garden, generating conversations with families about sexual diversity in the natural world and acknowledging that we are all

naturally diverse. In 2019, the booklet was transformed into a series of guided tours and outdoor workshops for eight public parks throughout the city, including the National Park in Bogotá, which was and continues to be a spot for gay cruising.

Also in 2019, the curatorial team of the National Museum of Colombia, a museum founded in 1823, renovated a permanent gallery where LGBTQ+ objects were introduced and displayed for the first time. Among them, a T-shirt used by Museo Q in the 2015 Pride march, along with the old and renewed ID of Katalina Ángel, an active member of Red Comunitaria Trans.[178] The T-shirt features a printed photograph from 1960 of a group of incarcerated queer people. Today, thanks to Katalina's work, imprisoned LGBTQ+ individuals have better humanitarian conditions. The vitrine, which is expected to last a few years, exalts lives and histories that were previously hidden, and which are now visible to all.

Far from creating a niche for queer people, Museo Q *queers* the space of others by being, knowing and doing otherwise. We believe that any museum, regardless of its collection, organisation, budget or location, can activate critical dialogues around the structures that have marginalised and eliminated LGBTQ+ lives and histories. And this, certainly, engenders queering architecture.

Above
In *A Kiss from Dick* (1992), the Colombian author Fernando Molano presents the National Park in Bogotá as an erotic space where the two male protagonists have sexual intercourse.

Left
Image for the digital publication *Devenir queer: al límite del patrimonio* ('Queer becoming: At the limit of heritage'), published in December 2020, available at www.museoq.org.

Clockwise from top

Incarcerated queer people at La Modelo prison in Bogotá, c 1960. At the time it was believed that prison overcrowding was turning men into homosexuals.

'Hacer sociedad' ('Making Society'), a permanent gallery at the National Museum of Colombia.

Leer las flores: breve historia (queer) de las plantas ('Reading flowers: A brief (queer) history of plants') – a guided tour at the Bogotá Botanical Garden.

Cats Adam and Huma miaowing in Javier's apartment.

Glorieta de los Insurgentes

MEXICO CITY, MEXICO

Sergio Galaz García

Either in the form of earthquakes, Aztec relics emerging from the earth or the slow but inevitable sinking of its buildings – the slow-motion vengeance of a lake dried out for the city's expansion – Mexico City has long had a special rapport with the ground over which it sits. Starting in 1969, a new dimension was added to this charged relationship: that of seeing flesh-and-bone humans descend into the ground, into a subway system that was inaugurated that year by the Mexican president on 9 September in a critically underappreciated but socially celebrated masterpiece of public architecture: the Glorieta de los Insurgentes, a public square, a subway station and a traffic roundabout.

Combining the curved formal language of late Modernism, the organisational rigour of early Modernism and the historicist bent of architectural movements that looked to the past for inspiration, the Glorieta embeds in three tangentially nested rings three wildly different urban circulation processes – the pedestrian, the motorised and the subway track – in a way that assures their successful coexistence, while also making sure that they don't ever step on one another's toes.

The Glorieta is curvy yet uptight, historicist and also forward-looking, massive and subtle. From an architectural standpoint, it is already quite peculiar. But its more potent queerness comes not from its spatial resolution, but from the uses poured into it by the uniquely diverse mixture of people who gather there daily: middle-class white-collar workers, tourists, basic cool kids, edgy cool kids, expats, punks, emos and, last but not least, working- and lower-middle-class gay people.

Housing a station on the main subway line connecting the city centre with the sprawling blue-collar districts of the east, and a few blocks away from Zona Rosa – Mexico City's flagship gaybourhood – the Glorieta has played for decades an unassuming but critical role in the sentimental education of millions of Mexico City gay people. During the day, it is a stronghold for sexual alterity, bringing together whoever comes in and out of the subway with those attracted to the zone by its wealth of gay-oriented services, like clothing stores or hair salons. Later in the day, as it turns dark after dusk, it becomes the main gateway to its clubs and bars, morphing from being a place of queer tolerance to one of queer celebration as it starts to be filled by gay couples and flocks of friends entering or exiting the subway station, spending time in the square, and proudly performing their sexual alterity as they get ready for a night out.

Over time, the neighbourhoods surrounding the Glorieta, which were originally built for the upper classes but degentrified over the course of the 20th century, have now been increasingly claimed back by the wealthy. The Glorieta, however, resists this gentrification, and remains a defiant champion for a democratic form of sexual alterity in the middle of the city.

Every day, as it has done for at least the past couple of decades, the Glorieta becomes a vast expression of everyday queerness, an open boudoir of gay subjectivity, where men of different upbringings emerge from the ground to prepare for their adventures in the night.

The Glorieta acts as a living physical objection to the commodification of queer alterities, and to the homogenisation of Mexico City's urban landscape as it progressively becomes integrated into the generic army of fashionably hyped global cities.

Above
The landscape of this complex work of urban infrastructure lends itself to groups congregating, and individuals who wish to linger.

Opposite, clockwise from top

Glorieta de los Insurgentes: access to the subway station.

The open space of Glorieta.

Aerial view.

Former Central V.I. Lenin Museum

MOSCOW, RUSSIA

Yevgeniy Fiks

Vladimir Ilyich Lenin's government decriminalised homosexuality in Russia shortly after the October Revolution of 1917. Although homosexuality remained taboo and never fully socially accepted, the period between 1918 and 1933 was characterised by a relative tolerance towards experiments in gender expression, and, to a lesser degree, towards nonconforming sexuality. However, male homosexuality was formally re-criminalised under Stalin in 1933 as part of a wider totalitarian conservative move, which included the criminalisation of abortion and the strengthening of the petit bourgeois values of the nuclear family and patriarchal gender roles.

The Central V.I. Lenin Museum, which opened in Moscow in the former building of the Moscow City Duma (the regional parliament) in 1936, became a popular site for clandestine homosexual activities in the decades between the 1940s and 1990s. In particular, the men's toilets located in the basement of the museum were covertly used for (often anonymous) gay sex. Located at the very centre of Moscow, within walking distance of the most popular outdoor gay cruising area in front of the Bolshoi Theatre, the Lenin Museum was open six days a week to the public, with free admission.

Additionally, the enormous museum featured several rooms and spaces that provided privacy for cruising and sexual activities, especially during weekdays, when the museum had fewer visitors. Of special popularity was the museum's large and mostly empty movie theatre, in which sexual encounters took place in the dark as Russian Revolution films played daily on loop.

A common modus operandi for Muscovite gays was to make an acquaintance by the Bolshoi Theatre and walk to the Lenin Museum toilets and occupy a toilet stall. The toilet attendants and cleaners there were usually older working-class women, who were often aware of the sexual encounters occurring in the stalls. Sometimes, the attendants would disrupt these encounters by calling the men out while they were in the stalls or threatening to call the militia (the police), after which the men would flee. By the early 1990s, however, Moscow gays became fearless and came to the toilets as if it were their own space. They would argue, with almost reckless confidence, with the toilet attendants for their right to occupy stalls in any numbers larger than one.

Aside from the queer history of the Central V.I. Lenin Museum in Moscow, Soviet gay men appropriated statues of Lenin during the time of the USSR. With a Lenin monument in every Soviet city, typically located in the city's main square, Soviet gays would often go on dates or cruise by those monuments, dubbing them 'Grandma Lena' in Soviet camp slang for Lenin.

The legacy of Lenin, the Soviet Union's founder, as a protector of Soviet gay men is just as contradictory as the relationship between 20th-century communism and nonconforming sexuality. Until recently, most communist parties around the world purged known gays from their ranks – marking them as 'security risks' – for fear that gay communists were vulnerable to blackmail and could become informants for unsympathetic governments. The official charters of most communist parties prohibited known gays from membership and stigmatised homosexuality as a 'capitalist degeneracy'.

Male homosexually was decriminalised in Russia in 1993, the same year that the Central V.I. Lenin Museum closed its doors; its closure was owing to the fall of the Soviet Union and the resultant change of ideology.

The former Central V.I. Lenin Museum in Moscow today is a site of queer history, where the post-1933 queer Soviet citizens were reduced to expressing their sexuality largely in the toilets of the museum, before both decriminalisation and the era of gay bars and clubs. At the same time, the museum was a physical space in the daily lives of Soviet gays, inadvertently providing them provisional shelter during those dark years of oppression.

Yevgeniy Fiks' installation *Untitled (The Lenin Museum)*, mixed medium, 2014, in his solo exhibition 'The Lenin Museum' at the James Gallery, The Graduate Center, City University of New York (CUNY).[179]

The image on the installation's façade shows the front façade of the former Central V.I. Lenin Museum in Moscow on the doors of the toilet stalls.

Soviet postcards published in the 1930s to 1950s, featuring the Central V.I. Lenin Museum.

Victorian Pride Centre

MELBOURNE, AUSTRALIA

Timothy Moore and Nicholas Braun

In May 2016, the Australian state of Victoria apologised for a law that made homosexual acts a criminal offence up until 1980. 'It's never too late to say sorry – and mean it,' said Victorian State Premier Daniel Andrews. 'On behalf of the parliament, the government and the people of Victoria: for the laws we passed, and the lives we ruined, and the standards we set, we are so sorry; humbly, deeply, sorry.'[180] The apology was one of several milestones for lesbian, gay, bisexual, transgender, intersex and queer (LGBTIQ+) rights in the state of Victoria during 2016. Alongside the apology, adoption rights for same-sex couples and a crackdown on gay conversion therapy, the government pledged A$15 million to construct the Victorian Pride Centre (VPC), a place that would champion diversity, equality and inclusion at the core of its mission.[181]

Opening in 2021, the VPC, designed by Brearley Architects and Urbanists (BAU) and Grant Amon Architects (GAA), creates safe and symbolic space across its 6,200m^2 gross floor area through uniting a spectrum of LGBTIQ+ organisations and individuals in the provision of office, commercial and cultural spaces. The architects evade obvious references to LGBTIQ+ cultures and communities in the design. The approach is driven by an exercise of subtraction where tubes, or extruded ellipses, are extracted from the maximum building volume. These ellipses allude to the ornate arches found in the Victorian-era grand terraces and amusement playgrounds in this seaside suburb on the traditional lands of the Boon Wurrung people.

The arches and vaults of the VPC make, and give form to, queer space. This is not only in providing a space for LGBTIQ+ communities. It is also in challenging the methodology in which the world, including its buildings, is materialised. This is evident in the creation of the threshold, where crossing it can be an act of coming out, which stretches over 26m long in this institution. This experience is amplified by a three-barrel vault where the enclosure of space is kept ambiguous, which shifts beyond binary notions: private and public, open and closed, solid and porous. The threshold, which includes a concierge, café, lounge and gallery, also prevents the dominance of one user group. This aids in making this entrance welcoming, alongside explicit sightlines and egress points that enhance feelings of safety.

At the termination of the threshold is a five-storey atrium created from the subtraction of an ellipsoid off-grid. The atrium brings light deep into the 58m-long site, with variations on solidity and transparency. A statement stairwell, with spotted gum plywood panels, at its centre provides a catwalk for the extrovert or a congregation place to gather for a performance or meeting. A theatre is tucked in behind the stairs; it is hugged by a lush velvet orange curtain that provides a flourish of pageantry to offset the austerity of the concrete blade walls.

Rising above and circling the atrium are tenancy spaces dedicated to LGBTIQ+ organisations, including Melbourne Queer Film Festival, Australian Queer Archives, Monash Health, Thorne Harbour Health, Joy 94.9 FM and Transgender Victoria, among others. Security lines block some access to these spaces and to the terraced balconies, while tenancy fitouts block some sightlines and sunlight. This shows the limits of queer spaces, where bodies can be regulated through clear boundaries. It also demonstrates the contradiction of LGBTIQ+ institutions that organise and contain identities while giving space to difference.

Above this complex is a 1,000m^2 terrace with expansive views towards the waters of Nairm (the Boon Wurrung word for Port Phillip Bay). A 15m flagpole tops the terrace, which is held by 10 smaller poles that pay tribute to individuals – parent, partner, mentor, sibling and others. (The poles also represent the 10 colours of a rainbow flag.) A plaque is located at the bottom of each pole. One reads: 'In remembrance of my lover and best friend for seventeen years John Paul McCutchan who died from AIDS on February 15th 2008.'

> As architecture strives to queer space, it also struggles to live up to this ambition, being a discipline that is mostly concerned with durable, containable and solid structures.

This is illustrated in the creation of a pride centre: it makes identities intelligible, but also more governable and consumable. Challenging this paradox is the approach of the architects, who intentionally created the project as 'unfinished'. The economical column-and-beam structure with minimal finishes leaves room for the user and their future uses.

Opposite, clockwise from top-left

The ellipses of the Victorian Pride Centre allude to the ornate arches found in the Victorian-era grand terraces and amusement playgrounds in the seaside suburb of St Kilda.

The Fitzroy Street balconies act as a viewing platform to watch the annual Midsumma Pride March.

An ellipsoid rotated off-grid creates an atrium across five levels, to break deep floor plates.

A scalloped façade along Jackson Street retains existing peppercorn trees.

The Pride Centre was opened on 11 July 2021 by the Victorian State Premier Daniel Andrews and Minister for Equality Martin Foley, with a welcome to country by Boon Wurrung Senior Elder N'arweet Carolyn Briggs.

The threshold stretches over 26m long – crossing it can be an act of coming out.

Aterro do Flamengo

RIO DE JANEIRO, BRAZIL

Ben Campkin and Rafael Pereira do Rego

Flamengo Park (Aterro do Flamengo) was conceived by Lota de Macedo Soares (1910–67), a self-trained landscape designer and architect.[182] In a city where public parks were not inclusive or accessible to many people, Lota's proposal was 'to offer to all the *Cariocas* [Rio denizens] and their families the opportunity to spend Sunday in the open air.'[183]

Lota was from a notable Brazilian political and aristocratic family.[184] Her personal life has lent itself to dramatisation, including her intimate relationships with women, including the US poet Elizabeth Bishop. She lived with Bishop for about 15 years, mostly at Fazenda Samambaia in Petrópolis, near Rio. The wider historical significance of Lota's work, including her important role in coordinating the huge and complex Aterro, has been overlooked. Her involvement is noted in a small plaque in the park, but its authorship is more typically ascribed to Roberto Burle Marx (1909–94).[185]

Burle Marx was undoubtedly more prolific; his works – including Rio's famous Copacabana promenade – have been hailed alongside those of other male Modernists, including Oscar Niemeyer and Lucio Costa.[186] Burle Marx's sexuality, and long-term relationship with architect Rino Levi, who accompanied his botanic expeditions, are, incidentally, also a matter of speculation. It is possible that the queer aspects of his personal life have been concealed or erased by his estate and academic historians.

At a time of major public works in the city, the park was built under the tenure of Carlos Lacerda – governor of the municipality and Lota's close friend – on the Glória-Flamengo landfill site, giving it the name *aterro* (landfill). The transformation of this site, on the Guanabara bay, created an important new public space, an emblem for the city. It was commissioned and realised at this location largely due to Lota's influence and curation of multiple practitioners and artists.[187]

Aterro has continuously been a location for varied activities and a social mix, and has been subject to debate regarding proper and improper uses. Today, its functions are diverse, albeit with an increased presence of park managers and security. It encompasses many formal and informal activities, whether vending, jogging or cruising, in its tree-lined and landscaped zones, next to a water-processing facility and popular beach. Trees and subways have been claimed by homeless people, mainly racialised

Brazilians, for shelter; Afro-Brazilian communities have used the park for religious rituals. A recent study by landscape architect Felipe Coral titled 'Informal Gardens' (2019) critiques the park's Modernist planning, along with the policies and policing practices of its management, as being oppressive to marginalised groups, including homeless, indigenous and LGBTQ+ people, who have long gathered in the park.[188] It is ironic that, after his death, it was Burle Marx's practice which conducted a study pinpointing the 'unwanted behaviour of marginals.'[189]

As well as its claims to queer authorship, the park has accommodated gender and sexual diversity and queer uses. In the 1980s, many community-led Pride protests took place here. The less illuminated areas of the park, with its dense canopies of trees, have favoured gatherings by these populations, away from the judgmental gaze of Rio society. It is a location for queer *Cariocas* to play Gaymado (a queer adaptation of Queimado, dodgeball, a sport associated with homophobia).

The whole process of the park's construction, the invisibility or visibility of its designers at different moments, and its management today, reflect wider power dynamics in Brazilian society, from the military dictatorship, to re-democratisation, to progressive governments and to Bolsonaro's far-right military 'democracy' – whereby public figures and institutions continue to marginalise outsiders with rhetorical and physical violence, favouring some uses and users over others.

ONE Institute for Homophile Studies

CALIFORNIA, USA

David Eskenazi

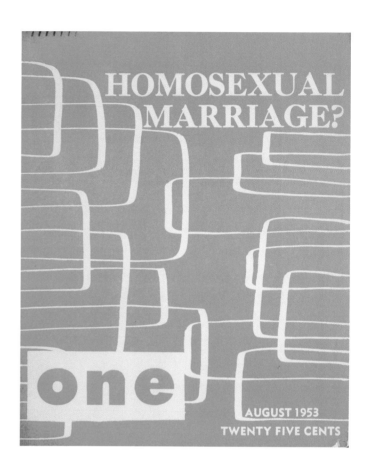

In 1953, the first issue of *ONE Magazine*, which would become the first widely distributed publication for homosexuals in the United States, was published in Los Angeles. At the time of its eighth issue, titled 'Homosexual marriage?', the postal authorities seized the publication until the US Supreme Court ruled in *One, Inc.* v *Olesen* (1958) that the magazine was not violating obscenity laws in a landmark ruling for free speech. It continued to publish for another 14 years, during which time the ONE organisation was founded.

The organisation began as an advocacy and publishing group that included *ONE Magazine* before acquiring numerous archives, starting with Jim Kepner's Western Gay Archive. During its history, it also included educational programmes that formed the ONE Institute for Homophile Studies and its associated publication. Beginning in 1981, it offered master's and doctoral degrees in homophile studies.

Today the organisation has split into the ONE Archives (hosted by the University of Southern California) and the ONE Archives Foundation (which operates educational programmes).

The archives claim to be the United States' oldest-running LGBTQ organisation and the largest repository of LGBTQ materials in the world.[190]

The archival collections range from drag show videos, posters and photographs of ACT UP protests, to collections from the pornographic publication *COLT Studio*, archives of gay and lesbian periodicals and books from throughout the United States, video recordings of performances and lectures held at ONE, correspondences, memos and personal papers of various activist organisations and individuals, such as records from *The Advocate* magazine, and personal papers of the Los Angeles-based artists Bob Flanagan and Sheree Rose.

Over its history, the ONE Institute's offices, archives and meeting spaces meandered around Los Angeles, from a downtown loft to a Pico-Union storefront, an archive location on the Hollywood Walk of Fame, a space in an elegant house in Arlington Heights, and eventually to its current location in a West Hollywood gallery, with the archives hosted at the University of Southern California's library.

With each location, we see a breadth of Los Angeles' everyday spaces and streetscapes. The downtown loft, the Venice Boulevard storefront, the large home in central LA: these are the spaces of everyday urbanism in Los Angeles. For every protest or ACT UP action in a public space, there were many more queer bars, activist meeting spaces and archives lingering in the background of 20th-century Los Angeles. The ONE Archive's meandering trajectory around the city mirrors the meandering ups and downs of coming out of the closet, of being loud or being quiet, being in the background or visible, and it's a trajectory that tells the story of an activist movement forming into an institution.

Above
Cover of *ONE Magazine*, Vol 1, No 8, 'Homosexual marriage?', August 1953.

Opposite
ONE founder Jim Kepner (left) and W Dorr Legg standing outside the ONE Inc. offices on Venice Boulevard, Los Angeles.

Inside ONE's Venice
Boulevard library, 1953.

Artist Joy Commander at the
National Gay Archives, looking
through the newspaper
collection, 1980.

Photograph of ONE
Inc.'s Venice Boulevard
headquarters, from
promotional materials, 1966.

An unidentified lesbian
meeting, 1970s.

Cover of *ONE: The
Homosexual Magazine*,
Vol 3, No 3, March 1955.

ONE, INCORPORATED

2256 VENICE BOULEVARD LOS ANGELES, CALIFORNIA 90006

Sappho Islands

KAMPALA, UGANDA AND STOCKHOLM, SWEDEN, AND...

MYCKET

In 2010, founder and director of the LBQ womxn rights organisation Freedom & Roam Uganda, Kasha Jacqueline Nabagesera (also known as Bombastic Kasha), together with other Ugandan LGBTQIA+ activists, opened Sappho Islands in Kampala, the first and only queer bar and nightclub in Uganda. The name is a tribute to the ancient Greek poet Sappho (c 600 BCE), an icon of love and desire between women, and her place on the fabled island haven of Lesbos. The bar was housed in a simple single-storey structure behind a sheet-iron fence. The construction is basic and painted white, but the pillars of unpainted wooden stems give it a vernacular touch. The space is open towards an uncovered backyard with straw parasols. It had a few site-specific design features, the lightbox sign being the most important.

For one year, Sappho Islands was a supportive and empowering space, a queer performative architecture which sustained lives in an oppressive culture.

The club triggered desires and generously supported bodies and brave political ideas. It was a playground for nonconformist feelings and unhabitual movements. Not least, it was a shared space of respect.

Sadly, Sappho Islands had to close in 2011 as a consequence of Uganda's crackdown on homosexuality. Uganda has one of the harshest standpoints on homosexuality in the world. Homosexual acts are prohibited by law and carry a potential penalty of life imprisonment. The queer community faces discrimination (arbitrary arrests, evictions, loss of employment and extortion), beatings, executions and vigilante torture – for instance, the hate-crime murder of the LGBTQIA+ activist David Kato, whose life and story is depicted in the movie *Call Me Kuchu* (2012) by Malika Zouhali-Worral and Katherine Fairfax Wright. The requiem of David Kato took place at Sappho Islands in Kampala shortly after his burial. The life of Sappho Islands in Kampala was temporary and brief, but the memory of it will linger in its participants' minds forever. And it can awaken again.

The nightclub is a performative architecture. It is in relation to the actions, the music, the style and the crowd that the spatial container of the club becomes significant. The relation between the social interplay and the material conditions are intimately connected. Queer nightclubs, to many the only place they can feel at home, are spaces and activities that have been, and still are, crucial to people who haven't had, or currently don't have, the freedom to act as they wish with their own bodies. The party cannot be separated from the political. This architecture is temporary (in that it exists at a certain place during a certain time); nevertheless, it can create an embodied spatial experience of belonging.

As part of their Club Scene research series, the art and architecture collaboration MYCKET reactivated this embodied spatial history by hosting full-scale enactments formed out of the dreams and debris of emblematic clubs. More than 200 activists from across the globe convened in Stockholm in 2012 for the world conference of the International Lesbian, Gay, Bisexual, Trans and Intersex Association (ILGA). They were invited to a tribute to Sappho Islands in which organisers and guests from the original club were present. Thus, this significant queer bar and nightclub came alive again, and for one night, in a shared spatial fantasy, everyone there became part of its acute history. In 2015, Kasha Jacqueline Nabagesera was awarded the Right Livelihood Award. She plans to reopen Sappho Islands.

Above
Sappho Islands, Stockholm, during the ILGA world conference.

Clockwise from top

Still from the film *Call Me Kuchu* (2012). The community sings 'Rivers of Babylon' on the karaoke machine after David Kato's funeral, changing the lyrics to 'Yeah, we wept, when we remembered David.'

Meeting at Sappho Islands, Kampala, 2011.

The kuchu community gathers after David Kato's funeral, 2011.

Still from *Call Me Kuchu* showing the sign at the front of the bar.

Comparsa Drag

BUENOS AIRES, ARGENTINA

Gustavo Bianchi and Facundo Revuelta

Comparsa Drag has been dragging streets since 2018. They've developed several ways of inhabiting public space as a diverse flock. They move around as a vagrant pack, wandering at queer speeds, under queer time, rubbing against the patriarchally constructed built environment, partying out in the open as a statement about the redistribution of pleasure, as a statement against violence, and work. Rumour has it that they've been painting city façades with stencils that question and stand against the patriarchal rule of compulsory production of goods and sexual reproduction.

Their queer wandering and excessive behaviour is the radical disruption of normative city manners, an urban practice that explores territories of sensuality and passion within ordinary spaces.

No le tenemos miedo a la noche (Not afraid of the night), 2018

Comparsa Drag was invited by Dagurke, an Argentinian photographer, to show Buenos Aires to a group of foreign artists, to whom they presented '*No le tenemos miedo a la noche*', a nocturnal city tour. Night-time in downtown Buenos Aires has often been described as dangerous by the mass media, as part of a campaign of fear, a way of sowing distrust among the population towards the nocturnal life of the city, and to justify an increasingly militarised control of the streets. Comparsa Drag's performance was a stroll around city landmarks that are still integral to popular neighbourhoods, dense places where otherness and difference coexist despite the homogenising influence of neoliberalism's bright lights.

Above, left
Frane Longo walking in the downtown streets of Buenos Aires after a group gathering at the Centro de Investigaciones Artisticas (CIA).

Above, right
Comparsa Drag marching alongside Martina Pelinco, Alma Fernandez and other LGBTQ+ activists at the first Plurinacional *Travesti*-Trans Pride Parade held at Buenos Aires' most emblematic slum, Barrio Mujica.

Derecho a lo cualquiera (Whatever's right), 2019

Back in 2019, Comparsa Drag were hired for a show at the city's government-backed art festival, Festival Internacional de Buenos Aires (FIBA). They took this as a chance to turn their form of dance into a political statement of resistance. The festival's spatial design was structured in several sequential stages aligned across the main street. Instead of performing tame fun on top of a stage, they marched along the street in a noisy protest that collided head-on with the public and with the other shows at the festival. Part of their display included protest banners against the organisers' plans for gentrification and surveillance, a funny songbook, an erotic nativity scene and a big flag calling out apocalyptic prophecies. They were never invited again.

Plurinacional Travesti-Trans Pride Parade

Pride parades are usually held in consolidated central neighbourhoods, but in 2019, a day before the XXVIII Pride March of Buenos Aires, an unprecedented event took place in a paradoxical territory that is both central, yet marginalised. The first Plurinacional Travesti-Trans Pride Parade was celebrated in the Barrio Mujica, one of Buenos Aires' main slums, surrounded by urban infrastructure and upper-class neighbourhoods. On this occasion, pride was about being trans and being a villera (slum dweller). Comparsa Drag was invited by trans activist Martina Pelinco to join this urban action, a parade that showed trans existence as a political force strong enough to lead a massive and highly visible occupation of the barrio's main streets.

This event is part of a larger phenomenon of the nationwide proliferation of LGBTQ+ protests and Pride parades that have resulted in the attainment of several political rights, such as same-sex marriage (2010), the right to decide name and gender depicted on official documents (2012), and the 'Diana Sacayán' law (2021), which states that at least 1 per cent of national administration jobs should be reserved for travesti-trans people.

Above
Diana del Mal wildly crashing official presentations at the Festival Internacional de Buenos Aires (FIBA).

Left
Fierce Dragstracta riding Barrio Mujica's lion at the first Plurinacional *Travesti*-Trans Pride Parade.

Opposite
'Mis armas, mis tacos' (our heels, our weapons): Marcelo Estebecorena carrying around a kart loaded with junk at the FIBA festival.